Highest Praise for M. William Phelps

NEVER SEE THEM AGAIN

"This riveting book examines one of the most horrific murders in recent American history."

—*New York Post*

"Phelps clearly shows how the ugliest crimes can take place in the quietest of suburbs."

—*Library Journal*

"Thoroughly reported . . . The book is primarily a police procedural, but it is also a tribute to the four murder victims."

—*Kirkus Reviews*

TOO YOUNG TO KILL

"Phelps is the Harlan Coben of real-life thrillers."

—Allison Brennan

LOVE HER TO DEATH

"Reading anything by Phelps is always an eye-opening experience. His writing reads like a fiction mystery novel. The characters are well researched and well written. We have murder, adultery, obsession, lies and so much more."

—*Suspense Magazine*

"You don't want to miss *Love Her to Death* by M. William Phelps, a book destined to be one of 2011's top true crimes!"

—*True Crime Book Reviews*

"A chilling crime . . . Award-winning author Phelps goes into lustrous and painstaking detail, bringing all the players vividly to life."

—*Crime Magazine*

KILL FOR ME

"Phelps gets into the blood and guts of the story."

—Gregg Olsen, *New York Times* best-selling author of *Fear Collector*

"Phelps infuses his investigative journalism with plenty of energized descriptions."

—*Publishers Weekly*

"This is the most disturbing and moving look at murder in rural America since Capote's *In Cold Blood*."

—Gregg Olsen

SLEEP IN HEAVENLY PEACE

"An exceptional book by an exceptional true crime writer. Phelps exposes long-hidden secrets and reveals disquieting truths."

—Kathryn Casey

EVERY MOVE YOU MAKE

"An insightful and fast-paced examination of the inner workings of a good cop and his bad informant, culminating in an unforgettable truth-is-stranger-than-fiction climax."

—Michael M. Baden, M.D.

"M. William Phelps is the rising star of the nonfiction crime genre, and his true tales of murderers and mayhem are scary-as-hell thrill rides into the dark heart of the inhuman condition."

—Douglas Clegg

LETHAL GUARDIAN

"An intense roller-coaster of a crime story . . . complex, with a plethora of twists and turns worthy of any great detective mystery, and yet so well-laid out, so crisply written with such detail to character and place that it reads more like a novel than your standard non-fiction crime book."

—Steve Jackson

PERFECT POISON

"True crime at its best—compelling, gripping, an edge-of-the-seat thriller. Phelps packs wallops of delight with his skillful ability to narrate a suspenseful story and his encyclopedic knowledge of police procedures."

Harvey Rachlin

"A compelling account of terror . . . The author dedicates himself to unmasking the psychopath with facts, insight and the other proven methods of journalistic leg work."

—Lowell Cauffiel

Also By M. William Phelps

Perfect Poison

Lethal Guardian

Every Move You Make

Sleep in Heavenly Peace

Murder in the Heartland

Because You Loved Me

If Looks Could Kill

I'll Be Watching You

Deadly Secrets

Cruel Death

Death Trap

Kill for Me

Failures of the Presidents (co-author)

Nathan Hale: The Life and Death of America's First Spy

*The Devil's Rooming House: The True Story of
America's Deadliest Female Serial Killer*

Love Her to Death

*The Devil's Right Hand: The Tragic Story of
the Colt Family Curse*

Too Young to Kill

Never See Them Again

Kiss of the She-Devil

DEATH TRAP

M. WILLIAM PHELPS

PINNACLE BOOKS
Kensington Publishing Corp.
http://www.kensingtonbooks.com

PINNACLE BOOKS are published by

Kensington Publishing Corp.
119 West 40th Street
New York, NY 10018

All Kensington Titles, Imprints, and Distributed Lines are available at special quantity discounts for bulk purchases for sales promotions, premiums, fund-raising, and educational or institutional use. Special book excerpts or customized printings can also be created to fit specific needs. For details, write or phone the office of the Kensington special sales manager: Kensington Publishing Corp., 119 West 40th Street, New York, NY 10018, attn: Special Sales Department, Phone: 1-800-221-2647.

Pinnacle and the P logo Reg. U.S. Pat. & TM Off.

ISBN-13: 978-0-7860-3277-8
ISBN-10: 0-7860-3277-4

eISBN-13: 978-0-7860-3376-8
eISBN-10: 0-7860-3376-2

First Printing: March 2010

10 9 8 7 6 5 4

Printed in the United States of America

For Dianne Manion,
Friend, neighbor, first reader

AUTHOR'S NOTE

For this project I reviewed thousands of pages of trial testimony, police reports, court records/filings, motions, trial evidence, divorce decrees, letters, cards, e-mails and various other documents, in addition to conducting over seventy-five hours of interviews. To protect some of my sources, I have changed several names. They are clearly marked in the text. I also changed the names of Jessica McCord's children, although I never spoke to them. Jeff and Jessica McCord, in addition to all the key players involved in this true-crime saga, had his or her chance to speak with me. Some chose not to. I commend all those who told their stories and added that additional layer of truth I seek when writing these books.

—M. William Phelps
October 2009

PROLOGUE

Friday evening, February 15, 2002. There was a slight breeze blowing in from the north, under partly cloudy skies. It was sixty-one degrees.

Warm. Mild. Pleasant.

Not bad for the South in the middle of winter.

Pam Walker worked for a division of BlueCross BlueShield in Birmingham, Alabama. Like clockwork, Pam returned home from a tiring day at 5:45 P.M. Her dog had been cooped up in the house all day. So Pam had a habit of pulling into the reserved parking space in front of her condo and immediately taking the pooch out for a walk.

The condo complex on Warringwood Drive in Hoover was in a quiet section of town, not yet affected by the overly congested, economically stimulated boom taking place in this popular suburb of Birmingham. The condo complex consisted of about twenty units connected in a line, like row houses.

As usual, Pam took the dog out back. There was a ditch there that dropped down into an area with a wall of trees lining the back of the condo units. It was the best place for the dog to take care of business.

Enjoying the warm winter air, Pam forced the pooch along the tree line to the opposite end of the condo complex, away from her unit. Across from where Pam stood, that thickly settled wooded area behind the condo units blocked what was a housing development—directly west—on the opposite side of the tree line. On a clear day, you could almost see through the trees, past a little ravine, into the corresponding neighborhood: a nice, cozy suburban denizen of middle-class homes. Sort of a white-picket-fence community.

Husbands. Wives. Children. Grandmothers and grandfathers.

Pam stood at the border of the wooded area. Her pooch went about its business. By now, it was, Pam remembered later, about fifteen minutes into her walk—or somewhere close to six o'clock.

Just then, as the dog finished, a loud noise startled Pam Walker. The sound was something out of the ordinary: two cracks in a successive pattern.

Pop. Pop.

"Directly across from where I was standing," Pam later said in court.

Firecrackers? Pam thought.

But the Fourth of July was months away.

Kids. Playing around. Maybe a car backfired.

Who knew?

There was a ravine in front of Pam. The sounds had definitely come from just beyond the wooded area, where all those seemingly perfect lives inside model-train-set houses were located on the opposite side of the trees.

After thinking about it, Pam hustled her pooch back inside and forgot about the strange noises—that is, until weeks later, when the cops came knocking, asking people in the neighborhood if they had heard anything close to "gunshots" back near the middle of February.

In every life, joy flashes gay and radiant across the sorrows of . . . which the web of our life is woven.

—Gogol, *Dead Souls*

PART I

A GRUESOME DISCOVERY

1

Joan and Philip Bates raised three delightful boys. They were as close as parents could be to their children. A solid family unit, the Bateses were one of those wholesome, old-fashioned Southern Christian families who believed strong ties, loyalty, respect, support and admiration for others were what mattered more than anything else in life. Married nearly forty years, Joan and Philip lived in and around Birmingham, Alabama, until 1991, when Philip took a job in Georgia, and moved the tribe to Atlanta. Philip was an engineer, able to get his degree, he was proud to admit, because Joan had worked her fingers to the bone and taken care of the family financially while he finished school. No doubt about it, the Bates marriage was a partnership.

Fifty-fifty.

In 1992, after twenty-nine years with BellSouth, Philip retired, relocated the family to Marietta, just outside Atlanta, where he went to work for an engineering firm, the Parsons Corporation. By 2000, the kids were grown and out of the house. Now it was time for Joan and Philip to settle into their "golden" years and enjoy the fruits of a life lived under the auspices of hard work and moral decency. There were grandkids and daughters-in-law these days. Family get-togethers and holidays.

Although the children were out of the nest, the three boys stayed in touch regularly with mom and dad. The Bateses lived in a modest home. Enjoyed life as the gift they felt it to be. Philip was like that: a dad who made his boys and wife a priority, not a *responsibility* that needed to be met. Philip did things from his heart, not some parenting playbook on the best-seller list. And the boys had picked up on this characteristic and had taken after their dad.

"Whatever we did," one of the kids said later, "Mom and Dad were there supporting us. Beautiful people."

On Friday night, February 15, 2002, as the ten o'-clock hour came to pass, Joan Bates was stressed and worried. She paced in the living room for some time, wondering what was keeping her middle child, Alan, who should have arrived in Marietta from downtown Birmingham hours ago. The day before, Alan flew from his home in Frederick, Maryland, into Alabama so he could give a deposition that Friday in a child custody matter he was pursuing. Alan had gotten re-married four years after he divorced his first wife, a marriage that had produced two wonderful girls. Joan and Philip had two extraordinary grandchildren, who made their hearts shudder every time they thought of them. Alan and his first wife, Jessica McCord, had been at odds over the children—more Jessica's doing than anything Alan had instigated. Jessica, who had custody of the kids, had kept the girls from Alan for the past several years, making his legal visitations a living hell. Alan had put up with it for years, only because he didn't want to hurt the children, but he had recently decided it was time to take Jessica to court and fight for custody. The trial was slated to begin in a few weeks, on March 5, 2002. Alan was in Birmingham that Friday,

February 15, to give his version of the events (deposition), same as Jessica. His plan was to pick the girls up after the deposition and drive them back to Marietta to spend the weekend with the Bates family.

Quite shockingly, Jessica had okayed the weekend visit.

Looking out the window, wondering where Alan could possibly be, Joan considered that maybe Jessica had changed her mind—it wouldn't be the first time—and reneged on an earlier agreement to allow Alan to take the kids for the weekend. Jessica often did that: told Alan he could have the kids and then disappeared, nowhere to be found.

At best, Marietta was a two-and-a-half-hour drive from Birmingham. Standing, then sitting, then standing again, Joan did the math: *Deposition ends at five, pick up the kids by six, get on the road and into Marietta by— the latest—nine-thirty.*

Alan had always called and said he was on his way.

Not tonight.

Philip and Joan expected them around nine, nine-thirty. Joan had dinner waiting, same as she always had.

Where in the heck were they?

Alan was never late. And he never forgot to call. The Bates were alarmed because they knew Alan generally would stop for fast food with the kids along the way and would call from that point on the road to give everyone an approximate time of arrival.

Not one phone call all night, however—and this alone, Joan and Philip believed, was reason enough to be anxious.

To worry.

"We didn't get the phone call," Philip said later. "So suspicions were such that we began to think that something was wrong, especially when they weren't there by ten-thirty."

Philip put his arm around Joan, consoling her the

best he could. "It's okay. He'll be here. Probably ran into traffic."

Joan looked at her husband. "Something's wrong." She felt it. That pang in the gut only a mother knew had been tugging at her: Alan had run into some sort of problem.

"I'll try calling him again."

Philip dialed Alan's cell phone.

No answer.

He tried Terra, Alan's wife. She had gone with Alan.

Again, nothing.

It wasn't that the phone rang and rang, like it had earlier that night when Philip tried calling both the same numbers. Now, hours after Philip first called, the line immediately rolled over to a computerized phone company message: "This phone is not in use at this time."

Things were skewed. Bad energy abounded inside the Bates home. Nothing was as it should be.

All they could do, however, was wait.

"I'll call Jessica," Philip said, patting Joan gingerly on the back again. He didn't like calling his ex-daughter-in-law's house. She was remarried to a Pelham, Alabama, cop. They lived in Hoover, a Birmingham suburb. They were crass people, Philip felt. Bitter and complex. Even arrogant at times. Definitely selfish. It was never an easy, friendly call. All Philip wanted to know was if Alan and Terra had shown up to pick the girls up, as scheduled, and, if so, what time had they left.

Simple questions requiring simple answers.

Philip dialed the number while staring out the window. He was obviously hoping the lights on Alan's rental car would bounce over the curb at the end of the driveway and, like two beams, hit him in the face as he waited for someone to pick up the line at the McCord home.

No answer.

Another dead end.

By 10:45 P.M., now certain something had happened to their son, his second wife and the children, Philip and Joan Bates decided it was time to call law enforcement. Philip had no idea how far he'd get, or if the cops would be any help. But he couldn't stand around and do nothing. So he called the Pelham Police Department (PPD) to see if Jeff McCord, Jessica's husband, had clocked in. Jeff worked second shift. Friday was his night to be on. He should still be reachable by radio or phone. Maybe he knew something.

"No, he's not here."

In fact, Philip was told, Jeff had taken the night off.

Philip could not go to sleep without trying to find his son, grandkids and daughter-in-law. He called the Hoover Police Department (HPD). He wanted to know if there had been any reported trouble over at Jessica and Jeff McCord's Myrtlewood Drive home. Maybe a family squabble. Alan was scheduled to pick up the kids there, Philip knew, somewhere between 6:00 and 6:30 P.M. It would be unlike Alan to engage Jessica in any sort of confrontation. But perhaps Jessica had pushed Alan over his limit. Or maybe Alan and Jeff had words.

Philip needed information.

Anything.

"Officer," Philip said, "do you have any report of a domestic disturbance at [the McCord's Myrtlewood Drive home] in Hoover?"

It was after midnight. Joan was dismayed by the course of events. If Alan had stopped and gotten a hotel or run into trouble along the road, Joan and Philip knew he would have called. He was a responsible son. Not calling would eat at Alan. Especially this late into the night. He knew his parents would be waiting and wondering, not sleeping. He would never put them through such a nerve-wracking ordeal.

As she thought about it, tossing and turning, trying to find any amount of sleep she could, there was nothing to convince Joan otherwise: Alan was in big trouble.

The Hoover PD told Philip they didn't have a report of anything taking place at the McCords' address, but they would send an officer over to the house to "check things out." Look around. See what was up.

Philip took a deep breath. Something was going to be done.

The case became known to the HPD from that point on as a routine "overdue motorist call." It happened a lot. People didn't show up where they were supposed to. Worried family members called in. The cops conducted a quick drive-by or knocked on the door. Generally, there was a simple explanation behind the missed calls—something that made sense later. A flat tire. A forgotten check-in phone call. A cell phone battery that had gone dead. Someone got food poisoning. A twisted ankle. The emergency room. *Forgot to call, Ma, sorry.*

There was a thousand and one reasons why people didn't—or couldn't—call. It would all make sense in a few hours. Perhaps Alan was stranded somewhere with no cell reception. No pay phone.

Things happened.

"We'll let you know what we find," the officer told Philip.

2

Hoover, Alabama, Police Department patrolman Scott McDonald was dispatched to Jeff and Jessica McCord's Myrtlewood Drive address. He had been told to check things out. Maybe Alan and Terra had broken down and were staying at the McCords' for the night while their car was being repaired.

Overdue motorist . . .

All cops know that these types of calls—nine times out of ten—turn into nothing. a misunderstanding, miscommunication. It was late. Alan and Terra were probably at a hotel somewhere in town. Sleeping.

Myrtlewood Drive is located in a residential area close to Baston Lake and Interstate 65. It's a quiet neighborhood, full of white picket fences and tarred driveways with the standard 2.2 cars, boat, lawn mowing on Saturdays, cookouts on Sundays, neighborhood dog walkers, and an overall feel that this small section of Hoover represented a broad brushstroke of what middle-class America should look like.

Little pink houses.

By the time Patrolman McDonald took a right onto Myrtlewood Drive and looked for the address, it was dark, desolate, and rather lonely in the neighborhood. Most families were asleep. A lone dog, which the cop could not see, barked at the night moon. But other than that, and a line of porch lights on for safety, the neighborhood was quiet.

Nothing much happening.

After pulling up in front of the McCords' house, the officer grabbed his flashlight—the house looked deserted—and walked up to the front porch.

Strangely, the window panels on the door were "covered up," McDonald later said, "with towels or sheets from the inside."

Huh.

It gave the windows a peculiar look. Like someone was trying to block the view of the inside of the house from anyone looking in. Or maybe there was work going on inside the house, spray painting or something.

That was it. Home repairs. The Home Depot and Lowe's had sent the suburban handyman into a frenzy of remodeling. Everyone was into changing this and painting that and falling farther into debt.

McDonald shined his light toward the windows to his right and left.

Same thing: the windowpanes were covered with towels and sheets.

Back on the porch, McDonald found a note of some sort—a handmade sign, Magic Marker written on a piece of cardboard: WE'RE HAVING SOME PROBLEMS WITH OUR FRONT DOOR. PLEASE COME AROUND TO THE BACK DOOR.

Now it made sense. In all likelihood, the family *was* having some work done to the inside of the house.

McDonald checked his watch: 12:21 A.M. Everything was magnified at this time of the night. Spookier and more mysterious. There was probably a nice, cozy family inside the home, all of whom were sleeping. Nothing more than a routine call.

Overdue motorist . . .

The officer rang the doorbell in front before heading out to the back. It was worth a try before walking away.

With no answer, he knocked hard on the door a few times.

Nothing.

Staring more closely into the house, his view obstructed because of the paper towels and sheets, McDonald saw the faint shimmering of a few lights left on. Was someone working in there now?

Of course not.

The officer found his way to the driveway and noticed that there were no vehicles parked in the yard.

He walked toward the garage. It was connected to the house. One of those you could walk from the garage directly into the house. He was hoping to look in through the twelve-by-twelve-inch square windowpanes on the garage door to see if there were any vehicles inside.

Once again, he couldn't see. The windows were covered with the same material: paper towels and sheets.

What in the world . . .

Beside the garage was a fence blocking the officer's view of the back door.

McDonald looked for the gate, he said in court later, not being able to see inside the fenced-in section, when he heard footsteps seemingly coming at him.

Fast and furious. Leaves cracking. Branches breaking.

Then came the barking. Ferocious and mean-spirited.

A dog. It was caged up inside the area. McDonald knew better. He wasn't going inside and having a showdown with some Cujo-like home protector. No one had answered the front door. What were the chances of someone answering the back?

So McDonald walked to his car and called dispatch. "Back in service," he said. "No contact with anyone at this residence."

3

During the early-morning hours of February 16, 2002, somewhere near 3:30 A.M., four friends traveled down Old Mill Road in Rutledge, Georgia. They were on their way to South Carolina to attend what one of them described as a "chicken show." In fact, inside the Toyota minivan they were traveling in were cages of chickens to bring to that show.

It was dark as motor oil out there that time of night. The men had just woken up. They were all a bit groggy still, the ruts in the dirt road bouncing them along, when one of them noticed a light. It was no common light. It had a red and orange glow to it. It came from off in the distance.

"Over there," one of the men shouted.

The others looked.

"I know someone who owns that land, y'all. Turn around and head over there."

There was a concern that the woods were on fire. A friend might lose acreage. Maybe even a barn. Animals. People. The closer they got, pulling onto Hawkins Academy Road, where the dark smoke and flames were centered, the more it became clear that this was not a small brush fire, but some kind of inferno. Something was burning out of control.

Pulling up to what they realized was a car engulfed in flames, the men got out of the van. As soon as they hit the outside air, they could feel the heat from the blaze push them back.

One of them was already on his cell phone calling the sheriff.

Morgan County, Georgia, deputy sheriff John Eugene Williams took the call. The man on the other end of the line reported that there was a car on fire in the woods near Hawkins Academy Road. Someone needed to get the fire department out there immediately, before the woods burned out of control. There were trees on fire already. The ground was charred and flaming. Rutledge is a suburb of Madison. It is a deeply settled region of Morgan County. Lots of trees and dirt roads and farmland.

Bucolic nothingness.

"It's rural," Deputy Williams later explained.

"There's a car on fire," the man said into his cell phone, "out here at Hawkins Academy Road. . . ."

Damn kids probably messing around again. After all, it was still Friday night, unofficially speaking. Bunch of punks probably tied a good one on and, after funneling beers half the night, got a little rowdy and decided to torch an old rusted-out junk vehicle sitting in some farmer's pasture. Deputy Williams needed to get the local fire department out there as soon as he could and get those flames extinguished before that common car fire turned into an uncontrollable forest fire.

Then he'd have big problems on his hands. A headache the deputy surely didn't need. Or wanted to deal with.

"Thanks," Williams said. He was on it.

* * *

Deep in the Georgia woods, standing there humbly among the flagpole-straight American beech trees, rotting leaves from the previous fall underneath your feet, you look up in the middle of the night and realize you are a witness to the immaculate grace of God's country: a blanket of diamonds sparkling against a perfectly black shawl of a sky that gazes back down at you. Off in the distance are the subtle, darkened silhouette outlines of mountains in the shape of a camel's back. Rutledge, Georgia, as Deputy Williams seemed to imply, is just a blip on a GPS screen, with a population of seven hundred. The town is located approximately halfway between Atlanta and Augusta. It is a forgotten place, essentially, there to serve its people. Rutledge and Madison are quiet and nondescript wooded areas off Interstate 20 that interlopers might assume are nothing more than lost, vast wilderness. Out here, good old folks live quietly. They bother no one. Their focus is on working the same land their forefathers have had for generations past.

Yet, during the late 1990s and early into the new millennium, for some bizarre reason few could ever discern, this same area of the state became a dumping ground for the dead, especially those who had been brutally murdered. There was an elderly woman, abducted and beaten with a tree branch, left there to be found by the animals; two teenage runaways who kidnapped a newspaper girl and left her mutilated body just off the interstate; and three teens who tortured and eventually killed a runaway.

Strange happenings, indeed.

Dead bodies popping up every now and then was no reason for alarm, locals knew. And law enforcement would say the same thing when asked why this area of the state had become such a refuge for murder victims: because it was between two major American cities, and the woods were easily accessible on and off the interstate.

It was either that, or Morgan County had the ghastly luck of being a quasi-burial ground for the murdered souls of the region.

Deputy Williams rustled up his jacket. Headed quickly out the door. Hopped into his Crown Victoria. Took off.

The Morgan County Sheriff's Office (MCSO) is located on Athens Highway. That's about twenty minutes from the fire scene. Hawkins Academy Road is in Madison, actually, a mere rock toss east of Social Circle, just north of Rutledge. Looking at the road on a map, you can easily see why one might drop off Interstate 20 and onto Route 11 (Covington Street), follow the train tracks toward Rutledge, then take that turn onto Knox Chapel Road and head toward Hard Labor Creek State Park, stopping off somewhere along the way to set fire to a vehicle. From a bird's-eye view you can see how one might be drawn to this area; that is, of course, if burning a car or dumping a body is in your immediate plans. The area is remote and yet effortlessly reachable, both in and out. The terrain is dense and thickly wooded and settled. If you wanted to cause mischief and not be seen, this would be an ideal place to get it done and get the hell out without anyone seeing you.

"There's very few houses on it," Williams said later, referring to Hawkins Academy Road. "It's fairly isolated."

As Williams drove, dispatch confirmed the call.

A 10-code. 1070. Vehicle fire.

From the main road, Williams turned onto Hawkins

Academy, a gravel road, heading toward a vast farming area. It was about 3:50 A.M.

When he arrived, Williams was pleased to see that the Rutledge Fire Department (RFD) was already on scene. Not only that, but to the deputy's great relief, they had extinguished most of the fire. It was under control. The ground smoking and hot. Trees blackened and bare. The car hissing, casting off an unhealthy smell of burned plastic and chemicals.

Chief Jerry Couch greeted the deputy as he pulled up and got out of his vehicle.

"Anybody in that vehicle?" Williams asked.

It was hard to tell by looking at it all burned up like that, but the car was a 2001 red Pontiac Grand Am. It had turned white, this after every last bit of paint had bubbled like blisters and melted from the vehicle due to the excessive heat and flames. Parked nose-first toward what looked to be a gate to let cows or horses into the acreage, a solid thirty years of the forested carpet in a circle around the charred vehicle was burned apocalyptic-like to the ground. Everything in that same area around the vehicle had turned to nothing but ash and black soil. Those skeletonized trees were just standing there, naked and charred like kindle wood.

As Williams walked toward the scene, he could see it was now nothing more than a smoldering mess of melted plastic and metal. Most of the rubber and plastic from the vehicle was gone. Liquefied. Cars didn't just catch fire like this and burn themselves unrecognizable. Williams was no rookie cop. He knew better. An accelerant had to be involved. Hell, you could smell some sort of fuel. A car fire will generally burn itself out without much help. But this: the entire inside and outside of the vehicle was completely destroyed, blackened and charred. Smoldering. There were no seats left. Inside and out, the vehicle was nothing more than a carcass, same as a frame at the beginning of an automaker's line in Detroit.

Having the fire under control, and more or less settled, was one less problem Williams had to contend with on what had turned into a frosty, excessively windy February night in the South.

Williams asked again: "Anybody inside?" There was the outside chance someone had torched the vehicle and a person along with it. Everyone had seen at least one episode of *The Sopranos* or a Martin Scorsese film. Burning bodies was a common way to get rid of evidence.

"No," the chief said. "Ain't nobody in there, but it . . ."

"Good . . . ," Williams started to say. Again, one less problem to contend with in the middle of the night.

". . . but it looks like somebody just slaughtered some beef or had some deer meat or something in the trunk," the fire chief finished spitting out.

"Well," Williams said, "let's have a look."

Poachers? Out here? What the hell? Someone trying to steal a darn cow in the trunk of a Pontiac Grand Am? The sheriff had seen people try to get away with more stupid things throughout his career. But this would be a first.

Williams could smell burning flesh himself as he approached the back area of the Grand Am. Waves of it wafted with the wind. Overtook his senses.

Indeed. Cooked meat had a very distinctive odor. Very potent. Very gamey.

To the sheriff, there was no mistaking what it was.

He walked over to the trunk. The plastic light housings on the rear end of the vehicle were gone, melted like candle wax, sponged into the black soil below his feet. The trunk was propped open with a halogen tool, a fireman's crowbar. The car's license plate had fallen off, but was on the ground, still intact, upside down.

That was good to see. Identifying whose vehicle it was would be easy enough.

The sheriff went in for a closer look.

The backseat of the car had burned into ash, spring coils popping up. This gave the sheriff a clear view from the inside of the trunk into the hub of the vehicle's backseat. There was definitely something bulky and large, all burned up, inside the trunk. There looked to be a blanket, or comforter of some type, underneath.

Williams leaned in for an even closer look. He knew right away what he was dealing with now. It was not going to be an uncomplicated night, after all.

The fire chief was off—but not too far.

"These are human beings," Williams said to the fire chief, "not an animal."

Both men stared at the mound of charred remains before them. It was hard to make out, but the cop was right. If you focused on the bulky entanglement of what looked to be two large animals coiled up together, you could clearly see the outline of two dead human beings, and what was left of the arm of one person. Williams believed, he said later, he was looking at a male and a female, or a man and a child. He didn't know which.

"I knew one was a male," he recalled, "but I couldn't tell if the other one was a female or a child. [It was] much smaller."

Either way, Williams was looking at the remnants of a heinous crime. A double murder. The vehicle was, obviously, the cover-up.

The crime scene.

Williams needed to clear the area. With help from several fire officials, he ran yellow crime-scene tape in a circular pattern extending to about thirty-five feet in diameter around the vehicle. He warned that nothing was to be moved or removed from the scene. Nobody should touch anything. Williams said he needed to get the Georgia Bureau of Investigation (GBI) out to start investigating. They needed to sift through what were the charred remains of two badly burned bodies and find out what had happened. It appeared a double homicide had been committed.

Williams went back to his car and got on the radio.

4

Philip and Joan Bates did not find much sleep throughout the night of February 15, 2002. Alan's parents spent long periods staring at the ceiling. Wondering. Waiting. Counting sheep. Their stomachs in knots. When was the phone going to ring? When was that news coming? Joan knew it wasn't going to be good.

A mother's instinct.

"I had done all I knew how to do," Philip said later, recalling that hectic night, "and went to bed for a few hours."

That morning Philip made coffee. The clock on the wall in the kitchen said 6:00 A.M. They had not heard from Alan since Friday afternoon. Not a word from anyone, for that matter. Philip called his son's cell phone again, same with Terra's. But he got the same voice message.

He put the phone down, he said later, and thought about it: *Darn. Those kids are in trouble.*

It was time to file a missing persons report, Philip knew. It was the only way to get law enforcement out and about, looking for Alan, Terra and the kids.

Sipping his coffee, Philip knew the first question

law enforcement would ask was a question he did not have the answer to. He needed to get some information first. Be prepared. Have what they need. Don't sound desperate. Appear organized. An engineer thinks through every contingency, every possible problem *before* it happens.

The worried father took out a pad. Sat down and called rental car agencies inside the Birmingham Airport terminal to see which company had rented Alan and Terra a car. Philip knew Alan always used one of the agencies from the airport. He just didn't know which one.

So he started with Avis.

"I told them who I was, what I was trying to do, and my concern," Philip said later.

The agent was helpful. Said he understood Philip's dilemma. Maybe he could help. Heck, he *wanted* to help.

Philip asked, "Have you rented a car to my son, Alan Bates . . . and if so, could you give me the color, make, model, maybe a description of it, so I could file a missing persons report?"

Philip knew he was probably going to have to repeat this same line to several different companies until he found the one Alan had used. But what he heard on that first call, he certainly did not expect.

"Um . . . hold on a minute, sir," the agent said. He sounded concerned. Worried. There was urgency in his young voice. "I need to get my supervisor."

Philip was shocked by this comment. Was there a red flag in the computer system on Alan's bill?

A manager came on the line. Philip told the same story. Then the manager made a suggestion that spiked the hair on the back of Philip's neck. "Sir, I was told to give this number out to anyone calling here regarding that rental."

The number was for the Georgia Bureau of Investigation.

Philip's heart fluttered; his stomach twisted.

"What?"

Here it was, Saturday morning, February 16, and Alan, Terra and the girls were a no-show. Philip had even called Terra's father, Tom Klugh, a man who knew just about every move his thirty-year-old daughter made. (Terra was set to turn thirty-one in about six weeks, on March 30.) Tom had not heard from them, either. And now here was some car rental agent manager telling Philip to phone the GBI.

"That's when I knew," Philip said. "That was it."

5

GBI crime scene specialist Todd Crosby was one of the first to arrive at the Hawkins Academy Road scene that morning. Crosby worked out of the GBI's Milledgeville, Georgia, office, a sixty-minute drive south of Rutledge. He had received a call at four forty-five that morning from the GBI Communications Center and hit the road in his crime scene van shortly after.

The GBI works on a "request only" basis, supporting all law enforcement agencies in the state of Georgia. According to its mission statement: *[The] GBI is an independent, statewide agency that provides assistance to the state's criminal justice system in the areas of criminal investigations, forensic laboratory services and computerized criminal justice information.*

The Bureau, as it's sometimes called, is split up into three divisions: investigative, forensic sciences and crime information. Each works to serve the other—and the corresponding law enforcement agencies calling on the GBI for help. It is an agency that has been operating in the state of Georgia in some form or fashion since 1937.

With two severely burned bodies in the trunk of a

car, there was a good chance someone was trying to cover up a set of murders. The mob did this sort of thing—although, they were generally a lot cleaner about it. If you know what you're doing, a fire is a great way to destroy evidence. The only problem is, you had better make sure you finish the job; because with the technology available today, a forensic team is certain to uncover bags of trace evidence in support of its case if the fire doesn't do the trick. Arson investigation is not as difficult as it may seem. Fire can sometimes preserve evidence and leave clues otherwise unavailable.

This was, of course, one of the main reasons why Todd Crosby was summoned to the scene. His job is to collect biological and fingerprint evidence. If someone left his or her DNA at the scene, or fingerprints somewhere on this vehicle, Crosby would find it with any one of his many forensic tools.

Crosby was briefed as to what was going on. The GBI Communications Center paged him and explained what it could. By 6:40 A.M., Crosby parked his van near the scene. Getting out of his vehicle, he was now among the commotion of flashing red and blue lights lined up along the road. Soon the sun would be up. Then the real work could begin.

Crosby first noticed that the original crime-scene tape was in an area too constricted and confined. It was awfully windy out, more so than it normally was on an average day. The scene needed to be expanded in case pieces of trace had drifted away with the wind. So Crosby ordered "approximately two hundred yards on either side of the vehicle" to be "roped" off. This area would be the "new crime scene." The idea was to begin a gridlike search of the ground for anything: cigarette butts, chewing gum, footprints, a fingernail, a piece of paper. Whatever jumped out. Killers are not generally prone to pick up after themselves and leave no evidence. Sure, the murderer generally thinks he or she is smarter than the rest of the world (especially law enforcement), but the reality is that *all* killers leave evidence behind. Crosby's job was to find what this killer had haphazardly left in his or her wake. That one clue. That one piece of the puzzle that might just make sense—and tie things together—in the coming days.

The wind picked up as Crosby began his duties. You get only one or maybe two shots at a crime scene before it becomes too overtaken and infested by people. "Contaminated" is the word they use. After a day, an outside scene like this wasn't going to be worth a damn.

Around the car, as the sun rose and illuminated the immediate area, pine trees were scattered, stuck perfectly in the ground like immense green arrows pointing toward the sky. There was not a house in sight anyone could see. As Crosby conducted his search, he photographed things. The initial area the technician focused on, which Crosby knew to be the most important, was the inside of the trunk, where both bodies had been uncovered. From the inside of the vehicle, looking toward the backseat, he noted it was an area of the vehicle that had been burned completely. So much so, Crosby could see into the trunk from inside the car.

As he glanced into the vehicle, a set of knees stared eerily back at him.

"Her legs," Crosby said later, "were bent back around, behind her. . . ."

It was a woman. She was small. Very petite. Moreover, it was easy to tell—and this would become an important factor as the case progressed—that the victim closest to the backseat of the car had been placed in the trunk first.

Were they dead before being placed inside the trunk? Chances were the victims had been murdered

by some other means—the fire had not killed them—
at a second location. Which meant there were likely
two crime scenes involved.

In front of the female victim, closest to the back end
of the vehicle, Crosby photographed and studied the
second victim's feet and legs. Both were somewhat visible if you stood over the trunk and looked directly
down. This victim was a man. They could tell by the
size of his left arm, which had been burned entirely
away from his fingertips, up to about his elbow. His
bone, near the bicep area, was visible.

Crosby took scores of photos. Flashes of light—*pop,
pop, pop*—paparazzi-like, one after the other. Crosby
studied how the bodies were placed and how they
might have been put inside the trunk.

"His legs," Crosby noted, talking about the second
victim, "come up and then bend back around the
thigh area . . . the right side of the body."

Crosby noticed that both of the victims' arms and
legs were discernible if you looked closely. The same
was true with regard to other parts of their bodies.
The back of the male's calves were, in the same way
as the female's, bent flush against the back side of his
thighs. These people were definitely, Crosby was now
certain, crunched up together and then placed into
the trunk—another indication that they were killed
beforehand at a second location.

As Crosby searched the trunk, another GBI technician combing the scene noticed something. There was
a comforter underneath the bodies that hadn't been
completely consumed by the fire.

They definitely needed that.

Hairs. Fibers. DNA.

Slowly, with the help of several additional investigators, including Susan Simmons, the deputy coroner of

Morgan County, Crosby removed the body of the male
and carefully placed him in a waiting body bag.

On the male victim's left hand was a wedding band.
Crosby photographed it before the body was zipped
away in the bag. As he did this, Crosby noticed what
appeared to be a bullet wound on the man's wrist.

Interesting.

The male victim had possibly held up his hands to
block an oncoming bullet, perhaps instinctively protecting himself. Maybe there was a bullet fragment
somewhere?

Looking at the female victim next, Crosby noticed
what he called "defects in the body," eventually finding
out that they were also "bullet holes." The female victim
had a wound in her lower back.

The comforter was now clearly visible.

When both bodies were placed in body bags, they
were taken to the GBI Crime Lab for further study and
autopsy.

Not too far away from the vehicle, one of the many
crime scene specialists who had shown up at the scene
found something else. It was a sheet of paper towel
with the imprint pattern of a little boy and little girl.
The corner of the paper towel was burned, but a majority of it was still intact.

A GBI agent bagged it.

Upon further investigation, GBI investigators found
what looked to be an engagement ring inside the
trunk, but the diamond was gone. It was underneath
where the female victim's body was placed. There were
all sorts of debris in the trunk. Then two duffel bags
were located: one contained partially burned clothes;
the other—on a quick glance—was full of what looked
to be court documents.

The theory was that the murderers had probably

hoped these duffel bags would be incinerated with the rest of the evidence.

No such luck.

There was a particular reason these two people were murdered. That was clear from the evidence at this early stage. Any cop worth his yearly salary knew that finding that reason would lead to a suspect.

Connect the dots. Despite what *Law & Order* and *CSI* portrayed on television, some investigators still viewed police work in that same simple, gumshoe manner. One piece of evidence leads to the next.

Baby steps.

As Crosby finished his work at the scene, investigators from the GBI and the Morgan County Sheriff's Office walked the scene looking for additional trace. At one point Crosby located and photographed a .44 Magnum Remington shell casing someone uncovered about ten to fifteen feet from the rear of the vehicle.

It was an odd find. A .44 would have blown the male victim's wrist off, not put a hole in it. Two weapons? Two different guns used in the same crime?

Another anomaly.

When he finished, Crosby was whisked up in the air by helicopter. This gave him the opportunity to take scores of aerial photographs before heading back to the GBI Crime Lab.

As investigators continued searching the scene, someone found a spent projectile that was mushroomed over on the top inside the trunk.

An important piece of the puzzle.

Not long after that, someone located a cigarette butt, a Marlboro Light.

Things were coming together rather expeditiously.

6

GBI investigator Kimberly Williams was at the Hawkins Academy Road crime scene in Georgia most of the morning. She arrived, along with several other investigators from the Morgan County Sheriff's Office and her GBI colleague Todd Crosby, near 6:30 A.M.

By late morning it was confirmed that the car was indeed the same red Pontiac Grand Am that Alan Bates had rented at the Avis airport terminal in Birmingham. Of course, this was not good news for Philip, Joan, Kevin and Robert Bates, who were now huddled together in Marietta, waiting for any sign of hope that Alan and Terra might be alive and well—that this entire episode was nothing more than a great misunderstanding.

GBI investigator Williams was familiar with the location in Rutledge where the bodies were recovered. She lived north of Milledgeville, about twenty minutes away. As she walked the scene, the wind picked up steadily, blowing the investigator's blond hair wildly around. With the wind came the cold, at least by Georgia standards. Williams was assigned as case agent; she was now in charge of the Bureau's side of the investigation from this point forward. By now, the seasoned investigator was aware that Alan and Terra Bates were supposed to have picked up Alan's kids outside Birmingham in Hoover and driven to his parents' house in Marietta. It was a good bet, considering the makeup and description of the bodies found in the trunk, that somewhere between Birmingham and Rutledge, Alan and Terra Bates had met with the violent hand of evil.

Williams had been with the GBI since 1995. A cop with her experience didn't need DNA and dental records to override her gut instinct. When all the cards were turned over, the only hand Williams could see was that the bodies in the trunk were Alan and his wife. Williams had been around her share of murder scenes, family arguments turned deadly, husbands and wives shooting each other for no apparent reason. Murder was not common, but it had a certain pulse to it that spoke through victims and the way they were found.

"I definitely would not say that I have seen everything," Williams said later, "but I have been exposed to a great deal by working narcotics and field cases."

The answer to what was now a mystery, Williams knew after realizing where the car had driven from, was in Birmingham. Or at least that was probably the best place to start. The other concern was the children who were supposed to be with Alan and Terra. Where were they?

Thank God—in some strange way—that there were only two bodies in that trunk—and both were adults.

"Once we identified who the car most likely contained, obviously the victims could not be identified formally," Williams said, "and once we talked to the Bates family and found out Terra and Alan Bates were overdue . . . we focused on where they were last seen."

And all roads led to Birmingham.

Backtracking, following Alan and Terra's footsteps,

Birmingham was the ideal location to begin that end of
the investigation. Seeing that it had been confirmed
that Alan walked out of a deposition downtown somewhere near 3:30 P.M. the previous day and hadn't been
seen or heard from since, Birmingham was the start of
the GBI's timeline—or, more like it, deathline. The
other arm of the investigation was going to be the hardest to go forward with right now: questioning Alan's
family. Searching for those important details and clues
without letting them know what, exactly, was going on.
The GBI couldn't come out and say they had found
Alan and Terra in the trunk. They needed positive
identification before that could be done. It was a catch-
22: because for positive identification to be made, they
needed dental records and DNA from those same
people.

"Vance," Williams called out to MCSO investigator
Sheron Vance, who partnered up with Williams almost
immediately, "can you come with me?"

Williams and Vance left the Rutledge scene for
Pelham, Alabama—this, while a second GBI agent,
Sherri Rhodes, took off for Marietta, Georgia, to interview members of the Bates family. They could discuss
developments via radio and receive updates about the
crime scene from the road. Best thing to do was to
spread out and begin putting the pieces together.

Jessica McCord's second husband, Jeff, was a Pelham,
Alabama, police officer. Cops helped each other. That
clichéd code of blue silence and brotherly love they all
lived by might come into play here. The brotherhood of
law enforcement. Jeff would be the best person to start
with. Williams and Vance decided that the Pelham PD
was as good a place as any to begin. From talking to Jeff,
they could track down Jessica and find out if and when
she saw or heard from Alan last—that is, if everything
went as planned, and Jeff was willing to help.

"Primarily," Williams told me, "[we selected an interview with Jeff McCord first] because we knew where he was supposed to be, which was at work." Jeff had swapped shifts, GBI found out, with another officer earlier that week; he was scheduled to be working that Saturday, covering for the cop. After speaking with the chief of the PPD, Williams understood the best way to approach Officer Jeff McCord was to arrive at Pelham before Jeff's 3:00 P.M. shift started. The chief assured Williams that no one would tell him the GBI and MCSO were on the way.

The focus in talking to Jeff McCord would be on what time Alan and Terra showed up at the McCord home. That was going to be very important. Once Vance and Williams had that information, they could continue to backtrack—and maybe find out who had last seen Terra and Alan alive.

7

Jessica and Jeff McCord arrived home early on the morning of February 16, 2002, a Saturday. They had been out all night. To the movies, Jessica later said. Dinner. Then a long drive. Some sort of romantic jaunt to one of Jessica's old hangout spots (they were celebrating Valentine's Day a little late) from her teen years. Then a stop at Home Depot—the first in line at the door before the place was even open. There to pick up supplies so Jessica's stepfather, Albert Bailey, could work on the house that day.

Both of them were tired. After putting her keys down on the kitchen table, Jessica scrolled through her caller ID to see who had phoned the house in their absence.

Philip and Joan's number popped up several times from the previous night and that morning.

Must be Alan, Jessica said she thought at that moment.

Alan had not shown up at the house as planned to pick up the kids, Jessica claimed. Maybe that was him, calling to give his excuse.

She dialed the Bates household in Georgia.

"Hello," Philip said. He sounded frazzled. Anxious. There were voices in the background Jessica could hear.

Although she didn't know it, the GBI had sent two investigators to the Bateses' home in Marietta. They were there to begin recording information and getting to know a little bit more about Alan and Terra's schedules and lives. They had just arrived and were getting settled. Alan's brothers, Kevin and Robert, had just recently shown up, too.

"Is Alan there? Can I speak to him?" Jessica asked.

"I wish I could let you," Philip said, a note of discomfort and confusion in his cracking voice. "But I don't know where he is."

"What do you mean?"

"I cannot find him."

"Oh," Jessica said. "Oh, my gosh." She later said this information Philip gave her was startling. It was unlike Alan to simply up and disappear. Alan was responsible. The do-gooder. The A student. The kid who never let anyone down. Jessica said she could never see Alan not alerting his parents to a new plan or his not showing up. When it came to her, she said that was a different story entirely. There were many times, Jessica later said, when Alan claimed he'd pick up the kids, but had never shown up.

Still, something was terribly wrong with this picture.

"I'm on the other end with someone important, Jessica," Philip said at one point during the conversation. "I'll have Joan call you back."

Jessica hung up. Stared at the phone.

Five minutes later, Joan called.

"Alan and Terra are both missing," Alan's mother said matter-of-factly. "They have not come to Georgia as planned. *Where* are the children?" Joan was stressed and impatient. She knew how Jessica could be. She'd slept very little the previous night. She did not need her ex-daughter-in-law's nonsense now.

"My mom's house."

"They haven't shown up. They're not here. . . ."

Jessica said she didn't know how to react to Joan's accusatory tone. Almost immediately, Jessica felt, Joan was condemning her. Poking a finger in her chest. She was only calling to threaten. Make the implication that Jessica had something to do with Alan and Terra's disappearance. ("It got ugly real quick," Jessica recalled.)

"You've harmed them," Jessica said Joan snapped at her. Joan was, obviously, upset. Uptight. On edge. Distraught. Crying. Saying things she would not remember later on. "They're missing. *Where* are they?"

"Please let me know, Joan, what's going on when you find out. I would need to tell the kids something." The kids were expecting Alan and Terra to pick them up. They had anticipated their arrival. But Alan and Terra never came, Jessica said. As she spoke, apparently trying to explain this to Joan, she could hear Philip in the background. He was giving someone her address and phone number. Jessica could hear him clearly, as if she were in the same room. She asked Joan, "*Why* is he giving out my address? What's going on? Why is he giving out my mom's address? Tell me, Joan!"

Joan wouldn't answer.

"Please, Joan. Please let me know, when you do, what's going on."

They hung up.

According to Jessica, the phone call upset her. She was bewildered and didn't know what to make of it. She went to Jeff.

"What should we do?"

"Well," Jeff said in his stoic Southern drawl, "let's just go about our business here. There's nothing that we can do. Sitting here, being upset, that isn't going to solve anything."

Jessica was unable to do chores around the house, she said. She was totally preoccupied with the situation. Pacing, waiting for Joan, Philip or anyone to call with some information. A bit of news. Some sort of word as to what in the heck was happening.

"Look," Jeff said, watching his wife fuss about, "it's not going to make them call any faster."

Jessica needed to know. She'd have to tell the kids something sooner or later.

After a time, Jessica recalled, she and Jeff went back to cleaning up the house so her stepfather could come in later on that morning, as planned, to put in a new kitchen floor. In fact, according to Jessica, there was all sorts of work going on inside the house. Wall plastering. Carpeting. Wallpapering. Furniture and toys being tossed out. Cleaning. Trips to the dump. Also part of the anxious nature in fixing up the house and getting things thrown away was the fact that the state was coming to look things over as part of the child custody matter Jessica and Alan were involved in. Jessica admitted she was no Suzie Homemaker, but she didn't want to give the state the wrong impression.

"Alan and Terra are much better housekeepers than I am," Jessica said later. "I mean, it certainly would have been an issue [for the state], had it been in the condition it was at that time."

8

Back at the Bates household in Marietta, the morning was a series of frantic, angst-filled uncertainties, disorder and questions. Philip called Robert early that morning to brief him about what was happening.

"I called the rental car company, Robert . . . spoke with GBI . . ."

Robert got the feeling something terrible had happened—he just didn't know what.

"Drop whatever you're doing and get up here," Philip said.

Robert called Kevin, explained what was going on.

"I'm on my way," Kevin said.

Robert, his wife and their kids were in Newnan at his mother-in-law's house. They had driven down the night before. Robert and Kevin planned to head over to their parents' house that afternoon—on Saturday—to meet up with Terra, Alan and the kids. They hadn't seen each other since Christmas. Alan had turned thirty on January 22. They planned a belated birthday party for him. They were going to spend the day and night together as a family. Laughing. Joking around. Telling stories. Catching up.

Just like old times.

Kevin arrived first. As he walked in, there was a terrible, cold silence in the house. A deafening hum of pain and emotional tension. His mother sat at the table. Joan was silent and sullen. She stared blankly, Kevin recalled, "her eyes covered in tears, her face red."

The progression of processing what was about to happen, Kevin recalled, was taking place in front of him. Both his parents were thinking things through. Facing facts. Trying to digest what was going on. What was coming. Accepting that a child is dead is not what parents are designed to do. It is a slow, wearisome transformation from protector to feeling like you're running to stand still. You want to do something, but you have to come to the realization that there is nothing you *can* do.

Then you're expected to open up and help an investigation that's going on around you.

It's as though the soul is being torn apart—slowly.

Philip didn't say much. But what he said stung Kevin as he acclimated himself to the house, the tone, and what was happening. It was like being sucker punched. You had no idea you had been hit until you felt your jaw begin to swell, turned and then saw someone running away from you.

"The GBI is on the way," Philip explained tersely, not pulling punches. His voice choked up.

The idea that Alan and Terra were in a car accident became the mainstay of thought. It was something they all considered, without verbalizing their feelings. That look Philip gave Kevin, however, told him something else. Staring at his father, Kevin considered: *The GBI would not be coming here if Alan and Terra were involved in a car accident.*

No way.

"At that point you realize something really wrong

has happened," Kevin said later. Before that, there was the hope that a hospital would call to say Alan and Terra were there. Alan was okay. Hurt, but okay. Terra was there by his side, holding vigil, befuddled and amazed. But safe.

When Robert walked in, he could see the look on Kevin's, his mother's and his father's faces: gloom and doom. A pale shade of white. Ghostly. The life had been drained out of them, the air sucked from the room. Philip Bates was not a man who broke under pressure. He was an engineer. He thought things through with a methodical sense of composure. He analyzed situations, came up with solutions. Here, though, at this moment, Philip was dazed. He didn't have the answer.

Kevin filled Robert in.

"Well," Robert said under his breath so his mom and dad couldn't hear, "I'm with you. The GBI doesn't get involved with just a traffic accident. This is bigger."

"We were just trying to think things through. What do you do?" Kevin later explained. "You don't know much, and what you do know is not good."

As they comforted one another, various emotions came in waves: hope, worry, dread. Up. Down. Tears. Then a happy memory. More doubt. Then a glimmer of optimism.

At this point they just wanted to know where Alan was. The GBI had not given them any specific details.

The GBI agents at the house were total professionals. They walked in. One of them comforted the family without giving away too much information. As they talked, another agent was getting details via walkie-talkie from the other agents at the crime scene and out in the field.

The agent asked the family for the spellings of names. Addresses. Phone numbers. Where? When? How? What time?

Everything seemed to be going at hyper speed.

Kevin and Robert gave the agent as many phone numbers as they had. Philip explained what he knew up to that point. And this was the reality about tragedy: in its early stages you're forced to go over the same stories again and again. The details are in the repetition.

"Where was Alan? Where did he fly into?"

Robert answered.

Then they'd ask how he seemed: Happy? Sad? Upset? Angry?

Slowly the pieces of the GBI's investigation began to emerge and come into focus for the Bateses. The GBI's questions, in turn, gave the family answers. The agents didn't need to say anything more.

"They handed the bad news out in bites you could handle," Robert recalled. He appreciated that immensely. This wasn't a movie of the week. No knock on the door by two state troopers with their hats in their hands and a mouthful of heartbreak. This was a process. A slow dance toward what was looking to be an inevitable truth the family was going to have to contend with, one way or another.

Knowing how distraught and upset Philip and Joan were, the agent called Robert outside. It was there, out of the earshot of Joan and Philip, that she explained how they had uncovered two bodies in the trunk of Alan's rental car. She wanted to let Robert know that they needed Alan's dental records.

Robert's stomach turned over when she asked. He knew, then and there, his brother was dead. He didn't need DNA or dental confirmation. Instinct grabbed hold of his throat, put a lump in it. The only silver lining—if it could even be called such—in the middle of this devastating news was that there had been only two bodies found in the car.

Not four.

That meant the kids were not with them.

The agent wanted to let Robert know first, before breaking the news to Philip and Joan. It wasn't corroboration that Alan and Terra were dead, of course—that's not what the GBI was implying here. The investigator said she'd seen more bizarre things happen in her career. But there was a good chance it was their bodies. The dentals records would answer a lot of questions.

"How do you think I should deliver this to them?" the agent asked Robert, meaning Philip and Joan.

"Dad likes to deal in facts. Give him the facts—however you choose to—and he'll manage."

As the morning carried on, bits of information came into focus. As they spoke, first the GBI let out that they had uncovered bodies in the trunk of Alan's rental; a while later, it became a car fire; then, "Can we have those dental records?"

One plus one plus one equals three. Every time. Kevin and Robert knew it. The slow walk toward the bitter, sad truth: Alan and his wife were dead.

Murdered.

The agent also mentioned that the GBI had investigators heading into Birmingham.

Kevin and Robert looked at each other. *Birmingham?*

"We may have another crime scene over there."

Philip came by. He seemed to be listening. "Alan was in Birmingham," he said, "giving a deposition in his child custody case."

That was important.

After a bit more going back and forth, some history of what was going on with Alan and Jessica, where Alan might have taken off to if he decided not to pick up the children, the GBI had what it needed and got ready to leave.

"We'll be calling you with updates, okay?" the agent promised.

Philip nodded his head. "Thank you."

What was left for the Bates family to do now? Especially because in their hearts they knew, deep down, that Alan and Terra were dead. This new dose of anxiety came in the form of an explanation as to what had happened, who had killed them.

Kevin and Robert went into autopilot, comfort mode, without even thinking about it. Stay busy. Do things. Make calls. Get Terra's family involved. Get family members over to the house so they could begin to put a support system in place for what they knew were going to be the roughest days of their lives ahead. Someone would have to tell the kids. Someone would have to sit them down and explain that their father and stepmother were gone. In fact, as Robert and Kevin and Philip thought about it, where were the kids?

9

Kimberly Williams and Sheron Vance made it to the PPD by 2:00 P.M. Of course, they had gained an hour as they passed over the invisible line of the Central time zone.

They waited around. Had some coffee. Explained the situation. "We talked to the chief and a couple [Pelham] investigators about Mr. McCord," Williams told me.

Through that, one thing became clear: Jeff McCord was not your typical cop. He had never been part of the blue crowd.

"They told us he was a loner. Strange person. Kept to himself." Not your traditional blue blood. Jeff was that guy who didn't say a lot but always seemed to have something heavy on his mind. We all know someone like this.

By 2:45 P.M., Jeff McCord arrived to clock in for his shift.

"His superiors told him to come in and talk to Miss Williams," someone close to the case later said. "There's a . . . question about whether or not it was voluntary."

Primarily, Williams and Vance wanted to create some sort of timeline for Alan and Terra, and find out what piece of the puzzle Jeff McCord could bring to the table. Simple stuff. Common questions Jeff had probably asked suspects himself as a police officer. There wasn't going to be any dark room, a chair in the middle of the floor, lights in his face. Just three cops talking. Getting to the truth.

At least for the time being.

Immediately Jeff came across as standoffish and aloof. He had an attitude about him that said, *You got a lot of nerve questioning me!* Kind of odd for a fellow cop to be so cagey and unhelpful. Then again, Williams understood, she didn't know the guy. She had nothing to base her judgment on. Maybe this was Jeff's general demeanor? The way he acted around everyone.

"You always want to try and build a rapport first with a witness," Williams explained in her clear Southern accent. "This way you can tell how he answers questions."

With Jeff, that was not going to be easy; he did not want to talk.

Jeff was concerned about speaking with two investigators from another state regarding a case that they did not want to divulge any information about. Jeff asked Williams why she needed the information, and Williams danced around that issue. She wasn't about to show her cards. Both Williams and Vance weren't saying much more than how they were looking for Alan and Terra Bates. On top of that, Jeff had been up most of the night with his wife. He was playing on a short fuse. He'd slept for a few hours that afternoon, but for the most part, he hadn't slept in the past two days.

Jeff's chief pulled him aside, according to what Williams later said. "You're under no obligation to talk to these investigators," the chief told his officer. Yet, there was something in the chief's voice, a look, letting Jeff know in not so many words that it might be in his best interest to tell them what they needed to know.

"I understand," Jeff said.

As the interview went forward, the tone remained informal. Very brief, too. Williams asked Jeff where the kids spent the previous night.

"The kids, oh," Jeff said as though he'd had a memory lapse, "I supervised them packing for the weekend. They were supposed to be picked up by Alan at six. When Alan failed to show up, we dropped them off at their grandparents [Dian and Albert Bailey, Jessica's mother and stepfather], somewhere near six forty-five." Dian and Albert lived on Whiting Road in Hoover, Jeff explained, about a half mile from the McCords' house on Myrtlewood. The drive took minutes.

Williams nodded and wrote that down. *6:45*.

They stood inside the same interview room the Pelham police used to interrogate suspects and witnesses. Jeff sat. He had his uniform on. His weapon holstered. He kept looking at his watch. He needed to get ready for his shift.

Williams asked where Jessica was at the moment.

"Her mother's house."

"What was supposed to happen yesterday?" Williams wanted to know. She asked Jeff for the day's schedule. What was the McCord plan and how had they carried it out?

Jeff shrugged. Didn't want to respond to that.

"Did the Bateses show up for the depositions?"

"Yeah," Jeff answered freely. "They did." But Jeff wasn't there. He said he was at home with the kids.

"Did you personally have any contact with them afterward?"

"Nope."

Jeff wasn't going to say much more than yes or no. He was either obviously hiding something or this was the way he reacted to questions from anyone. Williams and Vance had nothing to compare his reactions to. They had just met him. And the guy was easy not to like right from the start, Williams said. "We wanted to know about these depositions—what happened before, after, and so on," she explained later. "What he knew about them being in Alabama. What he knew about where they went, and what the plan was for them to pick up the children."

But Jeff McCord kept "talking in circles," Williams said.

"Just tell us, then," Williams stated at one point during the interview, now a bit frustrated and impatient with this fellow cop, "what *you* did, Officer McCord? What did *you* do yesterday since the time you got up? Talk us through your day until right now."

For Vance and Williams, they got the idea Jeff was being uncooperative. "We had no idea if this was the way he was or [if] he was actually hiding something. We had no idea how he processed things, or how to gauge when to be alerted about something. He was just very . . . very quiet."

Jeff's posture told another story—and this was something Williams studied furtively, intuitively. It stood out after a time. Jeff appeared defensive in his movements, especially the way he reacted to questions—which is something else entirely. A suspect cannot camouflage how his body reacts to questions put in front of him, no matter how hard he tries. It's instinct. All people do certain things with their hands, legs, maybe a crinkle of the brow, an eyebrow lift, a rub of the nose. Makes no difference how hard a suspect might try to conceal his actions and movements. His ticks. Cops just need to figure these out and they can give a lie detector test on the spot without a person even realizing it's going on.

"It was like pulling teeth," Williams said, "getting information"—even basic stuff—"out of him, and then when he decided to talk, he ran us in circles."

Did Jeff know this trick, too?

As the interview carried forth, Jeff rattled on and

on and seemed to be talking about nothing. So Williams interrupted him. "What point is it that you're trying to make, Officer McCord?"

Jeff lifted his shoulders and dropped them back down. Did he even know?

What is going on with this guy? Williams thought at that moment. "It was beginning to concern us, just because he was so matter-of-fact at times and jabbering at others."

Up and down.

This turned out to be another red flag. The fact that the guy was all over the place was cause for concern. He was apparently hiding something.

"What did you and your wife do last night?" Williams asked, breaking it down into bites. She decided to start back at the beginning.

Jeff went into a long "spiel, this convoluted" story, Williams explained, about what they had done.

"We saw *Lord of the Rings,*" he began. "Then snuck into *Black Hawk Down.* We went for a river walk and drove around. . . . Oh yeah, and . . . well . . . Jessica wanted to go to a strip club, so we went."

"Okay . . ."

Strip club?

"Well, look," Jeff said, reaching into his back pocket, pulling out his wallet, "I have the movie stubs."

How convenient, Williams thought. Time- and date-stamped movie stubs.

The GBI had already contacted the HPD and had gotten them involved. By now, both agencies had positive confirmation that the bodies were Alan and Terra Bates's. They had been murdered. As originally thought, they were dead before being stuffed into the trunk of Alan's rental car.

Once the GBI knew Alan and Terra were supposed to pick up the children at the McCord house the previous evening, they decided to put a surveillance on Jeff and Jessica's house. Philip and Joan Bates mentioned there was some animosity between the two families, and Jessica hated her ex-husband and was fighting him for custody of the children. Standing in front of Jeff McCord, questioning him regarding his whereabouts the previous night, Williams and Vance knew a good portion of this corrosive history. And now they had Jeff handing over—he just *happened* to have them on him—movie stubs. At best, it all seemed so staged. At worst, Jeff was just a numbskull and didn't really understand the ramifications of his highly suspicious actions.

"Can we see those stubs, Officer McCord?"

"Sure," Jeff said happily.

Jeff produced what Williams described as "two pristine movie stubs" from the Carmike Cinema on Lorna Road, in Birmingham. He took them out of his wallet. The date on the stubs was, sure enough, February 15, the previous night, 6:57 P.M.

How 'bout that.

Williams and Vance looked at each other. "This was a definite red flag," Williams told me later. "Generally, people leave movie stubs in their coat pocket, pants pocket . . . and here are these two pristine—in case I needed them, apparently—stubs."

"You cannot keep those," Jeff said. Then, with an overconfident smugness, "But you can go ahead and make a copy of them."

Why doesn't this guy want to help? Williams pondered.

Okay, so they had gone to the movies. "A night out," as Jeff put it. And he and Jessica were, in fact, gone until the break of dawn. That much could be proven. They had driven over to the Home Depot in Birmingham first thing in the morning, 6:00 A.M., to pick up materials to begin several long-overdue remodeling projects. Yet, they walked out of the Home Depot with basically nothing.

On the face of it, Williams and Vance considered, it sounded like, well, a story.

A carefully crafted alibi.

"The thing is," Williams said, "the truth doesn't change. It is what it is. No matter how you remember it, the truth does not change."

After they concluded the interview, Jeff took off to another part of the station house, one would imagine, as far away from Vance and Williams as he could get inside the same building. Williams and Vance went in to see Jeff's chief. They needed a few favors.

"Keep him here for his shift, could you?"

"Sure," the chief said.

"Yeah, we want to keep him off the road."

"No problem."

"Listen," Williams said, "if his wife calls, don't let him speak with her." The last thing they wanted was for Jeff and Jessica to talk. If they were hiding something, Jeff would spill what he had just talked about and they would have a chance to get together with their stories. The GBI wanted to speak with Jessica before she got a chance to speak with Jeff again.

Leaving the Pelham Police Department, Williams and Vance got hold of detective sergeant Tom McDanal from the Hoover PD. HPD was busy conducting surveillance at the McCord home, and from another room, several detectives monitored the interview with Jeff at the Pelham PD. Williams wanted to know if McDanal could go with her and Vance over to Dian Bailey's house on Whiting Road. They wanted to speak with Jessica McCord immediately, but at this point the GBI wasn't sure whose case this was going to turn out to be. On top of that, it would only help if a representative from the corresponding agency investigating the case was there.

McDanal said sure.

Now there were three different law enforcement agencies investigating the deaths of Alan and Terra.

Heading over to Dian Bailey's home, Williams and Vance received reports from the Pelham PD that Jessica was, as they had suspected, calling the station already— "repeatedly"—and asking to speak with Jeff.

But no one allowed it.

10

Williams and Vance made a detour. They stopped at the McCords' Myrtlewood Drive home to see what was going on before heading over to Dian and Albert Bailey's. The HPD informed both investigators that there was an older gentleman inside the McCord house. His van was pulled up to the back door. It appeared he was working on the house. Taking things out. Bringing things in. At this point anybody even remotely connected to Terra and Alan could know something. But inside the McCords' house—that was different. What was this guy doing?

Williams and Vance knocked on the front door. That sign—telling visitors to go around to the back—was still there.

With no response, they walked around. The man came out. "Can I help you?" He had a surprised look about him.

They identified themselves and asked what he was doing in the house.

"I'm Albert Bailey," he said. "I'm just doing some work on the house."

"You see Jessica around?" Vance asked.

"No . . . I don't know where she is. I think she might have gone over to the Home Depot."

They knew where Jessica was.

"Thanks," Williams said.

Then they left.

A twenty-nine-year law enforcement veteran, HPD detective sergeant Rod Glover was in charge of the surveillance at Jessica and Jeff McCord's house on Myrtlewood Drive. He heard that Vance and Williams had gone over to the McCord house and had spoken to Albert Bailey. But they had left to visit Jessica's mother, just blocks away.

The investigation of two missing adults had now spread out to include two different states, several towns, and various law enforcement agencies. It was midafternoon on February 16, 2002, a bright and cold Saturday in the middle of the most miserable month of the year. Williams and Vance were headed over to the Bailey residence. Glover, who was traveling down Lorna Road, was getting ready to make a left onto Chapel Hill and connect with Myrtlewood. As he did, Glover took a call from Chris Bryant, an officer stationed near the McCord home. Bryant was watching the house, waiting for Glover to arrive. It was Bryant who spotted Jeff McCord, hours earlier, leaving the house on his way to work, alerting the GBI and Pelham PD.

"We got a white van," Bryant said over the radio, "on the move, leaving the location."

Albert Bailey.

The white van pulled out of the driveway as Bryant spoke. Bryant got a read on the plate and called it in.

"Ten-four."

The van was headed toward Rod Glover. He had since

stopped on Lorna Road to wait for Bailey's arrival so he could pick up the tail.

Bryant sat in his car, down the block from the McCord house. Leaving, Albert Bailey didn't suspect a thing. Why should he? He had no idea, in fact, he was being watched and now followed.

Glover got behind the van. From Lorna Road—a four-lane, heavily traveled commercial route—the van made its way onto Highway 31, northbound. Then turned off and onto Southland Drive, traveling out of the city of Hoover and into Homewood, a neighboring town. From there, Albert Bailey headed toward Oxmoor Road, near the Birmingham town line, and made his way into a thickly settled industrial area, where Coca-Cola, Budweiser and several other large corporations had local warehouses and plants.

Where was this guy going?

Past a United Parcel Service (UPS) plant, Glover watched the van pull back onto Lorna Road and into the parking lot of Uncle Bob's Self-Storage. Albert Bailey was either picking something up or dropping something off. Either way, Glover knew, it would be smart to continue following him. By this point HPD had called the Birmingham Police Department (BPD) and Homewood Police Department, inviting both agencies into the tail. Depending on which town Bailey was eventually pulled over in, there would need to be officers from that town on site.

The van pulled out of Uncle Bob's parking lot a few minutes later and Glover followed.

Albert Bailey drove around the area, in and out of several businesses, before entering a warehouse parking lot. A minute later, he found his way back onto the main road, where he cut over to Green Springs Highway and proceeded into the town of Birmingham.

Glover lost sight of the van at various intervals, but
never entirely.

Following once again behind the van, now heading
down Oxmoor Road for a second time (now near a
strip mall), Bailey put on his blinker and moved into
the left lane to turn into the parking lot.

Birmingham and Homewood patrol cars following
Albert Bailey hit their lights and made the stop.

Glover pulled up behind the van and got out of his car.

He walked to the back of the vehicle and took a
quick look inside.

A couch?

Indeed. Bailey had one of the McCords' couches
(from the family room downstairs) inside his messy van.
The padding on the back support of the couch was
stripped clean, leaving the framework of it exposed.

The cushions were gone, too.

But why?

Glover walked over to the driver's-side door of the
van and had a few words with Albert Bailey. Then he got
back into his unmarked police vehicle and drove away.

Officer Glover told Bailey he was free to go.

11

The Baileys' modest-sized ranch house in Hoover stood on a corner lot, almost hugging an adjacent road. Toward the backyard there were several lots from a major industrial area of the city, completely congested with traffic and people. The neighborhood was middle-class. Modern, normal families locked in the bliss of enjoying their little slice of the American pie.

When GBI investigator Kimberly Williams and MCSO investigator Sheron Vance arrived, HPD sergeant Tom McDanal led the way to the front door. McDanal indicated he would knock. It was better this way. A local cop. As it was, the two dead bodies (DBs) in the trunk of Alan's rental were quickly (and clearly) looking to be the Hoover PD's case. The GBI and MCSO, Williams and Vance knew, were going to be supporting Hoover, but Hoover was about to take control of this investigation.

Dian Bailey answered the door; then she walked outside, closing it behind her, as if not wanting to disturb someone on the other side of the door.

"We're looking for Jessica McCord, ma'am," McDanal said. Williams and Vance stood in back of him.

"I'll get her." Dian walked back inside. It was clear she didn't want to be followed.

Jessica walked out the front door and toward the driveway. Dian followed her daughter. The three investigators behind them.

"Can we go inside and talk, ma'am?" Williams asked cordially. The Southern thing to do was to invite people into your home, not keep them outside during the winter. What was she so concerned about? Why the driveway?

Jessica snapped: "No!" She looked tired, pale. Her eyes were sunken. Her brown hair was knotty and unkempt. She wore glasses. She came across "extremely defensive," Williams said. They knew Jessica had probably been up all night. So she had every reason to be tired and, well, bitchy. The kids were inside the house. Perhaps she didn't want them to hear what was going to be said.

That would be logical.

Dian looked edgy, nervous. "You stay here," Jessica told her mother. "Don't go back inside." They stood in the driveway, yards away from the front porch. Dian was in back of her bossy daughter.

Dian had her arms folded in front of her chest. She was there, Williams guessed, for support. As they all stood together, there was this feeling that both knew, or had been expecting, the GBI and HPD would show up.

"What do you want?" Jessica asked sharply. She looked at Vance, then at Williams, bypassing McDanal.

Williams stepped forward, introduced herself and Vance. Then: "Can we ask you a few questions about Alan and Terra Bates?"

"She was short with us," Williams recalled. "Which we took as odd, simply because we're coming to ask about overdue people, specifically the father of her children."

Jessica snapped, "Why?" She didn't seem to understand

what the investigators meant. Was there a problem? Two children walked out the door. They stood near their mother, looking curiously up at the investigators.

"They're considered missing, ma'am . . . and we want to collect some information to help us in our investigation." Williams didn't feel right talking about this in front of the kids. Didn't Jessica care what the children heard?

"Oh," Jessica said. She seemed stressed by this revelation.

"Would you like to go somewhere else to talk?" Williams asked. She and Vance figured with the kids wandering around, they didn't want to burden anybody or make the kids or Jessica feel uncomfortable.

"No," Jessica said quickly. "This is fine."

"We were wondering about Alan and Terra—" Williams started to say.

Jessica interrupted. "They never showed up!" She sounded bitter and frustrated by the idea that it appeared Alan blew the kids off—and had never even called or given her an explanation why.

Williams asked Jessica where she was the previous night. She didn't phrase it with an accusatory tone. It was more of a casual question.

Jessica explained: dinner, movies, that walk with her husband. As she spoke, Williams thought how identical her story was to what Jeff had said earlier. But then, well, there came a point when Jessica made a mistake, or had a lapse in memory.

"We even came back here, near midnight, to pick up the kids," Jessica said, "but ended up letting them sleep over because they were already in bed sleeping when we arrived."

Jeff never mentioned this fact. He didn't say anything about stopping by Jessica's mother's house. It seemed to be an important part of the night. A pivotal point on which every moment after was able to happen. If they had the kids all night, they certainly could not have been out on the town until the wee hours of the morning. But Jeff had never said anything about this.

Williams and Vance put up their radar.

Vance watched Dian as Jessica explained how she and Jeff stopped by the house. Dian didn't see the investigator looking at her. Dian rolled her eyes when Jessica mentioned that she and Jeff came to the house near midnight. She had this *I can't believe she just said that* look about her, the investigator explained later. Dian actually cringed at what her daughter had just told three investigators.

Williams saw a door. "Did you take the children over here?"

"Yes."

"When?"

"Near five-thirty," Jessica said. "Alan was supposed to pick them up over at my mother's house."

"Did Alan ever make it into your house at all?"

"No! Alan is not *allowed* in my home. He has *never* been in my home. He's been there on one occasion to pick up the kids, only because I was directed to allow him by the court and my attorney." Jessica was firm on this point. She seemed to suggest that this was why they dropped the kids off at her mother's house— because Alan was not allowed at her house.

These answers struck Williams and Vance. Jeff McCord had said something entirely different. One hour and fifteen minutes different, to be exact. And the location of the pickup: Jeff was certain Alan was supposed to pick the kids up at the McCord home. How could they not know (or confuse) these two simple facts?

"Although they were close," Williams explained later, referring to how Jeff and Jessica responded to the same questions, "it shouldn't be difficult to remember where the kids were, what time, and all that." It had not even been twenty-four hours since the events had taken place. Why were two adults having such a hard time recalling detailed, straightforward facts that—on the surface—seemed so unimportant?

As part of their investigation, all Williams and Vance looked to do at this stage was lock people down to stories. Step back and take a look at any inconsistencies, if there were any, and see where each witness statement led. After all, Albert Bailey had been over at the Myrtlewood Drive home doing some remodeling. From there he was followed while driving around town with a couch taken from the McCord house. What was Albert's involvement in all this? What role did that couch play? Perhaps they needed to talk to Albert again? From the tone Jessica used, it was not hard to tell she was just about finished talking.

"Would it be okay if we searched your house on Myrtlewood Drive?" Williams asked, looking directly at Jessica.

"Absolutely not!" Jessica snapped.

Whoa.

With that sharp, direct answer, Williams explained why it was important to search the home. Exclusion was key. They needed to rule out people and scenarios so they could find out what had happened. Move on. Every little step would lead to finding what had happened to the father of her children.

"Look, this is what we've found." Williams decided to explain the scene back in Morgan County, Georgia, to Jessica. See what type of reaction she would give them.

"We think that it's Alan and Terra. But we're not sure yet."

"What do you mean?" Jessica asked. She was calmer now. Curious.

"Well," Williams said, "they cannot be identified."

At that, Jessica lost it. Her body dropped dramatically to the ground and she started bawling. She was hysterical—overly so, it appeared to Williams and Vance, who looked at each other as Jessica went into a crying fit. It was not a stretch to think that Jessica McCord could use a few acting lessons if this was the best performance she had in her.

Williams helped Jessica up off the ground. Then she made it clear that Jessica was the proverbial ex-wife in this unfolding drama. Having been given that status alone made her a suspect. They were checking things off their list. Simple 101 police work. They did it in every investigation. Procedure. 1-2-3. The basics. By searching the house, the Bureau could eliminate Jessica from its list of suspects and continue investigating. She would be helping them out immensely.

"Absolutely not," Jessica said again in a harsher tone after collecting herself and standing up. "You're not going in my house to search it."

Was she protecting her husband? Perhaps she believed that Jeff had been involved on his own and wanted to talk to him, get the story, before helping the cops?

"We just want to eliminate you as a suspect, Mrs. McCord. We need your cooperation. Your consent to search the house."

"The police are *not* going into my house." Jessica was very firm. No damn way any police officer was going to step into her home and poke around.

"Okay," Williams said.

Then, as the conversation seemed to reach an impasse, out of the blue, Jessica made a suggestion, which was rather odd.

"You should be going to Montevallo to search a house there."

"Montevallo?"

"I'd be happy to take you there," Jessica offered. "You know, show you the way."

So they all drove to Alan and Jessica's old house in Montevallo.

They found nothing, of course. It was a wasted trip in that sense. Leaving, Williams and Vance talked about the interview with Jessica back in Hoover, and how things had progressed from there.

"Did you see Mom when Jessica said she dropped the kids off at her house at midnight the previous night?" Vance pointed out.

"No, I was fixed on Jessica and her reactions. Why?"

Vance smiled. "Oh . . . well, there's no such thing happening that they went over there at midnight."

"Huh?"

"She was totally—you could tell by the look on her face," Vance said, describing Dian's demeanor, "rolling her eyes, like feeling, 'I can't believe you just said that.'"

Vance—and now Williams—were convinced Dian Bailey had things to hide.

When they had arrived in Montevallo, Williams asked Jessica, "Can you please clarify for us why you would allow us to search a place that Alan had been before, but not your house?"

This was something law enforcement couldn't understand. It actually made no sense.

"Because Alan has never been in my house. Sorry we don't see eye to eye on this."

This comment gave Williams a chill.

What a strange way to view things. What was Jessica so concerned about? Why wouldn't she jump at the opportunity to help find out what was going on with the murder of her children's father? What if her husband had killed them without her knowledge? There were so many variables possible. Jessica wasn't fazed, apparently, by any one of these—the least of which included finding out what had happened.

This, and that little one-act play of anguish she put on in the driveway, was an indication that the Bureau and the HPD were not done with Jessica McCord just yet.

12

In Marietta, members of the Bates family huddled together with friends and neighbors, holding vigil, waiting—and hoping—on the information as it came in piecemeal from the Bureau. As they talked things through, more questions than answers arose. And when they did, all fingers pointed at one person: Jessica McCord. She'd had something to do with Alan's disappearance, members of the Bates family felt strongly.

"Look," Kevin said, Robert nodding in agreement, "we knew where Alan and Terra had been, we had even made contact with Alan's attorney by that point, and we knew that the last place they were supposed to go was to Jessica's house—and no one had heard from them since."

Speculation. Doubt. Confusion. Empty spaces. Sure, you filled in the voids best you could, looking for any way to avoid the inevitable. But the end result seemed to be the same, no matter how you added things up. The mind colors in the blank spaces, creating its own finale. Yet, the available established facts of the case tell a story. If you played devil's advocate, the obvious questions would be: If not Jessica, who else? Was she involved? If so, had Jessica worked alone? Had she, prompting Jeff, sought out any additional help? Truth be told, the Bateses had not spoken to Alan the previous night. Robert's wife spoke to Terra earlier that afternoon. Terra said the deposition was going well, adding, "We're picking up the kids at Jessica's around six o'clock."

Terra's father, Tom Klugh, said he tried to call Terra that evening, after six, but he did not get an answer.

That was the dead space. The invisible moment.

And so between 3:30 and 6:00 P.M., family members figured, an answer resided. Inside that missing time. What happened took place during that window. If Jessica and Jeff could account for their whereabouts, how could they be involved?

Questions without answers. For a grieving family aware of the volatile history between Alan and Jessica, it was frustrating, upsetting and debilitating.

Terra's parents drove into Marietta. The Bates home became ground zero—an epicenter of mourning and uncertainty.

Things moved fast. Philip was able to get his brother in Birmingham—Uncle Randy, the kids called him—to pick up Alan's dental records. Then everyone turned their attention toward the children: where were they?

Philip called family members and friends. He needed to find the girls. Speak to them. Hear their familiar voices. Know they were okay. If Jessica and Jeff were involved, had the kids seen anything? Were they with Alan and Terra? Did they know what had happened?

On Saturday night, two additional Bureau agents rolled into Birmingham to assist Williams and Vance. They were there to help conduct interviews and build a case for a search warrant. It was clear that Alan and Terra left Birmingham somewhere near 4:30 P.M., which the Bureau confirmed by a videotape of them walking out of a local hot dog joint near Jessica's attorney's office. The restaurant just happened to be across the street from the Alabama Theater. Alan and Terra and every one of their friends from the theater knew the owner. It was a staple in town, a favorite place for friends to get together.

Then word came from the crime scene in Georgia that the bullet recovered inside the trunk of the rental was a .44 caliber. The battery in Alan's wristwatch—now a key factor in the case—stopped the bullet as it passed through Alan's wrist. He could have been holding up his hands, trying to defend himself, at the time he was shot.

Finding that bullet was a major break.

Great news for the Bureau and HPD. Now all they needed to do was find a matching weapon to the bullet, or some other piece of evidence tying that bullet to a suspect—a glass slipper, essentially.

Late Saturday night, February 16, HPD detective Laura Brignac was at a local Hoover bowling alley, enjoying a night out with her sister and a friend. It wasn't Brignac's weekend to be "on call." Detectives in her unit shared the responsibility. Brignac was off that weekend, out having some good old-fashioned fun.

She should have known better. Near midnight Brignac's cell phone rang. It was her husband.

"Tom's trying to get hold of y'all. He wants you to call him."

Brignac's husband was referring to her boss, HPD detective sergeant Tom McDanal, who was running the Hoover end of the Bates case. The HPD still wasn't sure whose case it was going to end up being. If the Bateses were murdered at that Georgia crime scene where their bodies were uncovered, it was the Bureau's. That detail had not been uncovered, as of yet.

Brignac called McDanal. Soft-spoken and cordial, she asked, "Yeah, Tom, what's going on?"

"Can y'all be at the office at eight tomorrow morning?"

A Sunday? Brignac hadn't heard anything about a case big enough to drag her into the office on a Sunday. She had no idea what the HPD had been involved with over the past twenty-four hours. But the HPD could certainly use her, seeing that Brignac had years of experience dealing with abused children and juveniles. Ultimately the McCord children would need to be questioned—and Laura Brignac was, unquestionably, the best cop for that job.

"What'a y'all got, Tom?"

"I would rather not get into that now," McDanal said. "Just be there at eight. I'll explain everything."

PART II

RED BOOTS AND WATER

13

A fine middle-class community of hardworking, good-natured people, Cahaba Heights, Alabama, is located in Jefferson County, inside the confines of the Birmingham-Hoover metropolitan area. Birmingham was one of several central locales during the Civil Rights movement of the 1950s and 1960s, led by the late American hero Dr. Martin Luther King. In fact, at one time, early in the movement, Birmingham was called "Bombingham," being the violent stage for eighteen unsolved bombings in black neighborhoods over a six-year period. This, mind you, on top of what became known as the "vicious mob attack," which was centered on the Freedom Riders on Mother's Day, 1961. There is a long history of violence in Birmingham; but also, perhaps more relevant to the peace Dr. King inspired, there is an air of redemption and civil obedience, there inside the internal framework of the community. Wrongs being righted. People being treated as the human beings they are, regardless of the color of their skin.

The Cahaba Heights section of Birmingham is just about in the middle of the state. The name was born from a Native American settlement originally located in the southeastern United States, the Choctaw ("water above"). Cahaba Heights has always been small-town. In the year 2000, there were some five thousand people living in this particular section of Birmingham, a metropolis with a population (including its suburbs) consisting of 1,079,089 people, making Birmingham the largest city in the state. Many of the people are assiduous, churchgoing, true-to-heart Southerners, living out the honorable moral virtues instilled in them by their ancestors. Cahaba has an ideal relation to the city, set on a perfectly placed cross section of Interstate 459 and Route 38.

Shades Valley High School has been part of Irondale's landscape, on Old Leeds Road, since 1996. Irondale is another fine Birmingham suburb that built itself up into a community of fun-loving, caring, pious people. One of its most famous residents is actress-turned-author Fannie Flagg, who brought fame to the town of just under ten thousand via her *Fried Green Tomatoes at the Whistle Stop Café* novel and a later Hollywood film version, starring Kathy Bates, Mary Stuart Masterson and Mary-Louise Parker.

Comparatively speaking, Shades Valley has a reputation among students and parents as being one of the best schools in the region, if not the state. Of course, this is an open-ended argument, rooted in the deep feelings locals in the South have for their high-school football and basketball teams. Yet, maybe a little bit of God's grace and goodness seeps into the pores of the people in Irondale, no matter what their take on reglion or spirituality is. The most recent Shades Valley location on Old Leeds Road is a literal neighbor to Mother Angelica's successful Catholic-based Eternal Word Television Network (EWTN) studios, where Catholic programming is aired worldwide to upward of 160 million households, twenty-four hours a day.

Alan Bates grew up as the middle child in a household of three boys. Alan and his brother Robert both attended Shades Valley when it was located in Homewood, just off Route 31, near the Birmingham Botanical Gardens. Alan excelled in high school. He was one of those kids every mother prayed their daughter would drag in through the door one day after school and announce as her boyfriend. Alan took Southern hospitality to new heights, learning all he conveyed from two fine and loving parents. Alan was an honor student. He was voted class president three years running, beginning his freshman year, in the tenth grade. (Shades Valley ran things differently than most schools. Junior high was seventh grade through ninth; high school tenth through twelfth.) Not only was Alan an active member of his church and his family, a God-fearing unit of reverent Christians, but Alan played drums in various bands, including gospel and Christian.

"[Alan] picked up an interest along the way," his father, Philip, later said, "in technical theater and was responsible for . . . his senior class having a stage production at Shades Valley, which they hadn't in years. But he was interested in the lights and the sound and the set design and the behind-the-scenes things that make a theater production go. He wasn't interested in the drama. But he loved that!"

Alan loved the theater so much, it wasn't uncommon for friends to stop by the Shades Valley auditorium during lunch hour and find Alan sitting there, eating, relishing the feel and smell of just being around the stage. One such friend, Marley Franklin (pseudonym), who had known Alan and the Bates boys since they were all in diapers, often sat and ate with her buddy.

"Alan and I," Marley said later, "were raised like brother and sister. He loved the theater, even then, in high school. He just felt so at home there."

It was during the summer break of 1988, Alan heading from his junior to senior year, that he met Jessica Callis, a local Hoover girl. Jessica was every bit the polar opposite of Alan. On paper they should not have clicked. However, they seemed to get along and shared several things in common (what, exactly, no one really could pinpoint, even years later). Jessica grew up the oldest of three children in what was a broken home, over in the Whiting Road section of Hoover. According to Jessica years later, violence was one way to solve problems in the Callis household. Sure, the family sought solace in God's word on Sundays in the form of the Edgewood Presbyterian Church on Oxmoor Road in Birmingham. But it was obvious the values preached from the pulpit by Pastor Sid Burgess must have gone in one ear and out the other of big daddy George Callis. There were beatings, Jessica later claimed, on top of openhanded slaps that left red marks and bruises; a week hardly went by without her parents getting into some sort of heated confrontation that ended in her mother crying, her dad taking off to go get drunker than he was already.

Jessica was a third-generation Edgewood Presbyterian churchgoer (though she rarely attended services as she grew older); her grandmother was a member of the church for some sixty years. "One of the saints of God's Kingdom," Pastor Burgess said of Jessica's grandpappy in one of his 2002 sermons. Jessica's mother, Dian, was the church treasurer at one time. Dian's second husband, Albert Bailey, was "an active elder" on the council of the church. It was inside Edgewood that Jessica was baptized and given the Christian name Jessica Inez, after her grandmother—a name Jessica would use for the rest of her life whenever asked.

The church—or religion, in general—was one of the fundamental differences Alan and Jessica shared. As Jessica later put it, "Alan was brought up in the Church of Christ, which is not my, I mean, it's Christian but, you know, the basic tenets are different than mine." Edgewood was more of a "liberal church," she said. "And the whole theory, different views on how girls should be treated, especially within the confines of the church. And I disagreed vehemently with [Alan's] family on that. . . ."

And so it would seem, at least in the realm of school-girl crushes and teen romances, that as "an item," Alan and Jessica would have not made a good match. Still, all that piety and good living was the social, public side of life Jessica led as a child. Living inside her home—keep in mind, this is according to Jessica herself—was a bit like stepping down into the fires of hell every day. And in that sense, unbeknownst to either of them, Alan and Jessica were like two magnets trying to stick together. Kids from vastly different up-bringings, with vastly different values and vastly different views of life, trying to come together.

A positive and a negative.

Sparks.

Nevertheless, Alan saw something in the young, auburn-haired girl with the cute smile, pudgy cheeks and boisterous, look-at-me disposition. Jessica was no knockout, like the more popular girls in school Alan could have snapped a finger and took out, but she had something. Maybe a twinkle in her eye Alan was attracted to. A flare for life. A subtle vulnerability. Perhaps a calming voice that made him feel at the same time both comfortable and defenseless.

Whatever it was, Alan liked the package.

Marley Franklin, who was hanging around with Alan every day during that period when he met Jessica, later said, "Jessica hated my guts."

As soon as she transferred to Shades Valley, Jessica made sure that people noticed her. Jessica did have a subtle beauty about her in high school; she stood out. Still, she craved and almost demanded attention.

"She latched onto Alan pretty quick, pretty hard and heavy," one old friend said. "She loved the fact that [Alan] was a 'band guy.'"

As Jessica and Alan became closer, Jessica pulled Alan aside one day and told him, "You stop hanging out with [Marley]. You *never* speak to her again."

It was about control. Jessica was stepping in and taking charge of Alan's life.

Marley got an uneasy vibe from Jessica and felt she and Alan were headed for trouble. Still, to Marley, Alan could make his own choices; he was a brother, not a lover. Marley wanted nothing to do with him romantically, or "in that way." Then again, it was unnerving for her that this new girl in Alan's life was telling him what people he could and could not hang out with.

"I got a really bad read of her," Marley said. "I mean, everybody that knew her got a bad read of Jessica. You could just tell she carried with her a negative energy."

It was like a cloud, former friends said. An aura about Jessica.

Perhaps Jessica fed a wild side of Alan that he rarely ever allowed to come out. She was aggressive. She was "different." Heck, Jessica was more than willing to put out.

"She was *fun*," said a former high-school classmate, "you know, and I am sure that was appealing to Alan."

14

Williams and Vance had a ring to it, maybe like *Cagney & Lacey*. The only difference being that Bureau agent Kimberly Williams and MCSO investigator Sheron Vance were focused on catching a real killer. A double murderer, in fact. Or pair of murderers. There was nothing Hollywood about any of that. Two people were dead. Two fine human beings had been shot and their bodies burned. Two families were now trying to understand what had happened. Trying to deal with this loss.

The ripple effect of murder—how it spread out so far and wide.

Forever.

Vance and Williams stayed in town on the night of February 16, 2002. They knew the answers to their questions regarding the murder of Alan and Terra Bates were most likely going to be found in and around the Birmingham region. Both had a feeling Alan and Terra never made it out of Birmingham alive. The Bureau was certain the crime scene was somewhere in town—not Georgia, which was, Williams said, clearly nothing more than a "dump site." Convincing the HPD of this was going to be a bit more complicated, Williams

and Vance considered. HPD investigators still weren't
sold on the idea that Alan and Terra were murdered
in their jurisdiction. After all, Alan and Terra could
have met their demise somewhere along the road between late Friday afternoon in downtown Birmingham
and early Saturday morning in Rutledge, Georgia.
There was over two hundred miles of roadway and
wilderness separating the two places. Anything could
have happened. And until it was clear, Williams and
Vance were sticking around to see it through.

   Contacted the previous night while bowling, HPD
detective Laura Brignac got to the station house first
thing the next morning, February 17, 2002. Detective
Tom McDanal explained to Brignac that there was a lot
to do. Interviews. Tracking down basic information.
Canvassing. Checking out cell phone records. Computers. Keeping tabs on the McCords, who seemed to be
moving from one place to another. Writing up search
warrants. Studying what type of evidence the Bureau
was processing and seeing how it fit into what the HPD
was uncovering in Alabama.
   Brignac was the perfect fit for the job. She grew up
in a town of about forty thousand, so there was that
shade of the small-town Southern belle in her demeanor; yet she understood the nuances of the big
city. She was the middle child of three girls. Brignac
had studied sociology and earned a master's in counseling and guidance from, of all places, Alan Bates's
alma mater, the University of Montevallo. Her main
focus in school, and later in life, became children and
families—troubled juveniles, specifically. Brignac
worked at various shelters with probation officers dealing with kids who ran away from home. She wanted to
help. She wanted to make a better life for kids who

never really had a chance. After college she went to work at a group home for children. Working there, Brignac became friends with one of the HPD's juvenile officers who brought kids to the home. One day the juvenile officer called Brignac to say good-bye. "I'm getting married and moving to St. Louis."

"Well, congratulations," Brignac said.

"You should go to Hoover and apply for my job," the woman suggested. She knew Brignac was the perfect fit.

That was 1985. Brignac didn't think twice about it and took the bait.

"The next thing I know," Brignac told me later, a mixture of humility and shock in her voice, "I'm being sworn in, given a badge and a gun and . . . I'm like, 'Wait a minute!'"

Brignac was fortunate in the sense that when she started on the job, she went to work for a progressive chief who just so happened to be in need of an investigator with some experience working with kids and families.

"So I am probably the only [detective] in the country who was never a patrol officer first," Brignac added. "He just put me right into investigations and the criminal unit."

Back in Georgia, inside the Division of Forensic Science morgue at Bureau headquarters in Atlanta, forensic pathologist Dr. Krzysztof Podjaski got to work on the autopsies. There was a lot riding on these examinations; the results of which could possibly provide several important answers to questions that would eventually help solve this case quickly, sparing the families a load of additional heartache and anguish.

A native of Poland, Podjaski had been in the United States for about fifteen years. He spoke English fairly well, having learned the language back home. Podjaski was well schooled in trauma surgery and orthopedics. He finished his two-year residency in Hartford, Connecticut, at Hartford Hospital. From there it was on to Atlanta, where he spent a year in forensic pathology and then joined the Bureau.

Some have a misunderstanding of the word "pathologist," bringing to it a certain Hollywood flare and connotation that we see today on crime television, vis-à-vis shows like *CSI, Law & Order* and *Bones*. Watching the television version of forensic pathology, a viewer might be inclined to think that pathologists are crime-solving wizards, or crime scene–inspecting sleuths—that one hair fiber or tooth mark can solve a case. Some think they run around town interviewing suspects and tracking down leads. But when you get inside the morgue and see what goes on, the reality is quite different: it's more tedious study and medical panache than *Star Trek*–like technology and *ah-hah* moments. Scientifically speaking, pathology is the actual study of, as Dr. Podjaski put it in court so perfectly, "bad things that happen to the human body that are of interest to law."

A careful dissemination of the facts (or clues) a dead body might reveal. The cause of death. The reason someone died.

It was so simple on the surface.

On the day Alan and Terra's severely charred ("burned to a significant degree") remains were brought in for the doctor to have a look at, he had been with the Bureau for a little over two years. Podjaski's focus was on the *cause* of death. All investigations began with a cause. The effect was gleaned from there. And so on.

Both bodies, zipped up inside black body bags, were brought in by deputy coroner Susan Simmons. By this point dental records had indeed confirmed just about 100 percent who the victims were. No surprises there:

Alan and Terra Bates. The backstory, however, one that pathologists try not to get involved with, was substantially different. Alan and Terra were a happily married couple in the prime of their lives. There was no reason for them to be dead.

And that's where a pathologist came into the situation. To unearth the why behind the tragedy.

The first thing Podjaski did was examine the outside of the bodies, or what was left, actually. He conducted what he deemed an "external examination." Multiple photographs were snapped before the doctor even put a finger on either of the victims. As needed, X-rays, especially when there was a possibility that the victim(s) had been stabbed or shot, were taken.

Podjaski wrote in his report that Alan's body exhibited *extensive charring, from head to toe, and has a pugilistic attitude with the right arm flexed at the elbow and the left hand at the wrist.*

Pugilistic attitude—or, as it is more frequently called, "pugilistic posture"—is a common occurrence found in victims of a fatal fire. What happens is that the body, as it heats up, is exhausted of most of its fluids. This loss of bodily fluids, mainly water, causes a restriction in the muscle tissue, which curls the tips of the fingers, the tips of the toes, ankles, elbows and any other place in the body where there is a moveable joint. Some say the body, when it is presented in this way, takes on a "boxer's position." The reasoning behind this observation is that the hands, wrists, elbows and knees are flexed and curled inward, due to the shrinkage of tissue. In homicide investigation this posture the body holds is sometimes mistaken for what is a "predeath attempt to shield oneself from an attacker."

Podjaski noted that Alan's right forearm was *burned away approximately 5 inches distal to the elbow. The lower extremities are contracted at the knees and ankles, with almost complete disarticulation at the knee and ankle joints.*

To look at a body that has been burned grotesquely in a fire is a ghastly reminder that the body is made up mostly of fat and muscle tissue, which burns fast and ferocious when subjected to an intense flame—much like the bristle on a steak flaring up on the grill.

"The charring of the soft tissues," the doctor said later, referring once again to Alan's body, "is most severe on the anterior portion of the face and the right side of the head."

Any exposed section of Alan's face, in other words, had been burned almost completely off.

One of Terra's extremities (arms) was partially burned, the other *totally, completely burned away,* the doctor wrote. Her *skin is completely burned away with some charred muscles and soft tissues.*

The doctor opened both bodies and removed the organs, one by one. Whenever he came across what he believed to be a wound of some sort, he used metal rods, or "probes," to figure out the trajectory any possible projectiles could have taken, pointing out a possible cause and direction for the wounds. Because the bodies were so badly burned, however, it was difficult for the doctor to figure out if he was looking at exit or entrance wounds. To find this out would take further examination.

With Terra, the doctor was certain the wounds on her back were "consistent with exit as opposed to entrance [wounds]," he said.

There was a second bullet wound, a "little bit closer to what we describe as axilla," or the armpit, directly underneath the position in the body where the arm connects to the shoulder socket.

Terra was shot, it appeared, as she lifted up her arm, probably as she instinctively defended herself. This was likely the first shot. A victim cannot necessarily put up her hands to shield herself if she has been shot anywhere else.

A third wound the doctor found was located in Terra's chest. A fourth in the "flank," or near the belly area on the side near the hip.

From the evidence available and the way in which the probes projected various trajectory patterns, it appeared to the doctor that Terra was shot four times, each hitting a different area of her body as she instinctively protected herself and fell to the ground. Terra's killer approached her with a weapon, began firing and didn't stop.

The poor woman never had a chance.

But then something odd stood out to the doctor—something quite significant. On both bodies there was an irregular, elongated area of the back side detailing a particular region of "dark discoloration." In the doctor's humble opinion, this subtle wound marking meant that the body was likely "pressed against something" when the bullet exited the body.

This was new information. Probably important, too.

"Maybe that person was sitting," the doctor explained. "I'm not sure. But there was something behind. That bullet exiting [the body] pressed the skin, and the skin hit that object and that caused [the] contusion."

The exit wounds the doctor referred to didn't have that familiar "blowout" starfish pattern of torn skin the doctor knew to be consistent with this type of exit bullet wound. Something was firmly pressed up against that area of the skin as the bullet passed through. This finding was common in the bodies of men executed by firing squad: because they were backed up to a wall and shot. The bullets had an extra layer of material to go through, allowing for the exit wound of the body to be clean.

In the end the doctor signed off on both deaths as homicide. Cause of death was determined to be *multiple gunshot wounds of the torso and upper extremity,* he penned.

So Alan and Terra were dead, as everyone assumed, before they were placed inside the trunk of Alan's rental car and it was set afire. Both were shot, seemingly execution-style, at close range, probably as they tried to defend themselves. In the doctor's final opinion, in fact, the idea that several shots were fired into each body was overkill. The fact of the matter, the doctor agreed, was that "one or two of these bullets would have been fatal in and of themselves without immediate medical attention. . . ."

Any good cop knew that overkill was another way to describe revenge or inherent, repressed anger. There was passion and vengeance behind these murders. Whoever killed Alan and Terra had a reason—no matter how vile and vicious or even insane it might seem.

15

Alan didn't run for class president his senior year. He met Jessica during the summer of 1989 and his life changed. Part of that change was a bit of rather sobering, shocking news Jessica hit Alan with, about six weeks after they met, which Alan had a hard time talking about with anyone else besides his best friend, Marley Franklin.

Alan took Marley aside one day in school and told her. "Jess is pregnant."

Marley was surprised, but not shocked. ("There's a difference," Marley observed.)

Some time went by. Marley beat herself up. She'd had a feeling something was going to happen between them. She sat talking with a mutual friend of hers and Alan's one day. "She trapped him. I should have told him before it happened. I *knew* it."

Alan heard what Marley had said. Upset about it, he called her. By this time Alan had made a decision about the pregnancy.

"Alan was such a good person," Marley said later. "He was always going to do what needed to be done."

Alan told Marley that Jessica had asked him never

to speak to her again. It was ridiculous, they both knew. But Alan was upset at what Marley had said. Maybe now was a good time to part ways, at least for a little while.

"I felt really, really bad that I hadn't sat down with him and truly told him how I felt about Jessica and the whole thing. So I said something about her that got back to him, and it hurt him and I feel really bad about that . . . but she hated me to begin with, because she didn't trust the relationship I had with Alan."

They were all so young. So immature and naïve. And here was Alan and Jessica bringing a baby into it all.

What was clear from that point on was that Jessica Callis was a girl who got what she wanted. Bates family members later agreed with this. When Jessica put her mind on something, nothing was going to stop her. It didn't matter what people said. Or did. When Jessica was determined, nothing was going to stand in her way.

And she would prove this—time and again.

"She set her sights on Alan the moment after she met him and wanted to have him, and that was it," Kevin Bates recalled.

Some saw Jessica as a person whose intentions were often misunderstood because she had a habit of always putting others before herself. Where friends were concerned, Jessica was "very selective . . . and only associate[d] herself with those who [were] good role models . . . ," a former friend said. Moreover, Jessica's independence, even at the puppy love age of sixteen, was evidence of maturity and a broad outlook on life in general. She was unique in that respect, the same friend claimed. An old high-school mate said Jessica's "honesty" and integrity was "sometimes misconstrued as arrogance or rudeness." It was the way she spoke: Jessica came across as crass and snotty, even though she didn't always mean to. While others were convinced that Jessica's abrasiveness and contentious attitude were products of her upbringing, it was, others stated, nothing more than her demeanor. Once you got to know Jessica, there was no mistaking the fact that she was different in so many ways.

If there was one thing about Jessica that stood out more than anything else in high school, it was her social skills. Jessica was not a shy person by any means, but she was not outwardly open in a social group setting, either. Like her friends, she hung with a group or "clique" of kids. From junior high on, Jessica had no trouble getting the boys to like her, and she thrived on the attention she got by giving herself sexually. One thing Jessica found hilarious, if not altogether a portent, she told a friend one day, was "that the last four digits of my phone number spell 'boys.'"

It was a joke, of course. But in the scope of her life, a harbinger.

Naomi Patterson (pseudonym) met Jessica in middle school but lost touch with her in ninth grade, hooking back up during their sophomore year together at Shades Valley. Naomi and Jessica became close. Ended up doing a lot of things together.

"In middle school," Naomi recalled, "Jessica was more normal. She never said much about her home life then, or got real deep." She held her cards close and was quiet—until she got to know a friend. "She was just your typical teenager at that point. Highly intelligent, though. Jessica was very smart." So smart, in fact, she was involved in a project called Research Learning Center (RLC). It was offered by the school system. Basically, it was a group established for kids with an obvious proclivity for higher learning. Alan was also invited into the RLC program, but opted out because it meant he would be isolated from the main campus of Shades Valley and the rest of the kids.

Naomi and Jessica didn't fit in with the factions of smart kids, the popular crowds or any of the other cliques.

"There was a whole group of us who were offset to the side," Naomi explained. "I teased somebody years later saying that, back then, we were Goth before Goth was even Goth."

They wore all black and stood out. It was the late 1980s. When most of the other kids wore their hair piled and teased higher than a beehive, formed solid as brick with cans of hair spray, Jessica and her gang wore a "flat and straight" hairstyle. Maybe just to be different.

By this point Jessica's life was spiraling out of control. She was only in the tenth grade. It got to the point where she was kicked out of the RLC program for not keeping up with her studies.

Jessica seemed to be living on her own. Although she lived with her mother and stepfather, it appeared that she could come and go at will. She was always going places, taking off in her car and not coming back for days. It was as if she had no supervision, Naomi said. No one to answer to.

"Rarely at home, if she could help it. And if she was home, she claimed there was always arguments. Especially with her stepfather." Albert was the disciplinarian in the house, clearly, Naomi observed. He wanted Jessica to do the right thing. "But he couldn't control her."

No one could.

According to some, Jessica saw Alan Bates as her golden ticket, a gateway—or free pass—into a better way of life. After all, Jessica hadn't grown up with all the benefits of a normal two-parent household. For Alan, he didn't know it yet, but there was no turning back once Jessica set her claws into him. "No" wasn't

an answer Jessica Callis accepted. And regardless of
what friends said, or what Jessica herself later claimed,
her behavior became the best indicator as to where
her life was heading.

Naomi was out of school by the time Jessica became
pregnant with Alan's child. Naomi was working, getting ready to attend college. Jessica called, however,
and brought Naomi up to speed about what was going
on in her life.

"I met this guy," Jessica explained one night, referring to Alan. "He's something." Jessica laughed.

"What is it?" Naomi wanted to know. What was so
darn funny about meeting a boy?

"We're sneaking around . . . messing around in my
car." Jessica thought it was funny that she and Alan
were having sex at will. It was as though she had
bagged herself a catch and used sex to keep him
coming back.

It didn't take a lot of work on Alan's part to get Jessica
to put out. She had no trouble attracting a flock. When
she met him, she was still seeing and sleeping with
another boy, several friends said. And yet, as soon as
she realized Alan could give her something more, maybe
something she wanted that the other boy couldn't, she
made Alan her focus.

The Bates family took most of their summer vaca-
tions down on the Gulf Coast. They stayed on the
beach at a condo they rented from a friend. During the
summer before Alan's final year of high school started,
weeks after Alan and Jessica had met, Alan explained
to Jessica that he wouldn't be around for a while. He
and the family were going away on vacation. He told
her they went down to the coast every year. Alan said
he enjoyed it. The vacation was the perfect place to get
his mind ready for the upcoming school year.

Alan told Jessica not to worry. They could hook

up when he returned. He liked her. He wanted to continue the friendship. He ended the conversation by letting her know the beach his family was heading to, but he never gave Jessica the exact address. They said their good-byes, and agreed to meet up when Alan returned.

Heading south, Alan felt good about this new relationship. It was the beginning of a typical high-school romance. Jessica showered him with attention and affection, sleeping with him willingly, and Alan was thrilled by it all. Most kids his age would be. He met a good-looking girl who put out.

Alan's older brother, Robert, was off at college. But Kevin, Alan's little brother, went to the Gulf Coast with the family. One morning Alan and Kevin stood on the condo balcony. No one else was awake. Two brothers just enjoying the early morning, looking out at the span of the wondrous water in front of them. They talked as two brothers might. Kevin looked up to his big brother Alan, six years older. He saw in Alan a role model on which to mold his future.

Standing, scanning the beach, Alan did a double take. He stopped and stared at two people sitting on the sand out in front of the condo building. It was early. Too early for beachgoers. The shore was pretty much deserted at this time of the day. These two looked like they had slept on the beach.

Alan took a closer look. No way. Couldn't be.

"That's Jessica," he said, surprised by his own words.

It certainly was Jessica. She was with a friend.

"No way . . . you've got to be kidding me," Alan said aloud, more or less talking to himself. "Why is she here?" Birmingham to the coast was a 260-mile trip, almost four hours of driving. One way.

When they arrived, Jessica and her friend traveled up and down the coastline in the town Jessica knew

Alan was staying in until she found the Bates family van. It was parked, sitting in a driveway with scores of other vehicles. After locating the vehicle, Jessica and her friend went out on the beach and stayed the night, knowing that Alan and his family were in one of the condos and would ultimately end up on the beach that day.

Alan had no idea Jessica was coming. She never said a word about it. In fact, they hadn't even been *officially* dating. They were "seeing" each other. Alan had slept with her a few times. That was the extent of the relationship.

Alan and Kevin ran down to the beach. Greeted Jessica and her friend.

"Hey," Alan said.

"Hey, yourself," said Jessica.

Alan invited them to lunch.

"He was a teenager. . . . He was flattered," Kevin Bates later recalled. "They didn't stay with us or anything like that. She just came down for that day."

An eight-hour drive to see Alan for a few hours.

Alan didn't think anything of it. He was a little puffy-chested at the notion a girl had gone to so much trouble to visit him. Here she was, all the way down at the Gulf Coast from the center of Alabama—a teenager, driving the entire way, scouting out the family van, just to see a guy she had just met.

Alan felt a pang of intimacy. Maybe even love. He was special. At least in Jessica's eyes.

"It was shocking to him more than anything that she could just . . . that she had this freedom (as a teenager) to just do whatever she wanted," Kevin said later.

Had Jessica's parents allowed her to travel all that way? She was sixteen. Out and about, running around the South.

Chasing a boy.

* * *

When Alan and his family returned from vacation, school was just about ready to begin. Alan and Jessica had some fun. The summer was filled with memories, but Alan wanted to refocus his attention on school. His future. College.

"They were on the verge of breaking up," one friend remembered later. "They weren't really dating at this time."

But Jessica wasn't going to let Alan get away. Not a chance. He was too good a catch.

It was here that Jessica and Alan's relationship took flight—that is, after Jessica went to Alan with the news of being pregnant. They were on the brink of a breakup, and Jessica just happened to get pregnant. Was it even Alan's child?

Soon after, Alan became more and more withdrawn from his family. He had always been a child—like his brothers—who felt comfortable going to his mother and father with the adolescent problems beleaguering most teens. They were a close-knit family. Philip Bates liked to tell his kids that any problem could be worked out: "Just come to us with it."

Be not afraid.

"We'll help you through anything."

As the fall came and school commenced, Philip noticed that the space between Alan and his family grew. Alan was clearly distracted. Something weighed heavily on the boy's mind. *What's bothering him?* Philip and Joan Bates, and even eleven-year-old Kevin, often wondered. They'd watch Alan walk about the house, his head drooped, shoulders slumped. They could tell his mind was buzzing with an obvious problem he was trying to solve alone. Alan had never been like this.

Joan encouraged Philip to talk to his son. Ask him what was going on.

But Alan said nothing. He was fine. He could work it out on his own.

The Bateses respected their son. What else could they do? Trust was an important family value in the Bates household. Alan would speak up when he felt comfortable. No need to push the boy.

"Something was upsetting him," Kevin Bates recalled, "and [my parents] kept trying to talk to him about it. But didn't get far."

On the other end of all this, Alan was likely feeling pressure from Jessica. There was no way she was going to abort this child, she had told several of her friends. Alan was going to have to stand up, be a man and take responsibility.

Alan needed his own time to process what it was that was consuming any serenity and confidence the kid had built up during his preceding years. Alan was a senior, heading into the year he had looked forward to since he was a freshman. It wasn't nerves about graduation and college and beginning life as an adult. Although that all probably added to Alan's sudden change. But there was more. Kevin, Philip and Joan were sure of it. Alan hadn't even put in his nomination for class president. He was backing off his music. All of this was so unlike him.

Alan made a decision to tell everyone. But he wasn't going to sit down and explain to his mother and father what had happened. So he wrote "a nice long letter" and left it for them on his dad's desk.

Picking it up and reading, Philip knew he had raised a responsible son. A boy who cared about others. Could he argue with that? Could he be angry at the boy for wanting to do the right thing?

Despite the uphill battle and obstacles Philip knew

Alan now faced, he was proud his boy had decided to handle it like a man.

"It was a very apologetic letter," Kevin Bates later commented. "Alan was saying sorry for bringing this on, sorry for making this mistake, that he was raised better than this, but he was also taking full responsibility. 'We'll make things work,' I think was one of the quotes Alan wrote to my dad."

Joan wasn't sold on Jessica as the mother of her grandchild. There was something about Jessica that Joan didn't like. She was upset with herself that she wasn't able to help Alan before things got to this point. But what could she do now? She had to support her son.

Alan's letter outlined the fact that he had—at least according to Jessica—impregnated her some weeks before and didn't know how to disclose it to the family. He thought a letter was the best way to address the situation. Part of what Alan wrote, however, was that he understood the values his mother and father had always instilled in him as he grew up. He was entirely prepared to take "full responsibility" for the pregnancy—abortion, of course, not ever being an option—by marrying Jessica. If he was going to become a father (a March 1990 due date was on the calendar), Alan Bates was going to provide for his child and the child's mother.

Make things right.

This didn't mean Alan was going to give up on his dreams of working on Broadway, behind the scenes as a technical director and stage person. Or that he was planning on giving up on his love of music or quitting high school to drive a forklift at some warehouse or work behind the counter of a convenience store and buy a mobile home. Those weren't bad things, but he had other priorities in life set in front of himself. Instead, this news meant there would be a bump in the road. Certainly. Times would be tough. Absolutely. But college was still part of Alan's future. Alan could see it. Feel it. He was not giving up on himself. In fact, maybe now more than ever, seeing that he was going to become a father and a husband, Alan Bates needed to turn his dreams into reality.

Jessica called Naomi to share the latest. Naomi stopped by Jessica's mother's house for a visit shortly after the call. Jessica was lonely. She was at home all day, with nobody around, her stomach growing. Alan still in school and working.

"You're keeping this one?" Naomi wondered. Jessica was showing by this point. It was strange to Naomi. Not that life was a choice, or abortion an option, but Naomi was confused by her friend's behavior: how had Jessica come to the decision? ("For whatever reason," Naomi said later, "Jessica decided it was okay to keep this one. . . .")

Still, why not the other babies? Why had she chosen to keep this particular child and not any of the other babies she had aborted?

Jessica explained that she and Alan were getting married, but it wasn't the flowery picture Alan was telling his family—at least from Jessica's point of view.

"The only reason I'm marrying him," Jessica told Naomi that afternoon, "is because Alan's grandfather has agreed to pay for me to have the baby at Brookwood." There were hospitals in town that those less fortunate, without insurance, checked into for treatment and births. Brookwood was a private hospital.

"Only if we're married, though," Jessica said, "he'll pay for it."

16

Investigators knew Jessica's stepfather, Albert Bailey, left Jeff and Jessica's Myrtlewood Drive house with a couch that Saturday, February 16, 2002. Then, for some odd reason, the man drove around town with it. Given the circumstances, knowing what the investigating law enforcement agencies now knew about the crime, it seemed peculiar that Albert would do such a thing. The timing was suspect. The pathologist said there was a good chance Alan and Terra were sitting down (or leaning against something) when they were shot. Could they have been sitting on the couch that Albert Bailey was tooling around town with?

The Bureau and the HPD were waiting for a judge to sign off on a search warrant to get into the McCord home. They wanted to see what it was Jessica had been so vocal about, and determined to keep from them. The fact of the matter was—at least from the side of the fence where law enforcement stood—that if Jessica did not have anything to hide, and Alan and Terra, as she herself had been so adamantly certain of, had never been inside her home, why wouldn't she willingly allow law enforcement to have a look?

After being stopped the previous day, the HPD followed Albert Bailey again. During that second tail, they witnessed him drive behind Uncle Bob's Self-Storage on Citation Drive for a second time, then take off back home. Albert was questioned later on that day and asked about the couch. After some prodding, Albert fessed up and told the Bureau where he had dumped it.

Asked why he did this, Albert said, "Jessica told me to."

Williams and Vance found the couch near Citation Drive, next to a large Dumpster. The couch was "turned up on its back . . . sitting next to" that Dumpster, Williams said later, "against a fence . . . upside down so the back would have been toward the fence."

The backing of the couch—what you would rest up against when you sat down—had been torn off. Actually, investigators observed, it was "cut out." It was a fairly new couch. Moreover, it was one of those sofa beds. But the mattress, along with the cushions, was also missing.

The timing of all this was incredibly suspect to investigators.

Williams and Vance looked through the Dumpster, hoping to find the remains of the couch or the cushions.

Nothing.

The two investigators went into a nearby building and spoke to several people who were there that previous afternoon when Bailey had dumped it. But they all said the same thing: "We never saw the couch with any cushions."

Williams ordered the couch to be picked up and brought in. Forensics needed to go over it. There were a few stains (dark spots) on one of the armrests. With a quick spray of luminol, it was determined those stains were, in fact, blood. The money was on whether it was Alan's, Terra's or a mixture of both their blood.

That afternoon, Williams heard the warrant had finally come through. HPD investigators had armed themselves and were headed over to the McCord house on Myrtlewood. The thought and speculation driving the search was that it wasn't going to be a pretty scene. Jeff McCord was a cop. That meant he had weapons. The McCords seemed like hostile, uncomfortable and tactless people. What were they going to do if they felt threatened?

Near one o'clock, on the afternoon of February 17, 2002, Jessica and Jeff walked out the front door of their Myrtlewood Drive home. The look on their faces before they spotted the police made it seem as though it were any other day. Jessica carried her youngest child in her arms. Jeff held the door for her.

No sooner had they stepped onto the front steps did she and Jeff hear some sort of a commotion going on around them.

A ruckus.

Several police officers, Jessica explained later, came hurrying around the corner, guns drawn, pointed at her and Jeff. They were "yelling" and "screaming," Jessica claimed. "Hands above your head . . . right now."

The focus was on Jeff, who had his "duty belt" with him. Jeff packed a service revolver.

"Put the belt down," one cop yelled. It was not hard to tell that the cop meant what he said.

Jeff was startled by this.

"Back up toward us, with your back facing us, and hand the officer your weapon, sir."

The tension was high and tight. Jessica stood, not knowing what to do or how to react. She was troubled by such a show of might. The HPD wanted to make an impression, make it clear who was in charge. But Jessica wasn't getting it.

What was happening? Were they there to arrest Jessica and Jeff? What was going on? Jessica had no idea.

Or did she?

The McCords' dog barked erratically, crazily. Jumped around. Ran up to the fence in the back of the house. He wasn't on a leash.

"Chain up the dog, ma'am," one cop said with concern.

Jessica tied up the pooch. "And that helped, too," she recalled, "because the dog was flipping out over all the people with guns and the voices and everything."

"Mr. and Mrs. McCord," said an officer, "we have a warrant to search your home."

Jeff and Jessica looked at each other. Jessica could not tell how many cops were present for the search, but, by her humble estimation a year later, she said, "It seemed like a ton. I remember when I looked up as we walked out . . . and, you know, all of these people standing there with guns pointed at us."

The HPD was concerned that Jeff McCord would draw on them; they knew he not only carried a weapon, but he had additional weapons inside his house. When you're dealing with guns and police and warrants, you don't take chances. Those days of brotherly blue were behind them. Jeff and Jessica were suspects in a double murder. They were considered armed and dangerous. If they had murdered two people already, what would stop them from going down in a hail of gunfire?

Sergeant Tom McDanal ran the show. He handed Jeff and Jessica the paperwork, saying, "You need to get those children out of here. They should not be here."

Jessica took out her cell phone. "I'm calling my father."

After a few moments, she hung up the phone.

"I'll have to give them a ride over to my mother's house," Jessica said.

Wrong answer.

"You cannot leave, ma'am," McDanal made clear.

So Jessica called Albert Bailey back and told him to pick up the kids at Myrtlewood.

Someone suggested Jessica, Jeff and the kids wait in the front yard. An officer would keep them company. Anyway, the HPD had work to do.

One of the children asked her mother what was happening. Why were the police going inside their home?

Jessica didn't answer. She stared straight ahead as a line of officers filed into the one place she had refused to allow them access.

Detective Laura Brignac stood out front with Jessica and the kids. "Do you mind if I talk to your children?" Brignac asked.

"No!" Jessica snapped. "No way . . . I don't want you talking to them."

Brignac pulled Jessica to the side, away from the children and Jeff. "Look, I'm not going to tell them anything about what's going on with their father. . . . I just need to establish a timeline." The seasoned detective paused. Then: "I'm going to interview the children, Mrs. McCord. Either right here and now. At your parents' house. Or at the police station."

The choice was Jessica's.

After a moment Jessica looked at the detective. Thought about it. "Well, my dad is going to take them and you can talk to them over there."

Albert Bailey showed up. Jessica and Jeff went into their Myrtlewood Drive home so they could watch the search. Brignac said she'd follow Albert and the kids and interview them at Jessica's mother's house.

Driving over, Brignac considered a few things: Kids, she knew, can be the most truthful of any witness. They lay out facts without thinking about them. Without even knowing it. This was going to be interesting.

As Brignac sat down with the kids out of Albert and Dian Bailey's earshot, she quickly built a rapport, chitchatting with them first about kid stuff. It was clear almost immediately to Brignac that Sam (pseudonym), who was almost twelve years old, and McKenna (pseudonym), closing in on ten years, could potentially break the case—without even realizing it.

"Y'all notice anything different about your house when you went back there yesterday?" Brignac asked both children. She knew the kids had been out of the home for almost an entire day, but they went back that afternoon. They had gone from day care on late Friday afternoon to their grandmother's house and hadn't left there until that Sunday morning. Brignac was already suspicious of Jessica's story of how Alan had never shown up at the house. The detective interviewed the day care provider earlier that same day and the woman confirmed that she, in fact, had dropped the kids off at Dian Bailey's, somewhere near 4:00 P.M. on Friday, not Jessica or Jeff.

So Brignac knew Jessica and Jeff had lied already.

The day care story was in total conflict with Jeff and Jessica's version of the same situation. Barring that, by Brignac's determination, this one discrepancy indicated to her that Jessica was not expecting Alan to show up at her house to begin with.

One of the children spoke up after Brignac asked if anything was different inside the house. "Yes," the child said, "the carpet was gone . . . in the den . . . there was a new floor . . . and the sofa was gone. . . ."

The other child chimed in, "Yeah, yeah, and . . . my momma had been talking about getting rid of that sofa, anyway. The den had been rearranged, too."

Brignac was floored by this revelation. She continued the interview, knowing exactly what she needed to do when she was finished.

D. C. Scively was one of the HPD's working technicians, there at the McCord home to "supervise the other technicians." Scively was also responsible for maintaining the integrity of the evidence collected. You know, making sure it arrived inside an evidence bag without a problem. Then onto the lab and wherever else, as it should. That whole chain-of-custody thing.

Throughout his time at the McCord house, Scively documented both on paper and with photographs the mess the HPD had run into as they approached the inside of the McCord house.

The place was simply disgusting. Housekeeping was definitely not a domestic skill Jessica could be crowned queen of; it seemed wherever you looked there was a stack of this, a pile of that: clutters of videos, DVDs, magazines, and even pure old-fashioned garbage. But more important to the search team, they confirmed that someone had been working in the home.

After the children left for Jessica's mother's, Jessica and Jeff walked into the house and began "observing different areas . . . ," Jessica later explained in court, "while it was being searched."

To Jessica, it seemed as though the cops were there to mainly ransack her home and invade her personal space.

"Oh, they moved things," she said agitatedly, "emptied drawers, made a big mess even worse."

HPD detective Peyton Zanzour was one of the investigators leading the team during the search. With nearly twenty-five years on the job, Detective Zanzour had surely seen and directed his share of search warrants. On this day Zanzour worked in the capacity of an investigator for the Crimes Against Persons Division (CAPERS).

Here, a group of cops was searching a fellow police officer's house. It happened. Didn't mean the guy was guilty. In fact, Jeff McCord likely knew better. Since that interview with Bureau agent Kimberly Williams at the Pelham PD, Jeff hadn't said much of anything, one way or another.

But then maybe Jeff was covering up for his guilty wife?

Several things stood out immediately to Detective Zanzour. For one, the fact that the house was "in total disarray." Cops couldn't walk through the place without stepping on something. One area was loaded with empty floor tile boxes. The carpet in the living room had recently been ripped up. With such a mess, it was almost impossible, without moving things around or dismantling parts of the house, to conduct the type of search the HPD needed to do. There was a lot of ground to cover, like the inside of walls, the basement, boxes, underneath carpets, and the garage.

Later, Jessica spoke of her reasons for maintaining such a messy house: "I have my days. We had been sick for—you know, we had been fighting the flu, back and forth, and, plus, I was pregnant. I had just gotten pregnant, and I was having morning sickness. And I hate to say it. I can't do dishes when I'm throwing up. I mean, it's just not in me to do that. And my husband does not help with the house. We've got four kids in the house, [one] a little baby. You know, I'm throwing up every other day. Lots of clothes. Bedding. And, yes,

I'm not a good housekeeper. I admit it. I would rather be playing with my children than to have a pristine house and no time for them."

Zanzour decided to take it slow and easy. Maybe just walk around for now and see what stood out. Look in drawers. Under beds. Closets. The attic.

They uncovered "some ammo" in a room downstairs. In the master bedroom upstairs, they hit a cache of additional ammunition and weapons: a Smith & Wesson pistol with a holster, two Smith & Wesson magazines, a box of shotgun shells. In the attic was a .38 Smith & Wesson pistol, a rifle and four magazines loaded with ammo.

Jeff McCord was ready for a war.

In one photo, taken inside the kitchen area, Scively photographed a roll of paper towels in the garbage. It seemed like it might be important.

Zanzour and Tom McDanal gathered everyone outside at one point, several hours later. It was near 5:30 P.M. Time to stop the search. It was difficult to find anything in such a jumble of garbage and clutter. On top of that, the search warrant they had did not cover tearing things up and looking in walls. Furthermore, out of all of the weaponry and ammunition they uncovered, there was no .44 caliber.

After she finished interviewing the children at the Bailey house, Laura Brignac called Tom McDanal. She knew he was with the team searching the McCord home. She was excited. She had a lead. An important piece of the puzzle, perhaps. Brignac knew where the focus of the search warrant should be centered. The kids had inadvertently mentioned several things that seemed to stand out. Now Brignac believed that if a crime had been committed in that house, there was no doubt where.

"The den," Brignac told McDanal. "Look in the den."

Standing outside the house, Tom McDanal went silent. That was information he did not want to hear now.

17

Though she had one year left of high school, Jessica Callis seemed overjoyed at the notion of being a mother. She had that glow about her face—a mother-to-be plumpness suited Jessica's large frame. To top it off, she had hooked herself a responsible high schooler and dedicated "family man." To boot, Alan was an active Christian. In addition to all that, a self-imposed shotgun to his back or not, Alan Bates planned to marry his pregnant girlfriend and make things proper.

The Bateses were a little taken aback by this new—sudden—fresh face in the family. Alan had known Jessica all of approximately six weeks. She was pregnant. She was having the child. They were getting married. The plan, for now, was Jessica would quit school and move into Alan's parents' house. All this, and no one really knew the first thing about the girl.

"What do we know about this person?" Kevin and Robert Bates later said the family asked themselves. Not necessarily in a derogatory fashion, but more out of curiosity and desire. "Who is she? We really don't know *anything* about her, and she is going to now become part of our everyday lives?"

It wasn't such a shock to the family that Jessica was into Alan as much as she seemed. Alan had a string of girls, throughout his junior-high and high-school years, vying for his attention. He never played into it, however, or abused the privilege of being popular with the ladies. Alan would just as well smile and be on his way. He dated—sure, he did. But dating was not something Alan focused on, as it was for so many of the other young men his age. Alan was busy with the bands he played in, studying, school politics, the theater. Girls were definitely not first on his teenage list of priorities.

"Our parents were young to become grandparents," Kevin remembered. "But they were smart enough to know that Jessica was still a kid, too. She had some growing up to do." No one in the family ever asked outright: "Was this the right girl for Alan?"

They simply accepted Alan's choice and trusted his judgment.

Jessica was a kid. Of course, she came across immature and a bit obsessive at times. Many teenage girls can be that way. This was a period before text messaging and the Internet and cell phones. Teenagers filled their days and nights with other things. That said, neither time, space nor electronic gadgets could curb what postpuberty hormones inevitably forced on kids: the need for companionship. Jessica wanted more than anything else what she herself never had: a stable environment. Someone to love her unconditionally. It was not hard for Jessica to tell that the Bates family could provide it all.

"You see red flags," Kevin said, commenting on those small outbursts in the beginning of Jessica's more bizarre behaviors, and the stories she began to tell about her own family, "and you think part of it's immaturity or her coming from a different background or different family."

Diversity. America was built on it. Part of the fabric and DNA of every community.

The bottom line for the Bateses was that they weren't about to judge this girl based on the fact that she had allowed herself to get pregnant. Or that she shared a few crazy anecdotes about growing up in the Callis household. Alan was not the type of person to have fallen for the blond, blue-eyed cheerleader, anyway, even though she might have fallen for him. In Jessica, Alan was attracted to what he viewed as her intellect. Jessica came across as very smart and intellectual. Alan liked that. She was also confident and wouldn't back down. Strong. He liked that, too. And then, on top of all that, she put out.

"She talked a big game," Kevin added later. "She had been, at one time, in the honors high school." She had the foundation of aptitude there, a chance to broaden her opportunities, even though she was raised—again, according to what Jessica claimed—in such a disturbing, violent, abusive environment.

As Jessica moved in and commingled with the Bates family, nursing her growing belly, complaining about the difficulty of carrying the child, Alan continued at Shades Valley, working toward finishing his senior year. Jessica stayed home, sat around telling the stories of her life. Philip Bates was fairly diligent about keeping a family log of every important event in the children's lives: baseball, soccer, football, whatever special occasion depicted the children growing up. When those albums came out and Alan shared the experiences of his formative years with Jessica, she countered with what were some of the most peculiar family tales of her own.

Jessica had tears in her eyes. They were sitting around,

going through a large binder of Bates childhood memories, bringing Jessica into the fold of the Bateses' lives.

"What is it?" Alan asked, concerned about the pain Jessica had apparently been whisked back into while thinking about how well the Bates family got along. How "normal" their family seemed.

"My father, he was *so* abusive. . . . When he left the house, he burned all of our family photographs," Jessica said, according to Bates family members. "We have no pictures of any of us left."

Alan and the others were drawn into this. Whether it was true or not, Kevin Bates later pointed out, "We never knew or questioned, not until years later."

Alan felt a pang of sympathy for Jessica rise in him as she told these stories. He was falling deeper in love with her. Which was, many later speculated, the way Jessica had planned it. She used the sympathies of others to manipulate her way—"or worm, actually," one source put it—into the good graces of the Bates household. She saw an opening and went for it.

"Alan felt— I know he did—that he could give Jessica a better life," Kevin said.

Alan developed deep compassion for Jessica as she took on the role of motherhood, acting like she was born for it. With the new family they were creating together, Alan said more than once, he could provide Jessica with the stability she'd never had. They'd break the cycle. With their child. Their marriage.

Make it work.

Together.

"There was the whole package that Alan brought to her," Robert later said. Alan's oldest brother had been out of college for several years when Jessica moved in. "There was nothing spectacular about her."

White picket fence. Three-bedroom house. Two-point-two

kids. Two cars. A dog. Maybe a boat. Family walks in the park after Alan got out of work.

It all sounded so good. So warm and fuzzy. Jessica could envision it all, as if writing the script of her life— all centered, of course, around the birth of her first child.

The day Samantha was born, March 20, 1990, was full of joy and love and caring in the hospital for everyone. Dian Bailey was there, as was Albert. Kevin and Robert, along with new grandparents Joan and Philip, were beside themselves with pride and adoration. Here was this new child in their lives. Such a tremendous bundle of joy. A gurgling, pudgy, red-faced gift from God, dropped from Heaven into their laps.

What a blessing.

"It was a shared family moment," Kevin said, recalling that day in the hospital. "An exciting first grandchild for both families."

This was the first time the two families had gotten together in the same room since the wedding back on January 26, 1990. There was a mild strain of awkwardness. Everyone was still getting to know each other. But things were okay. They all got along. Albert Bailey explained that he was a handyman, a local contractor with a small business. "If it was a deck to be built, he could build it," Jessica said of Albert. "If it was a water heater to be replaced, he could do it." He was a "very handy guy."

If Alan ever needed work, Albert suggested, he could throw the boy some hours, here and there.

Every dollar would help.

And so, they were an American family making the best of this unplanned situation. Alan was determined to be a great father, and he very likely would be, considering his pedigree. Jessica was steadfast in her desire to raise her children in stark contrast to her own upbringing. She was going to give the kid everything she never had.

Philip Bates lived by the common affirmation that "two wrongs never made a right." The family was happy to have Jessica and the child in their home. That traditional Christian upbringing, whereby you got married first, had children, climbed up the ladder of your career, had cookouts and birthday parties on Saturdays, attended church on Sundays, and subliminally counted down the moments until your death, was but a pipe dream. Yet, Alan was a traditionalist. Getting Jessica pregnant, he was determined to do whatever he had to do to give her and his child the life they deserved.

"My parents were worried that Alan felt pressured from his conventional upbringing to marry Jessica and be an honest man and father, and all those things," Kevin said.

Indeed, just like that, Alan was an adult. He was seventeen years old. Still in high school. It was the beginning of a new decade. The 1980s were history. Alan had a bright, prosperous future ahead of him.

Now he had a wife and child.

How things could change overnight.

Alan never viewed any of this as having a shotgun poked in his back, forcing him into a Las Vegas chapel. He embraced the idea of marriage and fatherhood. Took on the role as if he had been born to do it.

By April 1990, Alan and Jessica had lived with his parents for nearly two months. They decided to move, however. The best place was Hoover, into Jessica's mother and stepfather's house. Sam was a month old. Living in Hoover would be more convenient for Alan and school. Dian could help out with the baby. Jessica could begin to think about her future.

That lasted a month. It was said that a fight erupted

between Jessica and her mother. Whatever the case might be, Alan and Jessica were back at the Bates house in Cahaba Heights four weeks after leaving.

Jessica was different this time around. She pulled Joan Bates aside one day, for example, shortly after moving back in, and said, "Listen, you are not to answer the phone if my mother calls. You cannot invite my mother over to this house. I will say *when* she can see her granddaughter."

It was a control issue: Jessica had the power—the baby—to refuse her mother something she had apparently wanted. Payback *was* a bitch. It was as if Jessica was proving to her own mother how she had felt—the pain she had experienced growing up, being shuffled between her biological father and mother, and being put in the middle of what was a war between her parents.

Jessica was very much in the driver's seat of her life now. It was as if, as soon as she had a little bit of power over someone, she wielded it. And because of the tenuous relationship she'd had with her mother throughout the years already, Jessica was calling the shots now that *she was a mother.*

An eye for an eye.

For all those in the Bates household, the situation became volatile, not to mention uncomfortable and, at times, embarrassing. They had no real chance of seeing or understanding it at the time, but a pattern was developing in front of their eyes.

Robert was out of the house. He came home from time to time. Being away from the situation—distanced— Robert could see things the others couldn't. It was like not seeing your cousin for a year—you instantly noticed how much she had grown.

"I noticed immediately," Robert said, "that as Alan finished high school, things for him and Jessica were slowly beginning to become out of balance."

Out of balance, the family would soon come to understand, would turn into the understatement of Alan and Jessica's life together. From the moment Alan married Jessica, his life would be thrown into chaos. Because beneath a seemingly composed veneer that Jessica presented when around the Bates clan, coming out of her shell every once in a while to tell a tale of horror or to try to gain sympathy, lay an incredible brewing drama. Inside Jessica's soul, one could argue, she kept hidden an incapacitating, silent rage that would expose itself as she became more comfortable in her role as Mrs. Alan Bates. It was a fury, maybe even a woman's wrath, about to come to life.

18

After initial testing by the Bureau's forensic lab in Atlanta, it was learned the blood found on the Mc-Cords' couch that Albert Bailey had tossed out near that Dumpster across town was not a match to that of Alan or Terra Bates.

Indeed, the blood was someone else's.

Law enforcement had not expected this. The case had begun to look like a slam dunk. Most law enforcement involved would have bet that the blood was Alan's and Terra's. However, here was scientific proof it was not. A setback, sure. But no reason to abandon the hunch that Jessica McCord had something to do with the demise of her ex-husband and his wife.

As Jessica and Jeff began to accept what was going on in their lives, things seemed a bit surreal to Jeff. He was one of the cops generally involved in conducting the search and disrupting someone's life. Now the cops were focused on him. How quickly the tables had turned.

Jeff said he had always wanted to become a police officer. "Because I had been a fan of shows such as *Adam-12, S.W.A.T.* and *Hill Street Blues*," he told me.

Jeff had early "designs" and goals pre- and postcollege of being a probation officer. His dream then was to help children. Show wayward kids that there was life after crime. Prove that everyone deserved a second chance. He even once went to work for The King's Ranch, a Christian-based, adolescent-treatment center in Shelby County.

"I worked primarily in boys homes," he said. "My job entailed teaching or helping to teach social and independent living skills to 'at risk' youth with a variety of emotional, psychological and behavioral problems."

At one time Jeff McCord was a mentor. He believed children without a chance in life deserved a role model who could show them that achievement was a state of mind. Success was there for everybody, regardless of class, race, gender or social standing. You could do anything you wanted in life. This had always been one of Jeff's core convictions, on which he aimed to build his experience as a police officer upon.

"Cops, deputies and road troopers are in the best position to help people in need or distress," Jeff noted. "Be it by direct action or referral."

According to one of Jeff's high-school teachers from Opelika, Alabama, a man who later became friends with Jeff's mother, Jeff's problems did not start until he met and married Jessica.

"I observed [Jeff] as he attended church from a young child," Bobby Kelley, Jeff's former science teacher, later noted. "After he left home, I became acquainted with his mother, and close friends [with her] a few years prior to his involvement with Jessica."

The Jeff McCord that Bobby Kelley knew and taught was "an obedient child," Bobby said, "slightly introverted and very respectful of authority. He was an average student and average athlete. Although he was supported by his mother in his participation of sports, there was a noticeable absence of a father figure." Jeff's parents had divorced.

Bobby said there was no doubt Jeff was a "man's man." Jeff's sexuality "or sensuality" was never questioned then, but there were observations and issues surrounding Jeff's ability to bond with the opposite sex in a healthy manner. His fear of being rejected by a female he had "conquered" was likely, some suggested, one of the reasons why Jeff was easily influenced and controlled by Jessica. He had won her heart. To Jeff, that was the difficult part of the relationship—the challenge. Whatever happened afterward, whatever supposed hell he had to endure, was "the price" you had to pay in order to keep her.

"The way he changed after meeting Jessica was very strange to those of us who knew him," Bobby remarked.

Looking over Jeff's life, however, you could clearly see the correlation between the value he put on opposite-sex relationships and the choices he later made. Jeff's mother was there for him—always. She had raised a great kid. Without a male role model around, it was Jeff's mother who took him to baseball and football practices and cheered for him at the games.

More important to Jeff's future relationship with Jessica, there was a "conservative presence that permeated through other things," Bobby Kelley claimed, "like Jeff's inexperience with the dating area of his life, and the indirectness he dealt with confrontation and, to a degree, allowing manipulation to occur [in order to] prevent conflict."

Jeff had a "very healthy" relationship with his mother. He was allowed to grow, Bobby said, "and function without conflict" in the home. This is an important piece of a healthy upbringing. The idea that children learn to resolve disagreements in their lives with chaos is wired into their psyche at an early age. With Jeff, however, his character, or the impression of who he was as a young man, was never made that obvious or fully developed, Bobby Kelley speculated.

"If I have given the impression he was weak, that is not the case at all. He was able to function well on his own two feet. He had a . . . healthy communication with his mother during and after he left home."

That all changed, however, after Jessica was introduced into the dynamic of Jeff's life. Here was a dominating personality now taking over the role as authoritarian, in other words. Jessica was stronger than Jeff emotionally; she had been through more. If you believe Bobby Kelley's version, Jeff was just happy to have someone love him.

It was when he started dating Jessica that the communication between Jeff and his mom deteriorated rapidly, Bobby said.

"I don't want it to seem as if I'm saying that he left a dominant mother for a dominant wife. It wasn't that way. [Jeff's mom] is a strong woman, but [she] clearly wasn't a dominant, controlling, manipulative person."

Like Jessica.

Regardless, Jeff stopped responding to his mother's phone calls after he and Jessica married. No doubt, Jessica told him not to speak with his mother before consulting with her first.

When he heard that, Bobby Kelley suggested to Jeff's mom that she start sending correspondences to her son via the Pelham PD, bypassing Jessica altogether.

"It was during the time that [Jeff's mom] was unable to communicate with [Jeff] that she called me," Bobby Kelley said later. "The discussion was . . . that it would be very necessary to contact him at the [Pelham] PD, be it by phone or mail, to insure that [he] got the correspondence, whether he responded or not. I clearly told [Jeff's mom] that was the best way to insure communication avenues were open and we both agreed that [Jeff] would not have to suffer the brunt of having to deal with his decision to communicate. So it was [Jeff's mom] who initiated this activity with the desire to have a dialogue."

And it was Jessica who put the brakes on it.

At home there's no question Jessica monitored what was said between Jeff and his mother. She was keeping Jeff—same as she had with other people in her life—away from someone he loved.

Meanwhile, Jeff, instead of dealing with the conflict he knew it would cause between them, decided to go behind Jessica's back and, on the surface, pacify her insecurities.

Jeff's mother called the house one day. "He's not here," Jessica said.

"Have him call me," Jeff's mom demanded.

"Oh, I will. . . ."

But Jeff never called. When his mother finally did speak with him, he said he had never received the messages.

Jeff had a woman in charge of his life—one who felt threatened by the woman who had raised him. Jessica knew she could not control Jeff's mother. This caused a transference of anger and put pressure on Jeff.

"I truly [know Jeff's mom] feels that this factor played a part in the breaking of [Jeff's] spirit by [severing] family ties, to which, I regret, he had to make so many emotional disconnections," Bobby Kelley later said. "It is that point that led me to tell her that I felt [Jeff] was being manipulated to play her to get what Jessica wanted. And that, I expected, due to his passive nature, Jessica would or had learned the buttons to push to get [Jeff] to do whatever made her happy."

Jessica was the puppet master, that much is clear. She told the man what to do and when to do it—and he obeyed her. Former friends and relatives all agreed: Jeff was in the same boat as many others who had to deal with Jessica over the years. You agreed with her so as not to have to endure her wrath. It was easier to oblige than face a monster.

Except Alan. Alan Bates wasn't going to sit back and allow the woman to dictate his life, especially when he could or could not see his children. A line had to be drawn.

Standing with Jessica, watching all this attention being paid to his house, Jeff McCord thought about those moments when he valued the idea that his true calling was to help people in need. Now here he was, on the opposite side of that equation. His life had flipped over on him. The cops were chasing him.

"I grew up in the church," Jeff commented. "It would be safe to say I have done my share of 'back-sliding.'"

As Jeff and Jessica stood outside, Tom McDanal was on the telephone with Detective Laura Brignac, who had just finished interviewing Albert and Dian Bailey, as well as Jessica's children. Brignac knew where the search needed to be centered inside the McCord house. The den.

She explained her theory to Tom McDanal.

"We've released the house," McDanal said disappointedly.

Darn it.

Brignac's shoulders dropped. She knew that in order to go back into the McCord home once it was officially released, even with this new information from the children, the HPD needed a second search warrant. And getting a second warrant on a location you had just finished searching was going to take some time.

Which was exactly what Jeff and Jessica McCord wanted to hear.

19

Alan graduated from Shades Valley in June 1990. He enrolled in fall classes at the University of Montevallo, thirty-five miles south of Birmingham. Montevallo is spread out now across a 160-acre main campus, bordered by rolling hills, golf course green lawns, groves and colorful flower beds. It is a beautiful spread of land. Montevallo's academics and scholars are respected throughout the state. More than that, during Alan's time Montevallo offered excellent fine arts and theater programs for him to think about building on an already wide foundation of study in the technical side of the stage.

Being away from Birmingham and Alan's family was going to suit Jessica's growing needs quite well.

"She didn't like anybody who was close to Alan," a former friend said. "She felt threatened by *anyone* in his family, any of his close friends, and she basically wanted to pull him away from his whole life."

And here was that chance.

Jessica dropped out of school, with the intention of going back and getting her GED. As Alan got to know her better, he began to think that Jessica was either the most unfortunate person on God's earth, or she was making up stories about a tortured childhood that never was. One friend later said Jessica could spin the best yarn you ever heard, and she had a knack for making whatever story she told sound unequivocally true. "But come to find out," that same friend added, "she was nothing more than a pathological liar."

With a wife and child, Alan needed a home. Philip Bates purchased a "fixer-upper" for Jessica, Alan and Sam. It was a one-hundred-year-old ranch-style house that needed lots of TLC. But it was located just outside Montevallo. Regardless of the condition, it was enough room for the three of them. Cozy. Homey. The perfect starter home. Alan was determined to get a college degree. Find a good-paying job. Raise his family. When he wasn't going to class or studying, Alan was kept busy with odd jobs: landscaping, construction, anything else he could earn some quick cash from. He was still playing in a gospel quartet that paid, and it seemed the music became one of Alan's true outlets for his growing artistic expression. Jessica, though, was insecure about the band and rode Alan constantly about groupies and screaming girls vying for his attention.

Jessica's friend Naomi had Fridays off. Naomi often made the hour drive to Montevallo to visit with Jessica and the new baby. It was great to pop in and see how everyone was doing. Maybe help out. Bring a gift. Some food. Spread the love.

"I got a sense," Naomi recalled, "that they were, of course, struggling. Young couple. Recently married. New parents. Alan's in college. Working. In the band. It was *hard*."

For Jessica, the focus quickly turned to a notion that Alan was out and about, meeting women at school and at his band gigs, bedding them down. She accused him of sleeping with any female he crossed paths with.

The jealousy and insecurity consumed her. Ran their lives. Then it turned into chronic paranoia.

"He's seeing someone at the college," Jessica explained to Naomi during one Friday visit. Jessica said she was certain of it.

"Jessica, where's your proof?" Naomi asked. "Unless you have concrete evidence of you watching him go out with someone else, catching him in the act, you *have* to trust him."

What was a marriage without trust? Naomi stressed. If Jessica couldn't trust Alan to leave the house, how could she ever expect the relationship to grow?

Jessica changed the subject. Ignored the advice. Instead, she carried on about how she believed Alan was cheating. Naomi knew Alan took his wedding vows seriously. There was no way he would do anything to hurt Jessica. It just wasn't the person Alan was. If he wanted somebody else, Alan was the type to sit Jessica down and tell her it was over. Then go out and fornicate. But not while he was still married.

Nothing relieved Jessica's suspicions. She even showed up on campus one day with the baby, while Alan was in the middle of a production. As everyone working on the play with him turned, she yelled and screamed. Made an ass of herself. It was a scene. In front of everyone she accused Alan of doing all sorts of outlandish, sexual things with some of the women he studied and worked with at the campus theater. It embarrassed Alan a great deal. He didn't know what to do.

Finally he pulled Jessica aside, did his best to calm her down, then sent her back home.

Still, in many respects, during this same period, Naomi considered Jessica to be a "very good mother." "Homemaker" was probably a better way to put it. Jessica cooked. Cleaned. Made meals stretch for days.

She even went so far as to get cloth diapers so she could wash them and save money.

"She was very protective. A good mother. She tried to do everything she could. But at the same time, she was very insecure."

By 1992, Alan was cruising on autopilot through college, following his dream of working in the theater, now that much closer to living it. Jessica made the transformation to stay-at-home mom complete. She gained weight, watched soap operas and let herself go.

"They [were] a very young family," Robert Bates said of his brother and sister-in-law, "starting off under very trying circumstances. They were struggling. They were trying to figure things out."

On November 16, 1992, Jessica gave birth to her and Alan's second child, McKenna, and that's when things started to spiral out of control, members of Alan's family suggested. After a calm period Jessica's insecurities and abnormalities resurfaced on a new level—and Alan and his family were convinced now that maybe Jessica wasn't exaggerating when she told those stories of growing up in a chaotic, abusive household. Perhaps the environment in which she came from had affected her psychologically and turned her into the thing she so much hated.

What's more, one source noted, by this point in Jessica's life, she'd had no fewer than five abortions, using the procedure as a means of contraception. It got to the point, Jessica told one friend, where "there [was] no doctor in Birmingham that will touch me because I've had so many abortions."

According to a Forensic (Psychology) Evaluation Report conducted on Jessica in 2003, she claimed to have seen a mental-health professional when she was between the ages of nine and fifteen. *She saw someone,* the report indicated, *because her father was abusive. . . .*

Shortly before meeting Alan, Jessica admitted in that same report, she *saw a couple of licensed professional counselors because of domestic violence.* She was never hospitalized. Nor had Jessica been through any alcohol or drug treatment programs. This, despite admitting to having *used LSD between 500 and 600 times in her past with no history of flashbacks.*

"I agree with that," said a high-school friend. "She definitely used a lot of drugs later on in high school."

In addition, Jessica told the three doctors during her psychological exam, that she had a 50 percent hearing loss "bilaterally" since her teenage years, but she had never used a hearing aid of any type. She also reported having a history of "mitral valve prolapse," with occasional irregular heartbeats—in addition to hypoglycemia.

Jessica sat quite lucid during her evaluation, demonstrating normal eye contact, the report noted. She showed no "unusual mannerisms," and did not exhibit any odd gestures or facial expressions. In fact, doctors observed, Jessica appeared quite normal, with the exception of her tendency to—you guessed it—lie.

"Have you ever had any suicidal ideation . . . ?" one of the doctors asked Jessica at some point during the evaluation.

Jessica thought about it. "Not as an adult," she said, then broke off into a story from her childhood, adding, "but between the ages of fourteen and eighteen, I did."

"How so? Could you explain further, please?"

Jessica smiled. "I almost overdosed on Benadryl." Then, a while later, "And [drove] a car off the road."

The doctors weren't buying it.

In the same psychological report, one wrote: *She never required any medical attention and these should only be considered as gestures and judgment, if indeed they ever occurred.*

It was as if Jessica made up conditions, ailments and problems as she went along—illnesses that seemed to suit her needs at the time. According to the evaluation, the three doctors agreed that Jessica *came across as quite manipulative and self-serving. . . . She seems to be somewhat immature in her personal development and judgment but she had at least average intelligence.*

"She is the absolute queen of manipulation," an old high-school friend said.

There was no stopping Alan. Everybody around him knew the marriage to Jessica was wrong. Maybe even doomed. But friends and family could do nothing but support his decision and admire the guy for taking on the responsibility of being a father to his children.

One woman was hurt by the end of her friendship with Alan. All because Jessica would not allow them to speak to or see each other. It was a bit easier for this particular friend because she had moved away to another state to attend college. So the temptation to want to see and hang out with Alan wasn't always there.

And then Alan called one day. It was a total surprise. "Listen, I . . . I . . . Jessica said it's okay that we talk. And I really want you to see the kids."

Alan's friend was both appalled and excited. She didn't know what to say. She was back home on a break from school. Of course, she wanted to see Alan's kids. She and Alan were like cousins, brother and sister. She wanted to enjoy and share every bit of happiness Alan had in his life.

"But," Alan said, "Jessica wants to bring them over to see you. She wants to talk to you."

Jessica showed up at the woman's parents' house. They sat on the couch together. Jessica had failed to bring Alan. This first conversation was going to be just woman-to-woman.

"Here, hold the baby," Jessica said with that fake smile she had all but mastered by this point.

Alan's close childhood friend didn't know what to make of this.

"Basically, Jessica sat there and told me that she was going to 'allow' us to be friends again."

Jessica had once taken anything Alan's friend had ever given him—cards, stuffed animals, photographs, gifts, mementoes of their childhood together—and discarded it all in the trash because she wanted to wipe her out of Alan's life.

By the time Alan and Jessica were raising two kids, Alan worked full-time, while still managing a jam-packed schedule of classes. With that, Jessica milked her role as the stay-at-home mom, using the excuse of being young and strapped for money and home all the time as a means to drain Alan of any energy or serenity the man had left over.

Kevin Bates liked to spend time with his older brother and nieces whenever he could. He loved the children, of course, and was often driven to Monte-vallo on the weekends by his parents or Alan to help his brother work on the house. One weekend Alan made plans with Kevin to do several repairs to the front porch, which was in a state of rot and ruin. The two of them could knock it out on a Saturday and Sunday. Alan had a day off that weekend. He had been working himself ragged with school and a construction job. Just to hang out with his little brother and do some work on the house would be great.

Hammers. Nails. Laughs.

Man stuff.

But Jessica decided she needed to "sleep in" on Saturday. When Kevin showed up, Jessica went right at him and asked if he would watch the kids for her while Alan worked on the porch by himself.

"I'm not well," Jessica said, playing it up.

"Sure," Kevin agreed reluctantly. It was disappointing. He had so much looked forward to hanging out with Alan.

Jessica, Kevin explained, was well aware of that.

"Sorry about her," Alan said to Kevin, who sat in the living room, keeping the children busy, while Alan worked out front. "I'm really sorry. I've been trying to get her to get out of bed. But I'm not having much luck."

It was a recurring problem, expanding by the day. Jessica was getting lazier and more withdrawn, not wanting to do anything.

"It's okay," Kevin said. He understood.

"All she does is sleep, or want to sleep."

Kevin took care of the kids most of that day while Jessica slept.

"Whenever she could," Kevin recalled years later, "Jessica took advantage of a situation. She saw an opportunity that day and took it."

Alan never played into the drama of his wife's supposed "ailments." He internalized a lot of what bothered him about Jessica, realizing that bad-mouthing his wife or complaining about her behavior was not going to do anybody any good. It certainly wasn't going to help her or solve the problem. Part of Alan believed that it was a postpregnancy phase of depression Jessica was going to snap out of at any time. She would wake up one day and be an adult and a loving wife who wanted to participate in the marriage and raise the kids on a level compatible to Alan's busy lifestyle. Alan believed in her. She would want, someday, to work together with him to raise their family.

Inside the theater department of the university, there was a cot and an area where, at times, Alan slept. As much as he wanted to comfort his young wife, he just couldn't take her some nights. It got to a point where the idea of going home was too much to handle. He and Jessica, as the year 1993 came to an end, were having more problems. She was not getting better. Or so it seemed. Alan didn't know what to do. Was Jessica playing this game for attention? Was she truly ill? Did she need psychiatric help? He was willing to get her the help she needed, but enough was enough.

Something had to be done.

By the time Jessica sat and talked to three psychologists in 2003, she'd given birth to five kids: two with Alan (one of whom she'd later say wasn't his), one with a guy she met after Alan, and two with Jeff Kelley McCord. Not that having children is a crime, but Jessica seemed to blame the way her life had turned out on her own childhood, and then on the men she dated and later married. It was always somebody else's fault. She claimed her marriage to Alan began to suffer problems when Alan "wanted her to sleep with his friends."

It was an outrageous lie. So far removed from the person Alan proved himself to be. Jessica offered no proof whatsoever to back up this claim. It went totally against the grain of what Alan stood for and believed morally. What was more, every one of Jessica's and Alan's friends claimed otherwise: Alan had done whatever he could to save the marriage, while Jessica had done whatever she could to see that it failed.

If what Jessica said is true, and there was always a fine line between fantasy and reality, truth and lies, where Jessica was concerned, she had no ethical teaching growing up. Jessica was raised in Hoover, in the same house her mother, Dian, and stepfather, Albert Bailey, lived in at the time Alan disappeared and was found dead. The neighborhood was the same as any other middle-class locale in Hoover. Not a bad place to live out your formative years as an Alabamian. Yet, even though Jessica later said she hardly recalled much of her first five years, she claimed her life was nothing more than a wild, unstable and terribly abusive ride. She said her mother was constantly running away from an offensive, violent husband, a man locked in a perpetual pattern of destroying lives.

According to Jessica, George Callis, her biological father, was a brute of a man who seemed to think the answer to disciplining his children was to scare them into submission. Jessica related once that her father liked to lock her in the closet for hours when she was unruly or disrespectful. There was one time, she later explained in medical documents, when George displayed "snap judgment" anger. The Callises' dog, Champ, was down the block from their home, tearing it up with another dog, rolling around on the ground, biting and grunting.

Jessica ran home to get her dad, hoping he could do something to stop it.

George jumped in the family car, drove down the block, asked Jessica where the dogs were fighting.

"There . . . hurry," she said. Little Jessica was terrified that Champ was going to get hurt. Or worse, be killed by the other dog.

George drove into the yard and ran over both dogs, according to two reports of the incident, crushing them to death in front of several neighborhood kids.

This sort of violence has a lasting effect on a child;

they learn quickly to contend with stressful situations by resorting to violence themselves.

One of the Callises' neighbors, Dottie Gillispie, told *Birmingham News* reporter Carol Robinson that George hit Dian, but that Dian didn't want to do anything about it because she feared the man so much.

"He had beat the hell out of her," Dottie was quoted as saying.

George was abusive, no question. There is a paper trail of evidence left in the man's wake to support the fact that he liked to beat on women and children. Dian and George were divorced on March 6, 1978. Jessica was almost seven years old. George moved to Chattanooga, Tennessee, after living in Semmes, Alabama, for a short time. He drove into Birmingham every other weekend to pick up the kids for visits. As it was, Dian took George to court in hopes of him fulfilling his obligation as the kids' father and paying child support. She also wanted him to pay medical and "other" bills he was responsible for, per a court order—which was where the tug-of-war, the children at the center, started between Dian and George.

George used the kids as a means to seek revenge on Dian for the obvious hatred he harbored against her and the legal issues surrounding the demise of their marriage. Part of the divorce decree stipulated that George *shall pick up the children on the front porch [of Dian's home] when exercising his rights of visitation and shall not enter the premises unless explicitly invited therein.*

It sounded familiar, as Jessica later insisted on the same language in her divorce with Alan. The major difference, of course, was that when Alan Bates said he was going to pick up his children, he showed up. In Jessica's case, as a young girl of seven and eight, unaware of the bitterness involved in some divorce and custody matters, reports claim that it wasn't uncommon for Jessica to sit on the porch and wait for a father who never showed up. And when he did, he was loud, violent, drunk and accusatory, threatening that if the children—Jessica, her brother and sister—were unruly in any way, he would never pick them up again.

George's true madness unveiled itself after he and Dian separated. He kicked Dian and the three kids out of the house they lived in and sent them packing without any of their clothes, no money or accommodations. The kids missed school. Had nowhere to live. Very little food. No means of support.

George laughed at Dian. Made her look bad in front of the children whenever the opportunity presented itself. According to a civil action case Dian filed some years after the end of the marriage, she claimed the reason they'd separated was because George beat her. She was scared for her life. There were times when George struck Dian in front of the children: *in the face, slapping and beating her on her arms, back, and other parts of her body,* one court filing contended.

Dian sensed George would one day murder her. That killer instinct was there in his eyes. He was a wife batterer, sure. A drunk, no doubt. But there was something else about him when he snapped into a violent rage. He blacked out. His aggressive behavior escalated. And Dian's fear meter went off the charts.

Dian was able to get George kicked out of the house finally so she and the kids could move back in.

George moved to Tennessee during the late 1980s. It was then that he met a sweet woman, Olivia, who soon became his wife. Within no time, however, Olivia was now bearing the burden of George's insanity and violent nature as he started to hit her.

The guy could not leave women alone. It was something inside him. One drink led to two, which led to George walking into the home and abusing his wife.

But then, George took things to a new level one night. This happened just as Alan and Jessica, in late 1993, began to experience major problems themselves. Jessica had long ago written off her father as a deadbeat dad with whom she wanted nothing to do. But she was about to be rattled by a telephone call explaining what George had done—a crime that would turn out to be, in many ways, a prelude to what would take place in Jessica's own life.

20

Roger Brown was an old-fashioned Southern prosecutor who believed in the Joe Friday approach in a court of law: "I'm a cop. . . . All we want are the facts."

Brown was a tried-and-true Alabamian, right down to his deep-seated Christian values. For twenty years he served as the lay minister at Our Lady of Sorrows Catholic Church in Homewood. He prided himself on being a straight shooter. Liked to do things by the book.

As the chief district attorney (DA) for Jefferson County, Brown had his hands full with cases ranging from white-collar crime to child abuse, rape, theft and murder. A broad brushstroke of crime to contend with. Brown was a member of the Alabama Supreme Court Advisory Committee on Rules of Criminal Procedure, and he served as a member of the supreme court's Advisory Committee on Pattern Jury Instructions. When it came down to it, Roger Brown knew the ins and outs of a courtroom because he believed in the values that Lady Justice doled out—and he had spent a better part of his life experiencing it all firsthand.

Brown was contacted at his office on Monday morning, February 18, 2002, by the HPD. He was briefed about what was going on. If the case ever made court, Brown knew, he would be in charge.

Certainly, for the bad guys in Brown's district, you did not want to stand on the opposite side of the courtroom facing off against this solidly built man with the deep baritone voice. His Southern drawl casually accentuated an eloquence Brown had fashioned, and few could boast of sharing it with him.

The part of the job Brown didn't favor as much as actually working in the courtroom was supervising all of the attorneys in his district.

"I had administrative responsibilities for the office . . . and supervising those attorneys was like, ah"—Brown took a moment and thought about his choice of words—"herding cats, as they say. Supervising forty lawyers got to a point where it wasn't fun anymore."

Brown said he spent most of his time listening to the complaints of attorneys in the district. But when a hot case came around, he had no trouble forgetting about the shortcomings of the job and getting down to the business he was hired to take care of.

He jumped in headfirst

Detective Sergeant Tom McDanal called Brown and explained to the prosecutor what was going on with the McCords. McDanal went into great detail about the case, describing the evidence they had collected thus far, along with his thoughts, ending with, "This is what we got, Roger."

"Search warrant?" Brown wanted to know.

"Yes," McDanal said, explaining that the HPD needed that second warrant. "And we want to arrest her."

"Well, let's do the [second] search warrant first," Brown suggested, "see what comes out of it—and we'll make the arrest after that."

One step at a time. Be prudent. The guilty always make mistakes. Not that McDanal had suggested such a thing, but the idea was to make the case stick, as opposed to rushing into it.

Brown thought about things. There were a few aspects of the case that struck him immediately. Inside the trunk of Alan's rental car, forensics uncovered one bullet that had hit Alan in the wrist and went through his watch. A .44 caliber.

"Probably the only reason that it stayed in him," Brown said later, "is because it hit his watch. It's the only bullet we got."

Brown contemplated this fact: *We've got us eight bullet holes, four in each victim, but only one bullet that was removed . . . during autopsy.* That meant there could likely be additional projectiles somewhere. Maybe inside the McCord home. But the first search had not turned up anything. In fact, out of all the ammunition the HPD uncovered inside the McCord house during the first search, not one bullet was a .44 caliber.

Detective Laura Brignac weighed in with her thoughts about Jessica and Jeff McCord, Albert and Dian Bailey, letting Brown know where she was coming from. Brignac could tell by interviewing Dian and Albert, especially, that Jessica and her mother had some sort of pull on the men in their lives, which meant that there might be more people involved.

"Dian Bailey and Jessica," Brignac said, "definitely ruled the roost. What they said in that family went. As a matter of fact, the control they had over these men [Albert and Jeff], the more we got into the investigation, became obvious. Albert was henpecked. I don't know another word for it. Albert wanted to cooperate, say something, but you could tell that the wrath of Dian and Jessica would have been upon him. We wondered later what Jessica had on Albert to control him as much as she did. He was afraid. He feared Jessica. Heck, everybody feared Jessica."

From what Brignac could discern, looking into Jessica's eyes, talking to her during those early moments of the investigation, "There is no conscience there. It's all about her manipulating and controlling. She did that—and did it well."

Roger Brown was no wet-behind-the-ears investigating prosecutor. Analyzing a suspect in a murder case was all well and good, but he needed hard evidence to arrest Jessica McCord. He could not rubber stamp an arrest warrant without something tangible, concrete. That said, however, Brown and the HPD, now certain the case was theirs, knew there had to be spent projectiles somewhere. This was going to be the key here. Another bullet. The HPD needed to find it. Because the bottom line now was that all DA Roger Brown and the HPD had was, at best, a few spurious accusations and several circumstances pointing to Jessica killing her ex-husband and his wife. As far as something solid linking Jessica, Jeff or the both of them together to any crime, well, they had nothing. That first search of the McCord home had yielded no trace evidence.

There was a second problem. The house itself. The McCord home was trashed. The garage, for one, was cluttered from side to side, roof to ceiling. The woman was a slob to the tenth power. In having a close look at the inside of the home during that first search, the HPD considered that finding anything they could use was going to be like walking through a maze without an end.

"Literally," Detective Brignac said later, "we thought of [finding a spent projectile in that house] as finding a needle in a haystack, solely because that house was such a mess."

The one thing about cops, however, is that they are diligent and tenacious, and most have type A personalities. They don't give up. When cops smell the smoke

of a gun barrel, they keep searching for the source—
no matter where it takes them or how difficult the
search might seem.

DA Brown just had to convince a judge that a second
search on the same property was going to be worth the
court's signature.

21

Alan was distraught over the woman he loved. He was sleeping on a cot on the campus of the University of Montevallo. He and Jessica were arguing whenever they spoke. With all this turmoil surrounding him, Alan decided to fall into his studies in order to make sure he could at least provide for his children, should he and Jessica not make it. Alan wasn't giving up on the marriage by any means. But as he started his senior year, he was at his wit's end now, wondering if Jessica would ever change.

"He seemed to have the weight of the world on his shoulders," Kevin said, "from our perspective, simply because she wasn't contributing anything to the family. She wasn't doing anything but spending every dollar that he made."

Nearly two hundred miles north, in Chattanooga, Tennessee, Jessica's biological father, George Callis, was living with his second wife, Olivia. He was totally disconnected from the children he fathered with Dian. Not long before Alan started sleeping on the campus, a series of events in George Callis's life took place that gave rise to the idea that Jessica's stories of an abusive childhood might not be so exaggerated, after all.

It was near six o'clock on the night of November 11, 1992. George called the local Chattanooga Police Department. There was a problem at his house, he said.

"I need an ambulance," George said. He sounded resolutely calm and collected for a guy who needed medical help at his home ASAP.

"What's the problem, sir?"

A pause. Then, "I've been beating my wife," George said stoically. "She stopped breathing."

Officers and medical technicians arrived soon after the call to find George upstairs, standing over Olivia, staring down at her.

Olivia was laid out on the bathroom floor. Unconscious. Still as a rock.

"What happened?" one cop asked.

"Um, I, well, I beat the hell out of her," George stated.

The life, too. Olivia was dead. Her face was so badly beaten, cops could barely recognize a human being underneath all the blood and bruises. It looked as though George had taken a baseball bat to the woman's face. He had finally graduated—a wife beater had turned a corner and had become a killer.

George was arrested, found guilty of murder and sentenced to life in prison. It was there, amid the confines of cement walls and barbed wire, that George Callis, according to the dozens of pages of scribbled gibberish he sent me, found Jesus Christ and the Holy Spirit. Both of them were now guiding his every move. These days, you ask George a question about the way he treated his family back then, or why he killed his second wife, you get something along the lines of: *I have prayed about this and the HOLY SPIRIT has led me to recall what the LORD JESUS said at Matthew 10v8. . . .*

Then an extended quote from the Bible follows, with George stepping back in at some point, adding, *Also, at least this could be the avenue whereby I could expound on the fact GOD and HIS SON JESUS plus THE HOLY SPIRIT are <u>trying</u> to get people to see [how] abortion is, if it continues, the way SATAN is blinding people and that GOD will have to pour HIS WRATH on us. GOD uses base ones and despised ones too, anybody HE chooses, to do what HE wants. <u>Money</u>, or the love of it, is not my primary concern. . . .*

(Yes, George asked me for money in exchange for information, which I, of course, refused.)

This man, the same person who had raised Jessica and her siblings, arguably guiding them through those early, influential, formative years of childhood, sent me page after page after page of this "Scripture-inspired" nonsense, much of it entirely unreadable.

Despite all that had happened in their short lives together, Alan never stopped talking about the theater. The lights. The stage. All that went into the production of a Broadway play. It was part of Alan's DNA—his release from the doldrums and anxieties of a marriage on the verge of imploding. Alan was possessed with being the man behind the curtain; he didn't want anything to do with the spotlight. No notoriety or top billing. Instead, it was the lighting, the set design. Those aspects of a production that were done nearly anonymously.

"Alan is the one who will go on and win a Tony Award," Joan Bates said, knowing how dedicated her son was to what he believed God had put him on the earth to do.

"He actually had a deal with Mom," Kevin said later

with a humble laugh, "that he'd buy her a Jaguar when he did [win]."

As the Christmas holiday of 1993 approached, Alan and Jessica were like two cars heading in opposite directions. While Alan's collegiate life soared, Jessica's homemaking and attempt at taking on odd jobs slid down as she fell into an abyss of depression and self-pity. This depression, doctors evaluating Jessica in the years to come would say, and the tenuous mental state that Jessica was in, seemed to manifest into "a manipulative fashion for secondary gain."

She saw an avenue for which to blame others for her troubles and maybe get something out of it.

Married life was all about Jessica. Her world centered not on her children, Alan or what she could offer a failing marriage. Instead, Jessica focused on her own needs and the advantage she could take of the situation.

As Alan spent more time at Montevallo, harnessing his passion for the stage as a means to deal with a home life breaking apart, Jessica began to wonder once again what was going on. What was truly keeping Alan away from home? Was there someone else? Had Alan met another woman?

Jessica soon got a second wind and made some decisions. She went out and acquired her GED, as promised. Then decided to start taking classes herself.

Where?

Montevallo, of course. If Alan could be successful and graduate from college, why in the hell couldn't she? She was tired of staying home, taking care of his kids. Fed up with cooking his meals. Washing his clothes. Changing diapers. Playing the housewife. It was time she took control of her own destiny. What if Alan left her? Where would Jessica be then? What would she have to fall back on?

Heading into the heart of winter 1993, after about a year of living in a household of numbing relentlessness—doing the same things and getting the same results, fighting and arguing and not working together—by the beginning of 1994, Jessica was twenty-two years old and was now taking her life back. No more was she going to lie around the house all day and night wasting away.

It was time to get off her butt and become somebody.

Do something.

By now, Jessica told anyone who would listen that Alan was hitting her, that he was abusive and mean-spirited. That he yelled and screamed at the kids. He was this terrible, rotten man. She was also saying they didn't get along sexually. Didn't share the same religious beliefs. And, to top it off, their politics were so far separated from each other, she often wondered how they ever got along to begin with.

"We were very incompatible," Jessica commented later in court. "Between religion and politics and everything. Sexuality. I mean, just everything!"

Alan never once believed that couples should end a marriage or relationship because there were problems. He never felt that "rough times" were an indicator that the relationship was doomed. A marriage was a sacred bond. But also a living, breathing thing. It was going to experience ups and downs. Highs and lows. Love might even come and go, but Alan was determined. He was in it for the long haul. He hoped Jessica felt the same.

Jessica began to go out. As she did, she learned quickly that there was life beyond the four walls of her living room, the whine of two young kids and a television set. She was young. She could work at it and get her looks back. She could show Alan she wasn't some lazy-ass housewife who depended on a man for everything.

"Before [McKenna] was born, there were some troubles," Kevin Bates recalled, speaking about this period, "but Alan seemed to think that they were behind them, up until the new baby was born. When she was pregnant with [McKenna], everything was going forward." Indeed, the marriage was fluid, moving in a *direction*. It had purpose and meaning. "After [McKenna] was born, this was when Jessica decided that she suddenly wanted to go back to school."

Now the marriage was moving in two directions. Neither of them knew where the other was going. Or what the other wanted out of the union—if anything.

Alan did everything he could to take on more responsibility. He did not want to deprive his wife of her supposed "dream." He juggled two kids and two jobs and still found the time to study and continue going to school himself. The man never slept.

This, mind you, while Jessica took *a* history class. One course. Which amounted to about three hours of class time and study per week.

No sooner had Jessica gone back to school when she came home one night and began hootin' and hollerin' to Alan about a "new friend" she had met in school. Some guy. One of her classmates. They got along like buddies, she said. He was "helping" her through some tough times, both in school and at home.

To Alan, this was a major relief. "She's making friends . . . that's great," Alan told family members. It sure beat sleeping all day and feeling sorry for herself. Getting fat and angry and bitter.

Near Valentine's Day, 1994, after almost two years of working on keeping the marriage together, Jessica approached Alan with an idea.

"I need to take a trip to Washington, [D.C.]," she said, "for a class project I am working on in history." Jessica said she needed to do some research for a paper that was coming due. The trip would serve two purposes: schoolwork and a break from each other. It would help the marriage.

Alan thought about it. "Great," he said.

"Lots of research. I'll be by myself."

Alan believed the trip would do her (and him) a lot of good.

Time apart makes the heart . . .

So Jessica left.

At some point that weekend, while Jessica was in D.C., Alan was rummaging through the house, looking for something. He dug through drawers. Looked in closets. As he did, he came across several missing items in the house belonging to Jessica that made him question whether she had actually taken the trip by herself. He never said what was missing, but one would have to assume it was lingerie and/or female items that would persuade a husband to think his wife planned on having sexual intercourse while she was away.

Alan was hurt, obviously. They were having problems. But an affair was no answer. In his pain and frustration, Alan searched the house and came up with a phone number for that "friend" Jessica had been talking about—the guy she had met in history class.

He dialed the number.

The guy's mother answered.

"Hi, I was wondering if Steven (pseudonym) is home?"

"No," the mother said, "he's in Washington, D.C."

Alan called Jessica at her hotel later that weekend. Knowing she wasn't alone, he confronted his wife over the telephone with what he believed to be an affair she had premeditatedly planned and now executed.

Jessica screamed at him. Took to the defensive, as if she had nothing to explain. Nothing to hide. Nothing to talk about.

"I'm on my way home!" she yelled. "You had better be there. . . . This is *not* over, Alan."

This being the argument and discussion regarding what she was doing in D.C. How dare Alan question her. The damn nerve of the guy.

To several others, before she left, Jessica said she was going to D.C. for two reasons: one, to do research; two, to get an abortion. Why? Because no doctor in Birmingham, she claimed, or any of the larger cities surrounding it, would "touch her" again. As to who the father of the child was, Jessica never said.

"We all thought it was for an abortion," a friend later commented, referring to the trip to D.C. "That she didn't want any more children after having McKenna in 1992. I knew she was going with that guy, but I believed, or she made me believe, they were just friends."

Jessica worked at keeping the few friends she had apart from one another. It was one more way to manipulate the people in her life. Because none of her friends hung around together, she could tell lies to all of them, and not have to keep track of each fabrication.

Throughout the call to Alan, Jessica said several threatening things that convinced Alan there was going to be a "violent confrontation" when she returned. And if there was one thing Alan Bates did not want any part of, it was an aggressive situation, heated argument or contemptuous exchange with her. Alan understood that a day or two of silence could help a situation tremendously. Maybe make room for a better solution. He never hit Jessica. He never raised a hand to Jessica. It's safe to say, many of his friends and family agreed, Alan had never even *thought* about being violent with Jessica. Even after she attacked him, Alan resisted the temptation to strike back. Once, when Jessica was arrested for assault years ago, instead of defending himself, Alan held her down until police arrived. Contrary to what Jessica later told several people, there is no evidence to indicate Alan ever hurt her.

After Alan and Jessica hung up, he called his parents. "I must get out of here." He explained how he felt Jessica was returning from D.C. on a mission to do battle with him—and he couldn't deal with it. "I need to get the kids out of here."

After a call to Robert, he agreed to meet Alan. He said he would take the kids and drop them off at their parents' home.

Alan was on edge. Stressing over what was going to happen when Jessica returned.

"You okay, man?" Robert asked. He wanted to help.

"Yeah. Fine."

Robert could tell the wheels were spinning. Alan shared his deepest feelings only with Joan, his mother, but always after the fact. At the moment Alan would handle things himself. The main point, what worried Alan more than anything, was getting the kids out of the house—and that was done. They were taking off with Robert to spend the night with their grandparents. Alan could handle Jessica.

Jessica walked in during the middle of the night. Alan was packing. He made it clear he was leaving. Getting the hell out of her life. This time for good.

"It's over, Jessica. I'm through." They had gone around this track before. It wasn't going to work. The affair was the final blow.

Jessica paced. Then came that rage Alan later told his brothers about welling up inside her as she wore a hole in the carpet. Her demeanor changed. She was breathing heavily. Alan knew what was coming. The screaming and yelling. A fit.

Jessica—Kevin Bates explained later (both he and Robert got the story from Alan the following morning)—walked calmly into the kitchen. Reached inside a drawer and took out a chef's knife. It was one of those creepy stainless-steel jobs that horror movie types, like Jason or Michael Myers, use.

Alan saw what she was doing and went for the door.

Jessica ran at him, screaming. She wielded the knife. Headed straight at Alan.

He managed to slam the door on the tip of the blade, he told Robert—as Jessica went to stab him.

The knife stuck in the door.

Boing!

Adrenaline flowed like a drug through Alan's bloodstream. He wanted to turn around and confront her. Instead, he thought better of it and went for his vehicle.

"He left, and that was it," Kevin Bates said. "The marriage was over."

From Alan's perspective, it wasn't worth calling the cops and filing a report against his wife. He was moving out. He made plans to begin a new life—without this madwoman. The last two years had been torture on his emotions. The older the children got, the more corrosive the effect Jessica's insanity would be on them.

It could not continue.

On Sunday, Alan, his father and Kevin drove to the house to collect Alan's belongings. When they got there, the house looked as if someone had ransacked it. Jessica had pillaged the entire inside of the home, searching for anything belonging to Alan. She took every photograph, anything ever given to Alan by someone else, and either cut it up or smashed it with a hammer. The garbage can outside was full of destroyed items, many of which Alan had once treasured.

Alan stood over the garbage can and dug through it, salvaging anything he could, even if it was broken into pieces. The photographs were worthless— nothing but scraps of torn paper.

Expressing herself in this manner, Jessica showed how she dealt with the end of a relationship. This was her first serious relationship, as well as Alan's. Before Alan said he was leaving, Jessica came across apologetic and sorry for causing the marriage any distress. She appeared willing to work things out. But after she realized it was over for good, she went into revenge mode.

Snapped.

The war had begun.

"Indeed," Robert said, "from then on, it was Jessica saying, in not so many words, 'I am going to do everything I can to make you miserable.' Throughout this entire situation of the breakup, she tended to hide behind the kids and manipulate the kids, but it wasn't just limited to that."

The fact that Alan never played into Jessica's drama, Kevin and Robert said later, or engaged in any abusive behaviors, either before the separation or after, "made her madder. But he would never even argue with her. He was a peaceful person. Alan would sacrifice everything of himself to keep everyone around him happy—and often did."

* * *

Jessica was not finished playing games. She called Naomi, whose parents owned a Suburban SUV. "Can you come down here and help me move out?"

Jessica told Naomi that Alan had kicked her out of the house—that he wanted the house and she was going to give it to him.

"I actually helped her move into an apartment in Southside," Naomi said.

According to Jessica, the separation was mutual. Something they had both decided on.

"We'll likely divorce," Jessica told Naomi.

After packing everything they could fit into the Suburban, Naomi took the girls and got into the vehicle. She told Jessica she'd wait. Alan happened to be there that day. Jessica said she wanted to say good-bye to him.

Alan and Jessica stood on the porch. Naomi watched from the rearview mirror. The amicable end of the relationship that Jessica had laid out on the way to the house made sense to Naomi as she sat and thought about it. She watched Jessica and Alan hug. Jessica even kissed him. They seemed friendly toward each other. Just as Jessica had said.

Great, Naomi thought, watching, *this isn't going to be one of those messy divorces. They'll be okay.*

Jessica got in. She seemed fine. Quiet, but okay. She was upset about everything, yet eager to get to her new apartment.

When they arrived, Jessica complained about pains in her abdomen. "My stomach . . . it hurts . . . I've been bleeding all day."

The comment shocked Naomi, because she was under the impression that Jessica's trip to D.C. was for an abortion.

"Are you okay? Can I take you to the hospital?"

"No . . . I just miscarried. Must have been all the heavy lifting."

Didn't make sense: a miscarriage *and* an abortion?

Naomi was concerned. "Let me take you."

"No, it's no big deal. I wasn't that far along. I've been through this before. Don't worry about it."

22

Early Monday morning, February 18, 2002, detective sergeant Tom McDanal secured a second search warrant, partly based on the foundation that the HPD had developed new information. In that first search they might have missed something. So members from the HPD's forensic squad and CAPERS unit headed back over to the McCord house.

HPD investigators Greg Rector, Mark Tant, Laura Brignac, D. C. Scively and Peyton Zanzour were part of the team that arrived for the second search. Immediately it turned into a slog through the muck of the McCord home that would, this time around, prove to be far more productive than the first.

Lieutenant Greg Rector, commander of the Investigations Division of the HPD, walked into the garage. Sidestepping what was a heap of garbage piled around a plethora of "stuff," Rector began his search with his flashlight, combing the walls. He was looking for anything out of the ordinary. A good search team left no stone unturned. Officers checked every square inch of space, no matter how tedious and unnecessary it seemed. It took a special eye for this detail: someone with patience and a knack for the mundane. Rector admitted later (with a laugh) that he was perfectly suited for the job.

Within moments, the veteran investigator locked onto a wooden desk pushed up against the wall near a doorway that led into the McCords' den. The wall the desk had its back to was actually the opposite side of the den wall inside the home. Investigators noticed the wallpaper on the other side of the wall looked a bit askew. Maybe just sloppily installed. Albert Bailey, who said he was working on the house, prided himself a master craftsman. Jessica told investigators that her stepfather was one of those types born with a hammer in one hand, a saw in the other. Whoever had wallpapered the McCord den—presumably Albert—had either not watched enough episodes of *This Old House*, had downed one too many beers while working or had rushed to complete the job. There were two different types of wallpaper meeting somewhere in the middle, at waist-high level. The wallpaper line was crooked. The seams did not match up. Even more interesting, it was easy to tell that the wallpaper had been recently installed. Sure, Jeff and Jessica McCord said they were having work done on the house that weekend. But in the scope of the investigation, it all seemed too convenient. On top of that, the kids told Detective Laura Brignac that everything in the den was different.

Going back inside the garage, Lieutenant Rector took his flashlight and looked around the area where the wooden desk was butted up against the wall. While running his flashlight along the floor by the legs of the desk, staring at one section in particular, Rector noticed something.

A hole in the Sheetrock.

He looked down on the garage floor. There was Sheetrock dust and shards of broken plasterboard.

Next to one edge of the wooden desk, close to the floor, sure enough, there was a small hole in the wall. The back of the desk was away from the wall about three inches. Protruding from the hole in the Sheetrock was debris, broken bits of the plasterboard, a chalky white dust and a powdery substance that looked like confectioner's sugar. There was also a small bit of insulation from the inside of the wall that looked to have been pushed through. Something had been jabbed through the wall, from inside the den, and had popped a hole in the Sheetrock.

Rector panned his light down at the floor.

There it was: a spent projectile on the concrete floor of the garage, next to the baseboard, in near perfect condition.

One of the desk legs had an indentation, Rector noticed. Like a scar from where the bullet looked to have hit and bounced back. It was directly above where the bullet sat on the concrete floor.

If you looked down, it wasn't hard to figure out that a bullet had come through the wall, hit the desk, left a rather visible scuff mark on the desk leg, then fell to the ground.

Rector then went around to the other side of the wall, inside the den. Several investigators were in the room, looking around at various sections of the recent remodeling project.

Rector explained what he had found in the garage.

There was no hole, however, anywhere on the wall where it should have been. If a bullet had been fired from inside the den within the past week, say, and went through the wall and landed on the floor in the garage, there should have been a hole in the den wall. At least that's what the evidence in the garage seemed to suggest.

But there wasn't.

They knew why, of course.

Slowly investigators peeled back the new wallpaper.

And there it was: a small hole the size of a bullet in Sheetrock inside the den.

At some point one of the investigators put a trajectory rod through the hole; it indicated the bullet was fired from approximately the chest height of an average-sized human being who was facing the wall. The person would have been standing several feet away from the wall, pointing the weapon toward the garage. The aim was directly on the spot where the McCords' couch had sat before Albert Bailey removed it from the home.

Peyton Zanzour was in another part of the garage, poking around, when he noticed a bag next to the garage door. It was just sitting there on the floor, to the right of the washer and dryer.

To the right of the bag was a pile of clothes.

Inside the bag Zanzour discovered a "wadded-up piece of [old] wallpaper," about the size of a grapefruit.

He knelt down. Wearing latex gloves, flashlight in his mouth, the investigator took the piece of wadded-up wallpaper from the bag and unfolded it.

At first it didn't register. But then staring at it— *bingo*—there was the hole, about the size of a bullet.

Zanzour stood and took the wallpaper into the house. He held it up against the section that had been recently peeled back.

Like a Mylar overlay—a dead-on match.

Things made sense: someone had peeled off the old wallpaper and put new paper over the bullet hole, but did not plaster the hole first.

The HPD needed to get the bullet from the garage to the Alabama Department of Forensic Sciences (ADFS) lab and have ballistics check it against the bullet the Bureau had uncovered in the trunk of

Alan's rental car. That would be the real test. If the ADFS matched the two, the HPD could bank on those arrest warrants they were hoping to file against Jeff and Jessica.

Several pieces of furniture, including a small coffee table you might put in front of a couch, were taken outside the McCord home for the purpose of conducting luminol testing. Inside, parts of the rug in the den were torn up to display what appeared to be tile underneath—some of it new.

"The tile that was on the floor," Peyton Zanzour said later in court, "it was very dirty. There was dirt in places that was, like, in piles, a sandy type of dirt. It was very unusual, number one, that there was that much dirt."

The dog could have tracked that dirt into the home.

But the dirt didn't seem to be a collection from years of carrying it into the house on the soles of shoes; it "appeared," Zanzour testified, "to be as if it was dirt from the outside."

The theory, apparently, was that people were coming and going. Moving things around. In and out of the house.

Furthermore, when investigators took a closer look, they could tell that some of the tiles underneath the carpeting were new, while others were not. This did not make much sense. Especially seeing that there were plenty of other tiles underneath the carpet that could stand to be replaced. Why would a homeowner change only some of the tiles and then cover them with carpeting?

To hide something was the only answer the HPD could come up with. Jessica and Jeff were not providing any other alternative solution.

Zanzour found "gold-colored carpet" fibers near the

base of the hearth of the fireplace inside the den. It was clear upon careful examination that the fibers did not match the carpet the HPD had removed from the den floor.

There was an old carpet somewhere, the HPD was now certain. That carpet needed to be located. It was probably loaded with trace evidence, and possibly even blood from the victims.

"Shelby County Landfill," someone said. It was the closest dump site to the McCord home. Jessica, Jeff and Albert had admitted they had taken items to the dump that Saturday morning and the previous day. If the HPD could find the carpet, they were confident they were also going to find enough evidence to send Jeff and Jessica to Alabama's death row.

"As I recall," Jessica said later, "the carpet that was on the floor of the den went out with the trash."

Standing outside the home, D. C. Scively examined the coffee table that investigators had taken from the den. There was a small stain—about the size of a dime—on one of the coffee table legs. In addition, there were smaller "stains" on the glass portion of the table. All of these appeared to be red in color.

Scively sprayed a few mists of luminol on the glass and table leg.

Waited.

It took a few seconds, but there it was: that fluorescent shimmer, like a child's glow stick, exposing the blood of the recently departed.

23

Jessica alienated Alan from his children the moment he walked out of the house in 1994. One would have to assume that she believed if Alan had abandoned the marriage, why should she show him any respect where the children were concerned? He was the one who left. He had deserted them. He took it upon himself to leave. There had to be a price to pay for such a betrayal.

In the years to come, Jessica had no trouble expressing her opinions regarding Alan's responsibilities as a father; and it was clear that from the moment Alan was out of her life romantically, Jessica's goal was to make him look as bad as she could in the eyes of his kids.

Jessica didn't last long in the apartment she rented after leaving the house in Montevallo. She moved back into the house once she realized Alan wasn't going to be staying there. But even this act of hospitality on Alan's part—he *insisted* Jessica take the house because of the kids—was later turned around by her malicious tongue.

"Alan moved into an apartment in Southside," Jessica said in court, "and I was still in Montevallo at the time. And that fall [of 1994] and in the winter [of 1995], I came down sick. It was very, very cold in that house down there. I came down sick, and the kids were sick. And I just could not keep up by myself being sick with the two kids, so I went to stay with my mother."

Jessica tried to give the impression that because Alan had moved out, she had a hard time paying for heat. Alan gave her money from day one. There is a long, multipage computer printout detailing every payment Alan ever made to Jessica. The guy never missed.

It's clear Jessica needed to blame the people around her for anything that might have been even remotely considered her fault. She couldn't take responsibility for a failed marriage and begin a new life. It needed to be someone else's burden.

Friends became uncomfortable around Jessica as she routinely played the situation against Alan. Her whole life revolved around Alan. Everything was his fault. In front of the kids, she ranted and raved about Alan not paying her child support and not wanting to visit the kids.

None of it was true.

Bottom line: Alan gave Jessica more money than he had to. For example, Alan was paying Jessica child support even before the divorce decree was signed and sealed. Jessica took that money and spent it on herself, and then turned around and blamed Alan for not taking care of the kids financially.

Without being able to fend for herself and the kids as a single mom, Jessica moved into her mother's house in Hoover, abandoning the house in Montevallo. Her mother and stepfather could help out with the kids. Dian was about to start a new job as an accounting supervisor for the child support enforcement unit at the family court. At the time Jessica moved in, Dian was a cashier for the collections office of the court.

The Bates divorce was finalized in January 1995. If she chose, Jessica could take the Montevallo house, as Alan promised, until the kids were adults. The Circuit Court for the Eighteenth Judicial Circuit of Alabama gave Jessica, under Alan's complete blessing, the responsibility of the *care, custody and control of the minor children . . . ,* the Bates divorce decree stipulated. Alan had no trouble relinquishing primary custody. Kids belonged with their mother. He was all for it. At the time Alan believed Jessica was a competent adult mother who could take care of her children. She would get over the breakup. She'd realize what was important. Despite the violent nature she displayed and the negative attitude seemingly festering inside her, Alan trusted she'd snap out of it and come to terms with the notion that their lives were now about raising the children. He had no idea what was spinning inside Jessica—or what was in store for him in the coming months and years. Nor did he ever presume Jessica was capable of the behavior he was about to meet up with.

No sooner had a judge signed off on the divorce did the real problems begin for Alan. He knew it was going to be a fight, but he had no idea how bad it would become. Jessica routinely kept the children away from Alan, allowing him visitation only when *she* said so. And even then, it turned into Jessica purposely keeping the kids away from their father.

They weren't divorced a month and Alan was fed up. He was pulling his hair out, wondering what he had to do to see his kids. He'd call and no one would answer. He'd leave a message and the kids wouldn't call him back. He'd ask the kids, when he finally got to see or talk to them, if their mother or grandmother had given them his messages and they said no. There were times, family members and friends later explained, when Jessica took things as far as sending the kids outside to sit on the front porch with their bags, telling them Alan was "on his way." She would tell them this, knowing there was no scheduled visitation planned. After hours of sitting and waiting, Jessica would then call the kids back into the house, reportedly saying, "See, he doesn't care. He's not coming!"

Then came the men. Jessica hung around a popular local restaurant, J. Alexander's, in Hoover. One night she ran into someone she knew. Barry Cyrus (pseudonym) was older than Jessica. "The first time I met her . . . she was in high school, I was in college," Barry later said in court.

They never dated. Just friends, Barry insisted.

Now Jessica was giving Barry that eye, though—the look of a newly divorced woman out and about, prowling, looking for a man. She was going to show Alan that she didn't need him. She could go out and find herself somebody else.

The more they hung out together as platonic friends, Barry noticed how much Jessica had changed since high school. Barry also noticed the way in which Jessica addressed the children, especially when she talked about Alan. It was always in a negative light. Alan was the bad guy. The evil one. The cause of all Jessica's and the kids' problems. She constantly said vicious things about Alan to the kids, undermining his role as their father.

"I had mentioned to her a couple of times where she would say some things kind of unkind about Alan in front of the children," Barry said later in court.

"Try not to do that in front of the kids," Barry told

Jessica. He was unnerved by the way she spoke to them about Alan. It was not only uncomfortable and wrong, but it was having an ill effect on how the kids behaved and viewed life in general.

Then there was a phone call one day from Alan to Naomi.

"Have you seen Jessica?"

No one could find her. She was AWOL—again.

"As a matter of fact," Naomi said, "I haven't seen her for months."

Alan asked Naomi if she could call over to the Bailey house for him and find out what was going on.

"I will."

"Is Jessica there?" Naomi asked Dian.

Dian sounded discouraged, Naomi later explained. "Yeah, I've got the girls here. She's been gone a couple of months. I cannot find her. She's not coming to see the kids or calling."

Naomi asked around and finally found out Jessica was shacked up with some other guy.

"You need to go home and take care of your girls!" Naomi snapped at Jessica after locating her. Naomi was upset. The kids depended on Jessica. Here it was, Jessica's mother now raising her grandkids. It wasn't right. Naomi wanted Jessica to take responsibility. Grow the hell up.

Jessica said she was pregnant again. "Twins."

"Twins?" Naomi was floored. The last thing Jessica needed was more children. She couldn't handle the two she had.

Naomi didn't know what to say.

"I miscarried the twins, though," Jessica finally admitted.

"You get yourself home and take care of those girls."

* * *

As Jessica made Alan's life as unhappy as she could, most notably by turning the children against him, depriving him of the one thing she had control over (seeing the kids), Alan got busy with his own life—the one thing she couldn't control. Alan now had a degree from the University of Montevallo. He fell headfirst into his first real job in the theater as stage manager for the historic Alabama Theatre in downtown Birmingham. For the most part Alan's job consisted of what he loved more than anything besides his kids: reworking larger Broadway productions for the smaller stage.

The man behind the curtain.

In order to lead the new life she wanted for herself, Jessica spun more of her vicious and self-centered lies, using the children as weapons to get what she wanted out of Alan. Jessica refused to take a job. She told the court she worked for her stepfather as his secretary, but that was, at best, an exaggeration; at worst, a flat-out fabrication. The man didn't have that much work to require a secretary. The fact of the matter was, Jessica did not *want* to work. She believed Alan should support her and the girls.

By the end of 1995, it was clear to Alan that Jessica was taking the child support he paid her each month and using it for her own wild lifestyle of chasing and bedding men. All of this while telling the kids that "Alan wasn't paying her," Kevin and Robert Bates later said.

The entire situation tore Alan apart. From his engineering father, Alan acquired a trait that was now going to help him in his day-to-day dealings with Jessica. Alan grew into the most methodical, organized and thorough person many of his friends and family said they had ever met. He kept detailed records of everything in his life.

"He planned, organized, labeled and filed [things]

with amazing precision," Kevin Bates later said with admiration. "In fact, when things started going sour in the visitation, shortly after the divorce, Alan began meticulously recording, saving, labeling and filing every harassing or threatening voice mail he received from Jessica, and put them neatly in a box—which he labeled 'evidence.'"

24

There was still work to be done inside the McCord home as Monday, February 18, 2002, progressed. Wherever the HPD looked, another piece of incriminating evidence against Jessica and Jeff McCord seemed to pop up. There was now good reason to believe Alan and Terra Bates were murdered inside the McCord home.

Outside the den door, in the garage, a can of gasoline with an inch of liquid was uncovered. More ammo was found. A new bottle of Clorox bleach—empty. Several shards of wallpaper matching the old pattern, which were recently torn off the walls, were found crumpled up.

Empty boxes of tile.

And paper towels. Plenty of used paper towels were unearthed inside garbage cans throughout the house. No one knew then how important these paper towels would become.

Evidence tech Mark Tant, a seventeen-year-veteran law enforcement officer with the HPD, noticed as he took photographs of the outside of the house that there was no mailbox. It was the only house on the block without a mailbox.

Another anomaly. Why no mailbox?

The den was so crowded with stuff, Tant said later in court, "you could barely walk through there. You were stepping on things."

Boxes. Books. Clothes. Toys. DVDs. Tapes. Old newspapers. And trash.

In the far corner of one room on the main floor was a bookcase, later learned to be Jessica's. It was full of true crimes and thrillers. Dozens of them.

At some point that day, Tant was summoned to Pro Tow Towing, a service the HPD used to impound vehicles. The garage was located off Route 150, down on Lorna Road, not too far from the McCord home.

The HPD impounded Albert Bailey's white GMC van, the vehicle he had driven to transport the couch to that Dumpster site in town. The HPD believed Bailey might have transported the carpet, too, either knowingly or unknowingly. And there may well be additional evidence inside the van. Best thing to do was bring it in and process it.

On the back of the window of the beat-up van, Bailey had one bumper sticker, split into two sections: AMERICA, SEPTEMBER 11, 2001.

The guy was a patriot.

Inside the body of the van, Tant found several pieces of tile matching those found inside the McCord home.

He took the pieces out of the van and photographed them.

The HPD released the McCord home for the second time in three days. Jessica stayed at the house. Jeff was "escorted" to the HPD after volunteering to give another statement.

Inside the interview room Jeff made it clear that he

wasn't taking much of this all that seriously—which seemed rather odd, considering the stakes. He was cocky. Laughing and joking around. Acting like he had the situation under control.

Mr. Calm, Cool and Collected.

Peyton Zanzour and Tom McDanal started the interview by turning on the videotape recorder. First they asked about the couch. Who had removed it from the house? When? Why? "Who took the cushions off? Where *are* the cushions?"

This . . . seemed to confuse McCord, a report of the interview noted.

"Look," Jeff said after thinking about it, "I took the cushions off the thing so they would not blow off when the couch was removed from the house and taken to the dump."

But the couch was transported inside Albert Bailey's van.

Another lie.

"Which dump?" one of the investigators asked.

Jeff shrugged.

"Why was the leather stripped from the back of the couch?"

Jeff considered the question. "To make it lighter. And the cushions were actually taken to a charity drop-off at the Wal-Mart in Pelham."

"Where was the stripped leather disposed?"

Jeff said Jessica tossed it; he had no idea where.

The former cop continued to laugh. Apparently, two dead bodies and evidence pointing toward him and his wife was some sort of a joke. "Him being a police officer," Detective Brignac, who was in another room watching the interview on a TV monitor, said later, "you'd think he'd want to help us. But he kept saying he didn't know anything . . . and then he'd sit there and laugh."

"That carpet," one of the investigators asked, "when did y'all remove it?"

"Jessica removed that, too. I have no idea where it is."

As the interview went on, Jessica called the station house repeatedly. "I want to talk to my husband! Where is he? I need to talk to my husband."

"Busy, ma'am."

"I need to speak with him. Please . . . now."

"No. You can't right now. He's busy."

Getting nowhere, Jessica decided to pack up the children and head down to the HPD.

Back inside the interrogation room, one of the investigators asked again, "Jeff, where is the carpet?"

"I think she took it to the dump." Jeff named two different "public dumps in Alabama."

"Which one?"

He went quiet.

"We need to know which dump."

"Am I free to leave?" he asked at that point.

"Sure."

The interview was over. Jeff sat as they got the paperwork for the search warrant together and gave him copies.

"I need my gun and belt so I can turn it into Pelham," Jeff said. "I suspect I'll be placed on administrative leave until the outcome of this investigation."

McDanal left the room to go get Jeff's gun belt.

When he returned (*phrasing it as though there was bad news,* that same report indicated), McDanal told Jeff, "There's a problem with the evidence room door—we cannot retrieve the gun belt at this time."

Jeff went into a laughing fit in response to McDanal's explanation: *After learning what the actual news was, McCord laughed uncontrollably and then noticeably, physically relaxed,* the report noted.

Up and down. An emotional roller coaster for Jeff
McCord. He didn't know how to feel. Or how to act.

Jeff was told he could leave. Jessica was waiting outside in the parking lot.

"There was just so much going on, so much to be
done at this point," Detective Brignac said later, "we
had our hands full. We were all working sixteen-hour
days by then. . . ."

Jessica sat in the family van with the children and
their clothes. Jeff got in. They were heading to Pen-
sacola, Florida, to drop the kids off at Jessica's sister's
and maybe wait out the investigation down there.

Jeff made no promise he'd be back in town anytime
soon.

"If they stay in Florida," one investigator said, "we're
going to have big problems because of jurisdiction
issues."

As Jessica and Jeff pulled out of the parking lot, two
officers in an unmarked vehicle got behind the van
and followed them.

25

They lived in Cullowhee, North Carolina. Cullowhee is a quaint little village in between Rich Mountain and Pumpkintown, located at the base of Western Carolina University. Throughout the past half-century, Cullowhee has housed anywhere between two thousand and three thousand people. This is Blue Ridge–Smoky Mountain territory; Small-Town, USA, where neighbors watch one another's backs.

It was the early 1970s. Terra Klugh was three years old. It rained hard that morning, on and off. The torrential downpours were enough to swell the creeks in the region into fiercely powerful moving streams that could swoop in and swallow up a child of Terra's age in an instant. As an adult, Terra loved to travel. As a child, she was one of those kids who liked to go outside and explore—take off on her own and wander about, pick dandelions and blow them into the wind, maybe roll around in fields of flowers. Her parents were kids themselves, only in their early twenties then. Four years older than his wife, Tom was studying psychology at a nearby graduate school.

Terra's mother was busy doing some things around

the house one afternoon. Tom was at school, but he
called to say he'd be home soon. At some point Terra's
mother happened to call out Terra's name.

No answer.

Uh-oh. There was that honest-to-goodness heart-
pounding panic alarm every parent experiences at
one time or another. A pain burst and throbbed in her
chest as anxiety fueled a search.

"Sweetie? Sweetie?" Terra's mom said, walking hur-
riedly around the house.

Nothing.

She went from room to room.

Terra!

"Sweetie?"

Not a peep.

Walking toward the front of the house, Terra's mother
realized the front door was open.

Terra was gone.

And then the real panic set in.

"When I got home," Tom said later, "Terra's mom
told me what happened."

Tom walked down by a barn about a quarter mile
from the house.

"I saw some boot prints."

Terra had just gotten a pair of red rubber rain boots,
the shiny kind that a Hallmark card depicts kids
wearing while splashing around in summer pud-
dles. Because it rained so hard that morning, Terra
decided to put on her new boots and go out on one of
her adventurous walks.

Down by the fast-moving creek, Tom spied those
boot prints again—tiny molds in the mud stamped
all over the place. They led down to the creek, where
the embankment dropped off sharply into the water.

Then he saw barefoot prints walking away from the
water on the other side of the boot prints. They were

heading in the opposite direction. Little tiny feet that
Tom knew in his heart were his daughter's.

He took a look at the water. How fast the current
moved. Shook his head.

If she fell in there, she doesn't have a chance.

"Terra . . . my goodness," Tom said to himself.

"It looked as though she had walked down to the
creek and threw her boots into the water. If she would
have fallen in the water . . . Terra was gone."

Tom headed back to the house.

As it turned out, a neighbor found Terra wandering
around and brought her back home.

For Tom, the story epitomized what is, he says, "the
evidence of God." His wife had a hard time with the
memory, thinking she'd done something wrong. But
Tom (and later Terra) knew it was nothing more than
a curious child. The mother wasn't to blame. There
was no room for guilt or liability.

"It just happened."

One of those things.

Beyond that, "it wasn't Terra's time to part with the
world," Tom told me years later. "It would have been
an easy time for her to have parted the world, but there
was more for her to do."

Indeed, Tom Klugh's young princess, so stubbornly
foolish in her adolescence, so free-spirited and colorful, had other plans in life to fulfill.

In nearly every way that mattered, Terra Klugh was
the polar opposite of Jessica McCord. Terra was all
that Alan's first wife wasn't: quiet, kind, self-reliant,
warm, compassionate.

"She really, really liked Alan," Marley Franklin said
later. "What a doll of a girl. Just as sweet as you can
imagine."

Terra's formative years were spent in Clemson, South Carolina. She studied for a short time in London, where she pursued a degree in art history. Her minor was mathematics, which she pursued at Hollins University, in Roanoke, Virginia. Terra spent four years as an architectural historian for the Historic American Building Survey, and then became a project historian for the Alabama Theatre. One of Terra's goals was to begin work on her master of arts in historic preservation, an area of history she adored. Historic preservation was Terra's passion, and one of her primary focuses was to attend Goucher College, in Baltimore, Maryland.

Terra was conscientious, pretty, smart and extremely mature when, in 1995, as Alan and Jessica entered into a tumultuous, postdivorce phase of their lives, she started working at the Alabama Theatre. At twenty-five, Terra was career-minded, same as Alan. By then, Alan was in charge of "everything [technical] that happened on the stage . . . ," Alabama Theatre's executive director, Cecil Whitmire, said later. Whitmire was single-handedly responsible for saving the Alabama Theatre from destruction. Like everyone who met Alan, Whitmire thought the world of him.

Terra was sent to the Alabama Theatre as part of a restoration team put together by the Department of the Interior (DOI). The team traveled from D.C. to Birmingham to document the theater for the Library of Congress. Terra was living near Washington, D.C., at the time, and working for the government in one of its historic American buildings and structures programs. The last thing Terra was looking for was love. Her career was soaring. Plus, Terra had a way about her when it came to men. She was extremely private about this part of her life.

"I'm going out tonight," she'd tell her father over the phone.

"A date?"

"No, no, no."

"But you're going out with a guy, right?"

"Yeah. *Out,* Dad. That's all it is."

"You sure you're not dating?"

"No. No."

Next subject.

Ever since she was a kid, Terra had a strong will about her. She was her own person. Part of it, Tom Klugh believed, was from being raised an only child, and the family moving around a lot.

"Except for the first couple of years," Tom said, "we were in Fort Sill, Oklahoma . . . when I was stationed there during the Vietnam War, and then a little time in North Carolina when I was in school."

Terra left for Hollins with the idea of becoming a mathematician. She had a change of heart, though, and flipped her major to architectural history once she got to Roanoke. Maybe it was being in such a historic town with the ambiance of America's history at her doorstep. Who knows? The point is, Terra had found her passion in life and decided to go for it.

Terra took after her mother. Tom Klugh said his ex-wife was extremely artistically inclined. A ballet dancer. An expert potter. Whatever she did, it seemed, Terra's mom mastered.

"My ex-wife," Tom said, laughing admiringly, "has more talents than anybody should be given."

While Terra and her mom got along well and remained close, Tom said they seemed to always compete against each other.

"You have to understand," Tom recounted, "Terra was raised by two pretty immature adults. I was twenty-three when Terra was born, her mom just nineteen. But I don't think age says anything about our emotional stock."

The one thing Terra didn't appreciate was when she confided in her mother, and then her mom went back and told Tom. This exasperated her.

"I always told Terra, 'You know, you have *two* parents here. They're supposed to know these things.'"

While studying and working for the DOI, Terra took that trip with the preservation team in charge of restoring the Alabama Theatre. Not only was she staying in town, but she was working at the theater—where she soon crossed paths with Alan.

The moment she set eyes on him, friends later suggested, Terra "just fell in love with him."

"I had never really gotten the impression from her," Tom said, "that she was serious about anybody—that is, until she met Alan. Of course, there were others along the way, sure. But usually they tripped over their bootlaces if given enough time. And so that was it for them. But Alan . . . he was different."

They became friends first. But that didn't last long; the relationship moved quickly. Terra felt "at ease" around Alan, a feeling she'd experienced with no one else.

"She certainly talked about him a whole bunch," Tom added. "We did a lot of talking on the phone."

The impression Tom got after meeting Alan for the first time was that he wasn't this "warm, gushy person. . . . He was very nice. Certainly, he wasn't one of these toady people, who would 'yes, sir, Mr. Klugh' to everything I said."

An Eddie Haskell, in other words. A phony. Some guy trying to warm up to the dad in order to get in good with the daughter.

No, Alan was confident. Clean-cut. Quiet. Reserved. Determined. Liked to keep to himself.

"A lot like Terra."

Neither Alan nor Terra shared things about their

lives with other people. But they found each other—and with that, the ideal sounding board.

They hadn't even been officially dating when Terra turned to Alan one day after knowing him for only a brief time and said, "You know, I really see a potential here with you. I'm quitting my job."

"Quitting?"

Alan was frightened by this. He knew Jessica. He knew the turmoil he was involved in was just beginning. He knew that it was going to get a lot worse before it got better. Did he need to drag someone else into the mix—especially someone as loving and caring as Terra? She didn't need that in her life.

Terra's job would have taken her away from Alan after the company she worked for finished up at the Alabama Theatre. As the team she worked with moved on to other parts of the South to continue the work, Terra was going to have to leave Alan.

She thought about it. Decided she wanted no part of moving away from Alan.

Alan was thrilled. Exalted. Happy. But also scared.

"She was a beautiful, strong spirit," Kevin Bates remembered, "who just made my brother shine. She was the perfect companion for him." Terra Klugh brought out the best in Alan Bates; and they brought out the best in each other. "It made us realize we were looking at an adult relationship for Alan," Kevin added, "and this couldn't be a better situation."

Terra had short, straight auburn-brown hair. The most delicate, clear, white skin—smooth as paper— and a smile that woke up any room she entered. Terra loved to hike with Alan. She grew up with a penchant and passion for ballet, like her mother. Her voice, friends insisted, was distinct: soft-spoken, sweet in tone, gentle and kind. And yet, while Terra exuded an immense amount of femininity, certainly a woman from head to toe, she wasn't afraid to pick up a power tool and build a piece of furniture.

"She had a quiet strength," Kevin Bates said, "which was just the perfect companion to my brother."

Soul mates.

Alan was content romantically for the first time in his life—which would, he was soon to realize, only increase the hatred and dissension Jessica felt toward him already. If there was one thing that infuriated Jessica McCord more than anything, it was the competition of another woman.

26

MCSO chief investigator Michael Pritchett had been involved in the investigation since that burning car was reported in his jurisdiction. Pritchett, a twenty-five-year lawman, took on the job of locating a source for the "child's print" paper towel found on the ground at the Georgia crime scene. It was one sheet of paper towel, slightly crumpled, burned on one corner. The decoration imprinted on one side was a stick figure of a child, along with the simulated scribble of a preschooler learning his ABCs.

I ♥ DADDY.

A child's handprint was located directly underneath the writing. There was a smiley face sun figure next to rows of flowers.

Pritchett took a photograph sample of the paper towel and hit the road.

"I went to nine different stores, retail stores in the area of where the bodies were found," he said later in court. "As a matter of fact, there was nine closest stores to the scene. And the larger retail stores in the area, I went to check to see if they had in stock this pattern of paper towel. . . ."

Pritchett asked the clerk at several locations the same question: "Are you familiar with this pattern?"

All of them said, "No." They had never seen it before.

In fact, the sheriff testified, "No clerk remembered having sold that pattern." As the investigation would soon divulge, there was a good reason why.

Back at the ADFS Birmingham Regional Laboratory, Firearms and Toolmarks Identification Unit scientist Ed Moran got busy testing the bullet found at the Georgia crime scene against the bullet recovered inside the McCord garage. Here was the "smoking gun" evidence—nearly literally—that every prosecutor dreamed of. A match, without question, would tie Alan's and Terra's deaths to the McCord home.

Forensic expert Moran had sixteen years behind the microscope. He was rather blunt and realistic when explaining his often tedious job: "It's not like it is on TV."

Indeed. Matching bullets with lands and grooves was more complicated than putting two microscopes together on a granite lab table, looking into both of the glass eyes and, during a commercial break, coming to a conclusion.

With a master's in criminal justice from the University of Alabama, a bachelor's from Auburn University, Moran had been involved in firearms and toolmark investigation since 1990. He lectured and taught firearms courses. Few men in Moran's trade were more experienced.

"There are two types of markings I look for," Moran explained, referring to the science of figuring out if two bullets had been fired from the same weapon barrel. "The first markings are called general rifling characteristics. That would include the number of lands and grooves on the bullet, and the widths of the lands and grooves, and the directions of twists."

A bullet slides through the barrel of a gun, twisting and turning its way out, spiraling toward its intended target. This causes "special" tool marks left on the outer part of the jacket of the projectile. Think of a barber's red-and-white swizzle stick spinning outside his shop— that candy-cane-like pattern of stripes.

Same thing.

"Lands and grooves," Moran continued, "are machined onto the inner surface of the inside part of the barrel during the course of manufacture. They can be likened to ridges or valleys on the inside of the barrel."

Simple science. After all, no manufacturer can machine lands and grooves identical in each barrel. It's impossible.

"I cannot make a positive identification that two bullets were fired out of the same *gun*," Moran said, clearing up an assumption that television has promulgated into a fact of forensic science. "But I could eliminate whether two bullets were fired through the same *barrel*."

If, for example, a bullet had six lands and grooves, Moran said, which turn (or spiral) to the right, and a barrel has five lands and grooves rotating to the left, "there's no way *that* bullet could have been fired through *that* barrel."

Simple math.

There are also microscopic striations machined into the inner surface of a barrel during manufacturing. These cannot be duplicated.

"Those markings are to be likened," Moran insisted, "to a human fingerprint."

Moran lined up the bullets inside two microscopes. The one on the right was from Alan's wrist. The bullet struck Alan's watch, which slowed its trajectory, ultimately lodging into his wrist. A fragment of that projectile was found underneath Alan's body. If Alan had not been wearing a watch, the bullet would have gone through his wrist, and might not have ever been found.

The bullet on Moran's left was from the floor of the McCord garage.

Moran explained what he found: "When you look at this . . . I think we can somewhat readily see that the striations match up precisely. . . ."

Like a hand in a glove.

In Moran's opinion, which seemed to be backed up by the evidence, he was certain that the bullet extracted from Alan's wrist and the bullet located on the floor of the McCord garage had been fired from the same barrel. Moran guessed a Remington Peters— a gun, incidentally, that had *not* been recovered from the McCord home among Jeff's large cache of weapons.

As the investigation picked up steam in Alabama, a report came in from Georgia. There was a good reason why that particular pattern of paper towels had not been found in an approximately fifty-mile radius of the Georgia crime scene. Those particular paper towels were sold in the Birmingham region of the country.

27

Alan and Terra enjoyed the serenity of being in a mature relationship. They respected each other. Cared how the other felt. Talked things through like adults. This was new to Alan, who had lived a life of "romantic" hell for as long as he could remember.

Jessica, meanwhile, was busy holding on to Cupid's arrow for dear life, following it wherever the path led. If Alan had gone out and landed himself a catch with Terra, Jessica needed to find herself a man. Someone she could flaunt in Alan's face. Someone who could help her achieve whatever goals in life she now had.

Near the fall of 1995, Jessica visited the Lion & Unicorn Comics Games & Cards store on Lorna Road, not too far from her mother's house. It was one of those hobby shop/comic-book stores that sold various types of fantasy gaming items and other collectibles. It also advertised a line of vintage comic books and baseball cards.

Jessica later said she hung out in the store because she got involved in playing a game called Magic: The Gathering. (The game falls in line with the idea behind *Lord of the Rings*.)

It was a role-playing game—an appealing proposition to those who partake in fantasy, but also have an inherent need to control things. Essentially, Magic was the genre-breaking first in a series of card games that involved an ongoing plot, forcing players to buy additional products in order to continue playing the game competitively. An ingenious invention, in terms of marketing. The game was introduced in 1993 by a mathematician. The game revolves around your typical "good versus evil" plotline, in which wizards go up against "the dark side." Some liken it to an updated version of the popular 1980s phenomenon Dungeons & Dragons.

Jessica had other ideas, however, for heading into Lion & Unicorn. A man worked behind the counter, Brad Tabor (pseudonym), in whom she apparently saw potential. Brad lived alone and was content in his job at the card shop.

No one could understand why Jessica was attracted to the guy—that is, until it was later learned that Jessica believed Brad was going to one day inherit some money. Then it made sense: that "entrepreneurial" side of Jessica, in a perpetual state of looking for a free ride, a sugar daddy.

From Jessica's perspective, Brad fit into that mold.

Near January 1, 1996, Jessica and Brad started dating. Brad was taken with this attractive young woman who seemed to be not only full of herself, but confident, strong-willed and full of sexuality. To his surprise and delight, she was also into him.

Jessica knew how to manage what she had; she could doll herself up to look eye-catching and trashy hot. She owned the spotlight when she walked into that store, unafraid to shake her "thang" and play into whatever sliver of sexual sparkle she could conjure.

When Brad asked, Jessica said she had been married once and went through a divorce "several years prior."

It would be the first of many lies that Brad would soon hear.

Brad got Jessica a job at the Lion & Unicorn. They began spending time together. Brad liked Jessica. To him, she was a hot chick without kids who seemed to be interested in the same things he was. What was there not to like?

Indeed, Jessica failed to mention up front that she had two kids at home (or, rather, staying at her mother's house). Brad never suspected she was lying. Why would he?

In the years following, like most things in her life, Jessica viewed her relationship with Brad in a different light: "We slept together and dated," she said in court, "and the order varied. It was an on-and-off thing."

Not true. According to one of Jessica's former friends, as soon as Jessica and Brad started hanging out and working together, and Jessica found out Brad was going to "come into some money," she was all over the guy. She started sleeping with him voluntarily. He didn't need to work at it.

Ask Jessica, however, and you come up with a different version of how they met. "I worked there. And he worked there on occasion and came in basically to see who the girl was that was working in the store, because it was very unusual. And we became associated because we both played a game called Magic."

Setting aside the truth of how they met, regarding the idea that Jessica failed to tell Brad she had children, she said: "That's not true. I had been warned not to date him because he did not *like* children."

She never gave a reason (if it were even true) why Brad disliked children. Or why she would consider dating a man who felt that way.

"I didn't make it a policy," Jessica stated further, "to take people I went out with around my children. I thought it would be hard for them to have people, you know, going in and out. And . . . I had no intention of just getting divorced and dating one guy and getting immediately remarried. I didn't want the kids to suffer from a constant change of people."

Some wondered if that was motive enough *not* to share with a man that you allegedly liked that you had children. Like many things Jessica later said, her excuse for a particular behavior made little sense.

Brad lived in an apartment in the Five Points region of Birmingham. He had a simple life.

Work. Home. Work. Home.

Magic.

Jessica moved in with Brad. Her clothes and all. Six weeks went by, Brad later said, before she finally admitted she had two kids living at her mother's house. Two kids, in fact, who needed their mother and were not seeing their father on a regular basis because Jessica was so darn bent on spiting Alan.

This manner of conduct turned into a vicious circle. Jessica would leave the kids with her mother for long periods: weeks, a month, two months. Days, certainly. She would not see them—and sometimes, a friend later said, she rarely ever called them. She didn't care. Jessica wanted what she wanted, and nothing—not even her own flesh and blood—was going to stand in her way or stop her.

And now she had Brad.

Naomi called Jessica once in a while to see how she was doing. After learning Jessica was leaving the children with her mother, Naomi was upset. She wanted to reprimand Jessica and scold her into feeling guilty about it—and then demand she get over to her mother's house and take care of those kids.

Forget about Brad. The kids need you. This was a recurring thought, Naomi said.

Jessica got mad. Gave Naomi some excuse as to why she wasn't at her mother's with the children.

Then, as Naomi and Jessica were talking, Jessica came out with it: "I'm pregnant now, anyway."

Naomi expected to hear that Jessica was planning a trip to Mississippi or another state to get an abortion. Jessica claimed to have already had one abortion (Brad's child) after miscarrying twins.

But not this time. "I'm keeping it," Jessica stated.

From the sound of it, Jessica was looking at the new baby as a means to an end: another child support check from a guy who was, she believed, going to come into a healthy sum of money someday. Thus, all things considered, it would appear babies were a source of income for Jessica.

Not long after she moved in with Brad, Jessica went to him and announced that she was pregnant, adding, "I'm keeping the baby."

According to Jessica, Brad did not want anything to do with being a father. "I was not going to have an abortion," Jessica said years later in court, recalling this period of her life, "and I was not going to have my baby and give her away. I would *never.*"

But that's exactly what she did, Brad later explained. "Well, the first child. She aborted it."

About five or six months later, Jessica went to Brad again. "I'm pregnant."

This led to problems with the relationship. Brad and Jessica were not on the same wavelength about anything. So they split shortly before the child was born. Jessica moved out of the apartment and back into her mother's house—now back with her two kids . . . and pregnant with another child.

28

In Georgia, members of the Bates and Klugh families were not far from where the reclusive novelist Flannery O'Connor—a woman who seemed to set in bronze a long-lasting image of what a true "Southerner" represented—once stated that the "things we see, hear, smell and touch affect us long before we believe anything at all." The Bates and Klughs waited and wondered. Part of each of them leaned on that strong sense of family still so ingrained in the Deep South. The hardest element of it all was accepting that Alan and Terra would never again grace the dinner table at a family function. There would be no more phone calls just to catch up and say hello. No more of those million-dollar smiles Alan could flash to make you feel great. No more sharing of the good things in life. No more laughs or memories in motion. Terra and Alan were there one day, gone the next, as if they had vanished.

The other horrifying aspect of having to deal with a tragedy of such immense scope was that, of all the people in the world, the reality that Alan's ex-wife could have had something to do with his death was simultaneously sobering and appalling. In Philip and Joan Bates's wildest dreams, they could not have fathomed life to have taken such a terrible, personal turn. That inherent parental need to protect your child was there in every second of life. It was a challenge Philip and Joan took as the price of perfect love. And they had weathered the storm well—that is, up until this moment.

"Our parents had always put our needs before their own," Kevin Bates later explained. "They worked hard together to provide us each with everything we ever needed, and many (but not all) of the things we wanted. When we relocated to Atlanta in 1991, they chose our home for the best public-school system in the area for my benefit, despite the fact that this left Dad with up to an hour commute one way to work each day. Though us kids were all . . . out of the house, they remained very active and interested in our lives and looked for any opportunity to support our endeavors. They regularly traveled to see any show Alan worked on, whenever it would come within driving distance of Atlanta. And, of course, they looked for any opportunity to enjoy and spoil their grandchildren."

That flawless continuity of life was dramatically disrupted—all at once. Severed without warning. Both families asked themselves two questions as the hours passed: *What now? How do we deal with such an aggravated, abrupt end to two wonderful lives?*

By late Monday night, February 18, well into Tuesday morning, several facts were apparent to the families: (1) After some soul-searching, no one could discern any other known human being on the face of the earth who could have—or would have—wanted Alan and Terra dead, and (2) Jessica McCord expressed motive and had opportunity, two of the most important factors driving this type of crime.

As the families interacted while waiting for bits of news to trickle in, it was hard to push away the theory that Jessica had killed both of these beautiful people.

Roger Brown called Philip Bates early that week to explain "as much as I could at the time," Brown later told me, concluding the call with an apology for not being able to be more forthcoming with information.

"This is what we have, Mr. Bates. I'll call you as soon as I can give you anything more."

Philip, that engineering mind of his calculating things out its own way, understood there was a major investigation going on. Philip and the others would get the facts as they became available. The last thing anyone wanted to do was taint a future court case by pressuring Roger Brown to cough up particulars about his case.

"I understand," said Philip. It pained him. Sure. But he also knew how fragile and fluid the situation was and would be until an arrest was made.

Hanging up the telephone, Philip walked out of the kitchen and told Kevin, Robert and Joan, "We've got the *right* man working on this." Philip was impressed by Brown's matter-of-fact way of dealing with such a delicate state of affairs. Brown spoke in truths. Plain. Clear. Concise. Philip respected that. Brown didn't care to speculate. He rarely said anything, in fact, that he or his investigators did not know for certain.

Brown made a promise to keep Philip in the loop. And Philip appreciated it, knowing that when a Southern man—especially a lawman—gave his hand to shake on and his word, he damn well meant it.

The families had not yet come out and said to one another that *Jessica did this*. "But," Kevin commented later, "we knew the chances of it being a random act of violence kept diminishing. . . . Jessica was the only enemy Alan had in the world, and she was, after all, the last person he was meant to go see before he and Terra vanished."

Among them all was the sinking, sick feeling—like

some sort of virus they couldn't see, touch or get rid of—that Jessica resorted to murder to solve her problems. And then the confusing questions: Why would she do such a thing? How in the world *could* she do such a thing?

From where the Bateses stood, the scenario was clear and plausible. Alan and Terra were supposed to pick up the kids somewhere near 6:00 or 6:30 P.M. Jessica said they never showed up. She called Alan and left a message on his cell phone. Alan and Terra were found in the trunk of their rental car along the I-20, past Atlanta—heading in the opposite direction of his parents' home, near three-thirty that next morning.

When you stepped back and thought about it, what else could have happened?

As the days passed, Kevin and Robert Bates, along with members of Terra's family, converged at the Bates home, waiting for calls to come in. As they did this, the focus was put on the children. Number one, where were they? Two, had anyone told them what had happened to Alan and Terra?

Neighbors and friends sent food and flowers, cards and condolences, to the Bates home. The days became a foggy haze of puzzlement and melancholy. Some sort of dreamlike reality. It was as if they were all living someone else's life, just going through the motions of the day. You do things and later wonder how they got done. You don't recall conversations. Driving places. Eating or cooking meals. The body and mind seem to work together in unison, while the soul weeps.

Making funeral arrangements kept everyone busy for a few days. It was agreed that Alan and Terra would be cremated and memorialized together.

"As they would have wanted," said one family member.

"Everyone realized," Kevin added, "that no matter who killed Alan and Terra, they were gone, regardless.

We were focused on what we *needed* to do. What we *could* do. How do we honor them? We don't even have their bodies yet."

The idea that closure was going to come sooner rather than later was not a certainty anyone could take comfort in just yet. They all knew, understood and accepted that Alan and Terra were dead. Yet, officially, they were still waiting for "positive confirmation" that those two terribly burned bodies in the trunk of that rental car were actually Alan and Terra. Death's limbo. You know in your heart, but you still cannot stop holding out hope. Dental records were one thing, DNA another. Until then, that hidden optimism—a single strand of subtle brightness—hangs out there in the open, and you don't want to turn your back on it.

With the media stirring in Birmingham, waiting on the HPD's next move, reporting on the case, play by play, the families decided the best place to have the memorial service was Georgia.

The *Birmingham News* put one of its more esteemed, prized reporters, Carol Robinson, on the case. Carol had over a decade-and-a-half's worth of experience working the Birmingham crime beat. Most Hoover cops knew Carol. Appreciated her work. Valued her tenacity for printing the truth. "That is rare," one cop told me, "in newspaper reporting around here." If nothing else, investigators from the HPD knew that Carol would cover the story with a deference to the families and set her sights on facts. Carol had a reputation for not focusing on sensationalism but instead keeping her eye on what made the story important in the fabric of the local, social landscape. She was a reporter's reporter.

Carol was home, sick, on Monday. A source close to

the HPD called her. "Stand by, something big is coming your way."

She was interested, obviously, and the tip had a quick-recovery effect on the illness she was battling.

The attractive blond reporter, a native Southerner, was born and raised in Dixie. Carol and her family moved to Avon, Connecticut, for four years—from five to nine years old—but they had lived in the "Yellowhammer State" ever since. A graduate of Vestavia Hills High School in Birmingham, Carol went to Auburn University and started working for Alabama's largest newspaper, the *Birmingham News,* three months out of college, in 1986. It was her first and only full-time newspaper job. Heading into the McCord case, some sixteen years later, Carol was now the senior reporter, leading the newspaper's crime coverage. She had an understanding of covering high-profile murder cases: the slayings of three Birmingham police officers, the Birmingham abortion clinic bombing and the subsequent five-year hunt for fugitive Eric Robert Rudolph, as well as the reopening of the case of the 1963 Sixteenth Street Baptist Church bombing.

Getting out of bed and heading into work, Carol realized she had not even heard that two bodies with Birmingham ties had been found in Georgia. Still, she dragged herself into the office and wrote what would be the first of several stories the *Birmingham News* devoted to the case: KILLINGS FOLLOW CUSTODY FIGHT: PELHAM OFFICER, WIFE SOUGHT FOR QUESTIONING.

"As you can tell," Carol later told me, "it was made clear quickly that the McCords were suspects. . . . [The case] was a talker, but not, say, to the level of Natalee Holloway. That is, because there was not time for it to build as a mystery. . . . There was not much made about Jeff being a police officer because he was not much of a police officer, in that he was not some big, bad cop with a list of awards or disciplinary actions against him. He was just vanilla. Jessica became a popular villain as time wore on because she was trashy, crazy—and nobody could understand what she had that would attract so many men. . . ."

Carol's first story detailed the case up to the point of which it had been reported publicly, focusing on bare facts. It was enough to get the ball rolling so Carol could call on her sources and dig in.

"Had we been in Birmingham," Kevin commented, referring to the families, "we would have been right in the middle of the fire."

There was a lot brewing around town as Jessica and Jeff planned their next move. Part of the speculation was that Jessica fled—took off somewhere and could not be found. Investigators knew she and Jeff had driven to Florida to avoid the media and, presumably, the police, as well as to drop the children off at her sister's house. It was not uncommon for Jessica to head to Florida to visit her sister and, one former family member noted, "run away from her problems."

Jessica was an expert at avoiding accountability.

Word soon spread, however, that Jeff and Jessica had dropped the children off in Florida and had turned around and headed back to Alabama. One comfort to the Bateses in knowing this was that the kids were going to be spared all that was blowing up back home. The kids surely didn't need pressure of any sort. No good could come out of them seeing their dad's picture on the local nightly news, or their mother's name in the newspapers. The impact of the deaths alone was going to be hard enough. To think that their mother was being viewed as a suspect would be devastating.

Philip Bates called Jessica's sister's house in Florida numerous times. He wanted to speak with the kids. Then ask her to make sure they were sent to Atlanta in time for the memorial services. The funeral was planned for Saturday, three days away.

"I'll pay for their flights and your hotel room," Philip announced into Jessica's sister's voice mail that week during one of his many messages, "if you can bring the children here for the service."

The Bates brothers said Philip never got a call back.

Word was that Jessica's sister had some sort of problem in her house and it had to be fumigated. So she and the kids stayed at a neighbor's. She wasn't getting any of her messages. It was strange, bearing in mind all that had happened. Why wouldn't she check her voice mail during such a critical period of time? But investigators from the HPD backed up this fact.

By Wednesday, February 20, the kids had no idea their father and stepmother were dead. No one had told them. Instead, the news was given to them about an hour before the Birmingham police arrived in Florida to pick the kids up and transport them back to Alabama. Once they arrived in Alabama later that night, the children were scheduled to meet with grief counselors. After that, they would stay with an aunt and uncle.

"Jessica's sister told them [that Alan and Terra had been killed], right before we arrived," one investigator claimed. "Which we didn't want done. They still had to ride with us back to Alabama. We wanted them to at least have that ride back without having to think about it. But that was not the case."

29

One of the first things Jessica did during the spring of 1997, soon after giving birth to Brad Tabor's child, was summon him to court for child support. She was able to convince a judge to issue an order in the amount of a whopping $800 a month—nearly double what Alan was paying for two kids.

It was a paycheck. Between that and the money Alan was sending her, Jessica had the potential to collect almost $1,200 a month.

"She did whatever she had to do to get a free ride," an old friend said. "Everybody who knows Jessica will tell you this."

Everyone did.

Brad couldn't pay, so he was not involved in the child's life in any manner whatsoever. Sara (pseudonym) was born and Jessica took her home and Brad was not allowed to see the baby. At one point Jessica had Brad arrested for not paying child support. He was tossed in jail. Brad, in the meantime, proved to the court that he couldn't afford such a high amount. So the judge reduced the monthly debt to $463.

And guess what? Brad was able to swing it.

Before the second order was issued, Brad had no legal rights to his child. Jessica had made sure she controlled that end of things. Brad, however, was able to renegotiate the child visitation portion of the order and, heading into late 1998, convinced the court to back him up.

Still, the court's ruling meant little to Jessica. On top of that, Brad admitted later, he was afraid to go see his child.

"Personal-safety issues," he admitted in court. "After conferring with my family and my attorney, it was advised that it wasn't a good idea for me to be alone with her (Jessica)."

What was it that sparked this sudden fear?

Brad's attorney found out Jessica had put Alan in the hospital. Jessica showed up at Alan's apartment to drop off the kids one day and instigated an argument with him. Before she left, she hit and scratched him, then pushed him down the stairs.

"His face was bloodied," a friend of Alan's later said. "She messed him up good."

One of Alan's friends was there, as was Alan's mother, Joan. They were terrified. Jessica was wild and crazy that day. There was this look in her eyes: hate.

Jessica ran outside after the attack, but for some reason she didn't leave.

The cops came. Jessica was all scratched up herself.

"See what he did to me!" she told the cops.

The police figured out that Jessica had actually rubbed her body against a brick wall outside to create the appearance of cuts so she could blame Alan.

In addition to a battered face with deep nail scratches, Alan broke his arm during the fall.

This time he wasn't going to mess around; he filed charges.

When Brad heard about the incident, he didn't want

to find out what else Jessica was capable of. Nonetheless, Brad tried to maintain a relationship with his daughter. But no matter what he did, no matter how many times he called, Jessica found a way to sabotage it.

Brad was talking with Jessica on the phone one night. According to him, he could hear Sara in the background, "Let me speak to Daddy, Mommy. . . ."

Jessica became enraged. She absolutely despised the idea that the child wanted to even know her father.

"You hush, Sara!" Jessica snapped, according to Brad's version of the call. "He doesn't want to speak to you."

"Come on, let me talk to her."

"Never!"

By the beginning of 1999, Jessica was working for the Birmingham Police Department as a clerical secretary. The job, however, wouldn't last long, as Jessica lived up to her reputation as being lazy and disobedient. Not long after she attacked Alan, the BPD fired Jessica, citing her continued absence from work on top of, one letter noted: *the attack on Alan.* A termination message sent by the chief explained what happened, pointing out, *You went to the home of your ex-husband and you admitted you hurt him. . . .*

With no income coming in, save for the child support she collected from both men, Jessica needed more money. Near February 1, 1999, Jessica sent Alan a bill purportedly from SHR Incorporated, a contracting firm. On top of the bill, Jessica noted that she would soon be sending Alan all of the bills for the house and for dance lessons. It was Alan's responsibility to pay half of the Montevallo house repair costs and all of the dance bills for the girls. The list Jessica sent was long. According to the invoice, both hot- and cold-water pipes had burst inside the house, insulation underneath the kitchen had been destroyed, several "emergency calls" to plumbers ensued, and there were outdoor water pipes leaking. The place was falling apart. The total to fix everything, the invoice claimed, was $1,700. Alan needed to send his half immediately, Jessica warned.

Frank Head, Alan's lawyer, did some investigating. No one trusted Jessica. She was shady and a known liar.

Sure enough, Frank Head could find no such listing for a company named SHR. So he dashed off a letter to Jessica, explaining the problems with the bill. He said that after reviewing the statement from SHR she had sent to Alan, he could find no address or telephone number on the invoice. In addition, the invoice failed to provide the dates the work was completed. Head encouraged Jessica to provide *original* invoices so they could confirm the work with SHR themselves.

Frank Head never heard from Jessica about the bills again.

Alan was enjoying what could be considered a somewhat normal life. He had a decent job. He had met and fallen in love with Terra. He was working with Frank Head to get Jessica on the right track with visitations. His life was heading upward.

A direction—he came to find out—that infuriated Jessica even more.

Part of it was, whatever Alan had, Jessica wanted. It was a sport to her in some respects. She was all about keeping up with the Joneses. For example, Alan bought a brand-new Acura. Jessica went out and bought the same model, same year, same color, even though she couldn't afford it. The only difference in the two cars was that Alan's was a two-door; hers was a four-door, most likely because she couldn't find a two-door model.

"That was a big issue with her," said Naomi. "She had to have the *exact* same car, right down to the color."

Naomi had trouble keeping track of Jessica and the children. Jessica would drop the kids off at Naomi's, who loved to watch them. Naomi and her husband were McKenna and Sam's godparents, so it was like having their own children in the house. With Alan's life thriving, Naomi could hear the resentment and festering hatred building up in Jessica's voice whenever she got herself going on about Alan. Naomi and Jessica talked one day and Jessica blurted out, "Alan missed another visitation."

What? Come on, Jess, Naomi thought. She knew it was a lie. Alan loved those kids. If he could help it, he never missed seeing them. Especially since Jessica was so volatile and unpredictable when it came to allowing visitations.

There came a day when Jessica showed up at Naomi's house out of the blue. Unexpected, uninvited, there she was. It was dinnertime. Middle of the week. Naomi looked out the window and saw Jessica pulling in the driveway. No call. No warning. It was the first of what would be many unexpected visits, or pop-ins, by a woman hiding her kids from their natural father.

Jessica and the kids stayed for hours. Naomi and her husband fed them (they certainly didn't mind). They sat around after dinner. It seemed they were just staring at each other. Twiddling their thumbs.

Naomi finally asked, "What's up, Jess?"

"Nothing particular."

It was eight or nine o'clock at night before Jessica left.

Naomi thought about it later. These surprise visits were so strange—even for Jessica. Naomi would come to find out that Jessica was hiding out with the kids. Keeping them from Alan. He had a scheduled visitation, and Jessica didn't want to be home when he showed up.

For Alan, by June 1999, it got to the point where he was forced to ask Frank Head to file a grievance against Jessica. The motion outlined the nature of Jessica's disregard for the Final Judgment of Divorce. She wasn't following the court's ruling. She was playing games again. Same as she had for most of her adult life, Jessica was making up rules as she went along.

But Alan wasn't going to stand for it anymore. It was time to let the courts decide what to do with the woman and her stubborn ideas regarding visitation. Alan had tried. He gave Jessica chance after chance to conform. He put up with her screaming and threats and even violence.

But no more.

Now it was going to be up to a judge.

Jessica met Jeff while working for the Birmingham PD. She called him by his middle name of Kelley. Jeff was sort of an oafish guy. Quiet. Subdued. Easily manageable for Jessica. It was not hard for her to tell immediately that it was going to be effortless to manipulate Jeff any which way she wanted.

Not long after meeting Jeff, Jessica called Naomi, who hadn't seen Jessica for quite a while because of work and a conflicting, busy schedule.

"How are you? How are the kids?" Naomi asked, excited. It was good to hear from Jessica. She wondered why the pop-in visits had suddenly stopped.

"Good." Then Jessica went into how she had met this new guy, Kelley. How great he was. They were considering moving to Birmingham and buying a house together, but they didn't have enough money. She was still living in the house Alan had left her in Montevallo.

"Really?" Naomi said, shocked by this statement. Here's this new guy in Jessica's life. Out of nowhere.

It was apparently serious. And now they were talking about buying a house together.

Jessica had that schoolgirl-lust quality to her voice. "He's great," she explained. "How's this—we had sex in the living room . . . all over the house."

Naomi was horrified. "The kids, Jess? What about the kids?"

"They were asleep. Don't worry." Jessica laughed. That sarcastic I-know-something-you-don't-know tone that meant she was holding something back.

Part of Jessica's excitement was that Jeff McCord was a cop. This gave her a sense of protection, an overpowering feeling that she could play her games with Alan and turn around and say, *See, I have a cop to back me up! Alan's the bad guy. Not me.* The other part of it became that Jeff was naïve and could be talked into things. Her own little puppet. Jessica plied the guy with the best sex of his life and he took the bait.

Part of this new relationship spoke to Alan getting serious with Terra. Jessica needed to settle down so, in the eyes of the court, she could appear to have a stable environment in which to raise her children. Jessica had to play up the façade that she was a good mother. That she had a peaceful, family-foundational household. That she could provide for them. With Alan involving the courts now, she knew that social workers would be poking around. She would need to put on a show.

But there was also something else working in the background—a developing storm—something Jeff Kelley McCord could provide to Jessica that, she believed, all the others couldn't.

30

According to Jeff McCord's version, on Monday morning, February 18, 2002, he and Jessica took off to Opelika, Alabama, a town about 140 miles, or a 135-minute drive, from Hoover. Born in Tallahassee, Florida, before living in Cairo, Georgia, for a brief spell, Jeff moved to Opelika with his mom after his parents split up (and later divorced). Jeff had graduated from Opelika High School.

As police searched his home back in Hoover that day, Jeff and Jessica cruised the streets of Opelika. At the center of their conversation was what Jeff was going to do about his job: call in sick or show up? His house was in the process of a second search by the HPD. Cops talked, Jeff knew. The Hoover PD had a full report on Jeff, his entire life and career as a police officer. More than that, Jeff heard that his Pelham PD patrol commander was looking for him and wanted to talk before his shift started later that afternoon. Hearing this, Jeff knew darn well what was going on.

At 10:00 A.M. Jeff called work.

"Hold on," dispatch told him. The call was rerouted

to the chief's office. Jeff had a feeling dispatch had been waiting for his call.

"McCord," the chief said, "you need to be in my office today at four. Bring in your badge and ID. You're going on administrative leave for the time being."

Jeff hung up. Dropped his shoulders. He realized how serious the situation had become. When he met Jessica, she had seemed so boisterous and fun and bossy—which he liked. A woman in charge. She knew what she wanted. That was all well and good when dealing with laundry and food shopping and picking colors of drapes and styles of tile and wallpaper. Maybe even when it came to parenting. Jeff didn't mind standing aside to let Jessica take the wheel. In many ways, Jeff later said, Jessica was the first "real" relationship he was involved in. He had dated a beautiful woman for two-and-a-half years during college, and for a short time afterward. But that woman, Jeff later told me, was rather "normal," as compared to the relationship he later got mixed up in with Jessica.

"At the same time," Jeff added, "if [a] 'real' [relationship] means the other person is divorced, has three kids and [a] trainload of baggage, then I guess it may well depend on one's definition and one's perspective. I readily concede that cluelessness and ineptitude on my part may well have made things worse or at least different than they were and/or turned out to be. Also," Jeff cleared up, "Jessica was not the first woman with whom I had had sexual relations."

Some claimed she had been.

Jessica and Jeff headed back to Hoover from Opelika on Monday. Jeff stopped by the house after dropping Jessica off (one would guess at her mother's) to pick up his uniforms and badges. Then he took off for Pelham.

A Hoover police officer got behind Jeff as he left the

Myrtlewood Drive house and followed him as other officers joined the motorcade. Jeff drove a U-Haul truck he and Jessica had rented (for no apparent reason he could later give—"We just needed it").

"We weren't hiding the fact by then that we were following Jeff McCord," one law enforcement source told me.

Near Route 31 and Lorna Road, the HPD hit their lights.

"Anyway," Jeff recalled, "I get pulled over by half of Hoover's evening shift." It was funny to him that the HPD had no fewer than six officers tailing him.

Tom McDanal and Peyton Zanzour were part of that team.

"License and reg," one of the patrol officers asked Jeff after he rolled down his window and asked what was going on.

Jeff nodded. Did what he was told. What else could he do? He knew what was going on.

"Give us a minute."

Some time later, Jeff got his license back. "Where y'all headin'?"

"Pelham," Jeff said.

They let him go.

Jeff walked into the Pelham PD about ten minutes later and went directly to the chief's office.

The chief had a written notification of Jeff's administrative leave on his desk, waiting for Jeff's signature.

Jeff paused. Reluctant, he took the pen and signed.

"You need to contact me, [the captain or the lieutenant] at some point during the day, until you're told otherwise, McCord. You understand?"

Jeff nodded his head. He knew the routine. He was being babysat. Watched. Told what to do and when to do it. Guilty before innocent. Jeff was well aware how things worked once law enforcement got a whiff.

A burned Pontiac Grand Am was discovered in the woods of Rutledge, Georgia, at 3:30 A.M. on February 16, 2002. *(Photo courtesy of the Hoover Police Department)*

A different angle of the same vehicle. *(Photo courtesy of the Hoover Police Department)*

Inside the trunk were two severely burned bodies.
(Photo courtesy of the Hoover Police Department)

A paper towel, charred on one end, was found near the torched Grand Am. It would turn into a key piece of evidence. *(Photo courtesy of the Hoover Police Department)*

A spent projectile taken from inside the trunk of the burned vehicle was one clue that lead to solving the case. *(Photo courtesy of the Hoover Police Department)*

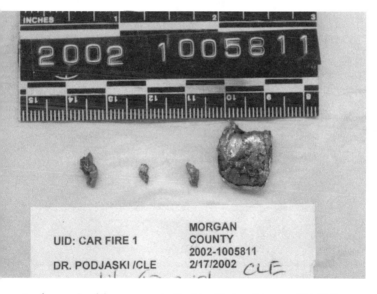

Another angle of the same projectile, identified on February 17, 2002, as a .44 caliber bullet. *(Photo courtesy of the Hoover Police Department)*

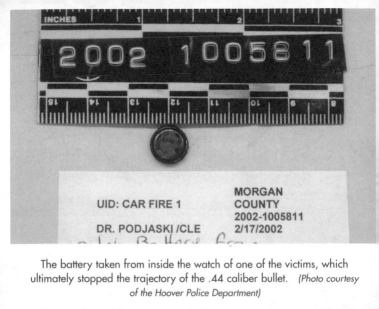

The battery taken from inside the watch of one of the victims, which ultimately stopped the trajectory of the .44 caliber bullet. *(Photo courtesy of the Hoover Police Department)*

A couch, stripped of its leather backing, taken from the home of an Alabama couple suspected of being connected to the crime scene in Georgia. *(Photo courtesy of the Hoover Police Department)*

Jessica Inez Callis in eighth grade in Hoover, Alabama. *(Photo courtesy of Gresham Middle School yearbook)*

Heading into high school, Jessica was an honors student who claimed to have taken between "500 and 600" hits of LSD during her high school days.

Alan Bates was a popular student with a passion for the theater when he met Jessica. *(Photo courtesy of Shades Valley High School yearbook)*

Still in high school, finishing his senior year, Alan Bates married Jessica after discovering she was pregnant. (Jessica had dropped out.)

Months after getting married and welcoming their first child in 1990, Jessica and Alan appeared to be a happy young couple enjoying the senior prom.

Hoover Police Department investigators look at a piece of floor tile inside Jessica's home, searching for any sign that a double homicide had occurred. *(Photo courtesy of the Hoover Police Department)*

Investigators later talked about how messy Jessica's house was when they went in to conduct the first of two search and seizure warrants in 2002. *(Photo courtesy of the Hoover Police Department)*

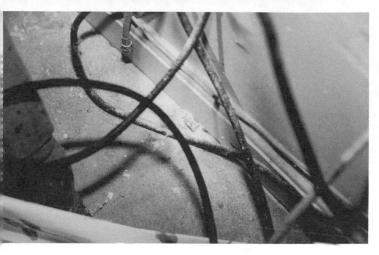

A break in the case came during a second search on February 18, 2002, when investigators discovered this single spent projectile on the floor inside the garage of a home owned by Jessica and her new husband, Jeff McCord, a police officer. *(Photo courtesy of the Hoover Police Department)*

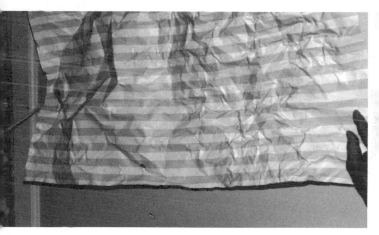

Moments after the bullet was uncovered, investigators found this piece of balled up wallpaper inside a garbage bag. *(Photo courtesy of the Hoover Police Department)*

This coffee table, taken from Jeff and Jessica McCord's home, was later found to contain blood evidence. (Photo courtesy of the Hoover Police Department)

After investigators moved the couch and focused their search in the messy den of the McCord home, the pieces of a double homicide fell into place. (Photo courtesy of the Hoover Police Department)

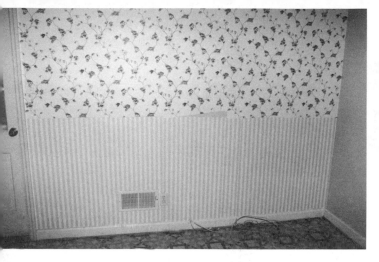

Investigators were at first perplexed that the wallpaper seams in the McCord home did not match. *(Photo courtesy of the Hoover Police Department)*

When both spent projectiles—the bullet found in the trunk of Alan Bates' burned rental car and the one found inside the McCord garage— were put side by side, a clear match was made. *(Photo courtesy of the Hoover Police Department)*

An only child, Terra Klugh hammed it up for this Norman Rockwell-like photo. *(Photo courtesy of Tom Klugh)*

Many friends recalled the warmth and comfort of Terra's smile. *(Photo courtesy of the D.W. Daniel High School yearbook)*

As a young woman, Terra fell deeply for recently divorced father of two Alan Bates after meeting him at the Alabama Theatre in Birmingham. *(Photo courtesy of Tom Klugh)*

Alan Bates and his father Philip were quite the pair as Indian Guides during a campout. *(Photo courtesy of Kevin Bates)*

Together, Alan and Terra Bates enjoyed all that life had to offer. *(Photo courtesy of Kevin Bates)*

Alan loved nothing more than taking photos of his second wife, Terra, whenever they went on hiking trips.
(Photo courtesy of Kevin Bates)

Terra enjoyed capturing this moment of her husband doing what he enjoyed.
(Photo courtesy of Kevin Bates)

After Alan's first wife, Jessica, destroyed Alan and Terra's initial wedding plans, there was nothing she could do to stop the wedding a year later.
(Photo courtesy of Kevin Bates)

As a youngster, Jeff McCord loved football. *(Photo courtesy of Bobby Kelley)*

Jeff graduated from the University of Montevallo and wanted to help wayward children. *(Photo courtesy of Bobby Kelley)*

Family and friends were proud of Jeff, who had never been in any trouble, expecting "big things" from him post-graduation. *(Photo courtesy of Bobby Kelley)*

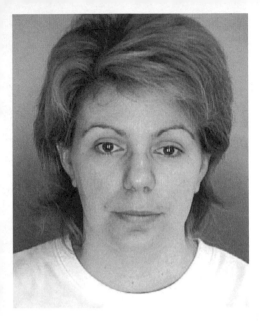

Jessica's look transformed through the years. Here she is after being arrested on double murder charges in February 2002. *(Photo courtesy of the Hoover Police Department)*

Friends say Jeff McCord was a passive, reserved puppet, who was easily manipulated by Jessica. A police officer at the time of his arrest, Jeff was also charged with double murder. *(Photo courtesy of the Hoover Police Department)*

Although he was upset and somewhat angry for not being granted the benefit of the doubt, he could not deny the fact that there was a double-murder investigation going on that was mainly focused on his wife. If he hadn't been part of the actual murder, he was connected to it by marriage. Either way, he couldn't do his job as a police officer.

From there, Jeff drove back to the house, watched the HPD finish that second search and then voluntarily went down to the HPD to answer questions. He was then picked up by Jessica. They drove to Florida to drop the kids off at her sister's house.

While in Florida, Jeff called the chief's office as part of that daily ball-and-chain order he had signed.

"You need to be in my office at nine tomorrow morning," the chief told Jeff that Tuesday.

"What is it? Disciplinary matter or what? *What's* going on? Something come up?" Jeff wanted details. Thought he deserved them. He hadn't been charged with a crime. Neither had Jessica. Now the Pelham PD was pulling his strings, making demands. He didn't have to do anything he didn't want to do.

"Look, McCord, you just need to be here."

Jeff thought about it. He didn't like the tone. He was upset that the chief was so steely and not giving him an opportunity to explain. Nor was the chief forthcoming with any information. In addition, it was clear there was going to be a disciplinary hearing on the day Jeff returned.

"Screw it," Jeff said. "Fire me if you want."

The following afternoon, a Wednesday, the Pelham PD fired Jeff McCord. This occurred as the HPD made it public that Jeff and Jessica McCord were its chief suspects in the murders of Alan and Terra Bates.

When Jeff heard he had been canned, he and Jessica drove into downtown Birmingham. HPD investigators tailing the couple watched as they parked near a professional building. The media was there waiting. *Birmingham News* journalist Carol Robinson was among them. Word was that Jeff and Jessica were going to hire David Cromwell Johnson.

"[Johnson] was the highest-profile defense lawyer in town at the time, and we all camped outside his office that day, waiting to get a glimpse of Jessica and Jeff for the first time," Carol told me.

Carol wanted a comment from Jessica to fill in a story she was working on. Carol didn't know quite what to expect.

As Jessica started for the building, Carol got up next to her and announced, "I'm from the *Birmingham News,* Mrs. McCord. My name's Carol Robinson. Can I get a statement from you?"

Jessica took one look at the reporter. Stopped. Snubbed her nose. Then sneered, "You're a liar!"

Carol had no idea that she was so popular in the McCord household.

"It was the only time she ever spoke to me."

Heading into Cromwell's office, Jeff and Jessica were apparently getting themselves lawyered up and ready to do battle with Roger Brown and the Hoover PD.

31

For the Alabama Dance Academy the annual recital is one of those yearly events signaling the unofficial start of summer. All the bliss of hot days in the pool, walking along the beach, a day in the park, as well as barbeques and family picnics, is right around the corner. Soon schools will pop their doors open and unleash the children. They'll turn giddy and bored and begin to look for things to do. For the dance studios all of this summer folly begins on recital day. It is a time when little girls and boys dress up in their colorful patent leather costumes, down feathers, silk scarves, spandex pants, then take to the stage for that one day when the spotlight is all theirs. They two-step and tap, do hip-hop and ballet. They smile until their blushed cheeks hurt. Mothers busy themselves backstage making sure every seam is pressed, every hair in place, every dance routine remembered. The culmination of ten months of rehearsals.

Over in one (long) afternoon.

And so it was in late June 1999 that nine-year-old Samantha Bates found herself inside the historic Alabama Theatre, backstage. She was there to take part in the Alabama Dance Academy's "Evening of Dance," waiting for her chance to enter stage right and perform a routine she had practiced since the start of the school year. Standing in line next to Sam was her dance instructor. Sam had been taking classes since 1996, McKenna having joined in 1998. Sam could feel the excitement in the room. Raw nerves. The anxious butterflies flapping their wings inside the tummies of all the girls and boys.

The lights.

The music.

Grandparents.

Moms.

Dads.

Friends.

Everyone there to cheer on their favorite dancer.

"Miss Pamela," Sam said to her instructor, Pamela Merkel Sayle, tugging at her blouse, "can you say hello to my daddy for me?"

Alan felt at home inside the theater, having worked in the building now for years. As part of a deal he had made with Pamela Sayle, Alan took care of the recital's technical details. Although he was working, Alan had that proud smile only the father of a little dancer can muster. He was going to watch his little girl perform today, and Jessica was not going to be able to stop him or interfere.

Alleluia.

Kneeling down eye level with Sam, Pamela pointed to Alan. "Well, Sam, he's right over there. You can get out of line and go say [hello] yourself."

The well-liked dance instructor smiled. What was the big deal?

Sam stared at the floor. Paused. Then, "But I can't, Miss Pamela. My mommy said I was not allowed to speak with my daddy."

Little Samantha couldn't help herself. Like her sister, she loved her father. She was a child—like millions—caught in the whirlwind swirling amid the selfishness some parents harbor when battling over issues that have little to do with the children's well-being and everything to do with getting back at a spouse because of some deep-seated resentment. It's pure torture on kids. Yet so few parents are able to see beyond the self-centered ideology of themselves. Where the kids were concerned, Jessica created every possible difficulty she could for Alan. It was as if the court did not exist. Jessica believed she could do whatever she wanted and she would not have to answer for it.

To anyone.

Standing so close to her father as he worked backstage, Alan glowing and beaming, having not seen him for some time, Sam decided to walk over and pay her pop a visit.

Alan smiled when he saw his little girl coming toward him. Held out his arms.

Still under her mother's spell, however, Sam was true to her keeper: she hugged Alan, but then got back into line with the other dancers—this, mind you, without speaking one word to her father.

Pamela Sayle was surprised. She hadn't realized things had spiraled so out of control—that the communication between Jessica and Alan had broken down so badly. Indeed, many later said that Jessica warned Sam and McKenna not to speak to their father. Under no circumstances were the kids to exchange words with Alan—unless, of course, Jessica gave the order. Pamela Sayle knew Jessica and Alan were having problems. It was not uncommon for Jessica to show up at Sayle's dance studio and announce to the instructor and her aides that they were not to allow Alan to pick up the kids from dance.

He was never to take them.

Court orders.

It was a lie. But no one questioned Jessica—why would they?

But now, Jessica wasn't allowing the kids to even speak to their father.

One evening, Pam recalled, when Jessica picked up Sam and McKenna at the Alabama Dance Academy, she babbled about her (supposed) latest dilemma with Alan. It was right after Alan and Terra hooked up. Alan informed Jessica he was taking the visitation situation to family court to get things settled. It wasn't what he wanted to do, but Jessica had forced his hand.

Jessica was incensed at the notion that she could lose custody of her kids. As far as she could tell, Alan's plan all along was to get sole custody and take the kids away from her.

And that, she decided, was never going to happen.

"What's wrong?" Pamela asked Jessica, noticing how on edge she seemed. Pam was curious why Jessica was so irritated.

A smirk flashed across Jessica's face—that Joker-like grimace Jessica could call up in a moment's notice, the one that screamed revenge. She was up to something.

"I'll take the girls to Florida," Jessica snapped back at Pamela, "if he *ever* tries to get them!"

Knowing Alan was involved in a long-term relationship with Terra, and might marry her one day, Jessica needed to act. She was a single mom. Alan was working on creating stability, which Jessica knew the courts would look at favorably.

One other time, Pam later testified, some weeks after that first incident, Jessica was in a rage over Alan and his desire to take her to court. The court had set a trial date and Pre-Trial Order for September 14, 1999. The judge had asked each party to file "a list of all [their] personal and/or real property," among other actions. This grated on Jessica's unstable temperament. She hated the idea of being told what to do. The court even "encouraged professional counseling" to rectify the issues of visitation and child custody. After all, it could only help. A trial was going to turn things nastier.

Apparently, however, Jessica had a new plan.

Pam asked if everything was all right.

"If he ever tries to get the girls," Jessica said, helping one of the kids put on her jacket, "he'll regret it."

Jessica was not going to allow her ex-husband to have his way. Nor was she going to permit another woman, especially someone she saw as prissy and prudish, to step into her role as the mother of her children. Just wasn't going to happen. In her mind Jessica was undoubtedly prepared to do everything in her power to see that Alan and Terra never got custody of the kids. Thus, the situation—a war Jessica had waged—wasn't about Alan not seeing the children anymore.

It was about winning.

Beating Alan.

Alan's plan, up to this point, had never involved taking legal full-time custody of his kids. Jessica was telling people this—one could only assume—to draw sympathy and make Alan out to be an aggressive, uncaring monster. Alan was known as the proverbial "peacemaker" in his family. Many of his friends agreed with this. Alan never once vocalized a desire to take the kids away from their mother—even when Jessica was at her worst. To the contrary, Alan was all for the kids staying with Jessica. Providing, that is, she could raise them in a way he saw fit. Part of that upbringing needed to include Jessica fulfilling her end of the divorce decree regarding visitation.

From old friends and family, Alan got word that Jessica routinely dropped the kids off at the houses of friends and family (her mother included) and took off for an indeterminate amount of time. Jessica pushed the responsibility of raising their kids, it seemed, on everyone else but Alan. This made it clear to Alan she was punishing him. No other reason. She wanted to hurt him.

"Alan just wanted to see his children," Robert Bates later explained. "But she kept shoving him back."

Alan and Terra planned to get married at the end of June 1999. They talked about having the wedding on the stage of the Alabama Theatre, a building they had grown to love throughout the years of their relationship. Invitations were printed. The caterer hired. Flowers purchased. Limos. Gowns. Little wedding favors picked out.

But Jessica wasn't about to let Alan go through with it. If Alan got married, what would a judge say about his situation? Alan would have that lock on stability first. Terra would be the kids' stepmother. Both Alan and Terra had clean records, something Jessica couldn't claim. Jessica feared the worst. So she kept the girls away from Alan the week leading up to the wedding.

No one could find them.

"No kids, no wedding," Alan said.

Terra had no trouble with the decision. She understood. There was no way she was about to marry Alan without his kids being part of the ceremony.

"Instead of going through with the wedding," Kevin

Bates later said, "Alan and Terra decided to postpone
it. They weren't about to get married without the girls
present. Whether or not Jessica was responsible for
keeping the kids away, Alan knew it would send the
wrong message to them."

Some weeks later, as the subject of when to reschedule the wedding came up, something else happened.
The last year and more had taken its toll on Alan. He
was ready to give up. He felt there was no way he could
drag another human being—suffice it to say, a woman
he loved deeply—into such a mess.

It wasn't fair.

Terra hadn't been feeling herself lately. She was
tired a lot. It turned out to be Crohn's disease, a debilitating disorder that causes inflammation of the digestive tract, as well as a host of other symptoms that
make life uncomfortable at best, miserable at worst:
frequent abdominal cramps, dry skin, joint pain, stress.

She flew to Iowa to work on a special project one
weekend. Alan met Terra at the Birmingham Airport
a few days later. He looked glum, Terra noticed as she
walked into the terminal. Alan had his head down.
Seemed preoccupied. Not himself. Terra knew him
well enough by this point. His demeanor. It was different. Something was going on.

"What's wrong?"

"Nothing."

"Alan, what is it? I know you."

"I don't know that I'm—I'm"—Alan had a hard
time getting it out—"ready to get married."

There it was: out in the open like an exposed secret.
She'd asked for it.

Terra was astounded. Hurt. She didn't know what
to say.

She called her father later that night and told him the story.

Tom Klugh loved hearing from his only daughter. They had weekly talks. Tom thought only the best of Alan. Knew he was the perfect husband for his daughter. Terra expressed how happy she was with Alan, and how much she loved his kids.

Terra explained how she felt about this latest incident. Every detail.

"I'm so sorry, sweetie," Tom responded when she was finished talking. "What can I do to help?"

"That is going to be it."

Tom didn't understand. "What do you mean?"

"Alan and me. I think I'm done."

Terra didn't have the energy to go back and forth with Alan on a relationship seesaw: seeing him, not seeing him; getting married, not getting married. It wasn't her. Terra was all about yes or no. She didn't want to be with someone who didn't want to be with her.

Not a week later, Tom talked to Terra again and things seemed better.

"I think I'm going to give him another chance," she said. "I really love him, Dad. If it can work out, I want it to."

It wasn't that Alan didn't want to marry Terra—his decision had nothing to do with love. Nor was it a reflection of Terra's character. Alan adored Terra more than any woman he had ever met or dated. They were perfect together. Alan felt torn that his ex-wife was torturing their lives. Day in and day out. Jessica ran their emotions. Now she had gone and destroyed their wedding day. What else was she capable of doing? What else would she do? Alan didn't want to drag such a sweet person as Terra into the chaos of his life dealing with Jessica. Terra had endured it long enough already. Didn't matter what Terra said. That unconditional love she showered on Alan and the kids was something Alan did not want to take advantage of. Enough was enough. Jessica wasn't going to hurt anybody else.

On the flip side of Alan's decision was the notion that he did not want to play into Jessica's hand. If Alan and Terra went forward with their wedding—without the children—Jessica could turn around, take the kids aside and make a case: *See, Daddy* doesn't *love you. . . . He went and got married* without *you*. Alan knew Jessica pounced on any opportunity to bad-mouth him. He understood that Jessica was filling the kids with this sort of rhetoric, anyway, telling them he had run off with Terra and was creating a new life without them, that he really didn't care anymore. Saying it was his fault they never saw him, not hers. Why give the woman more ammunition?

So Terra and Alan talked it through and agreed to wait. It had been four years since they met. What was another month, or two, or even three?

32

The idea that Jeff and Jessica were on the run during the week of February 20, 2002, was the result of circumstance. Because they had not returned to Jessica's mother's house, or to their own home, it appeared they were running. When, in fact, the couple was just trying to avoid what was turning into unneeded attention swelling around them in relation to the deaths of Alan and Terra Bates.

As it turned out, Jeff and Jessica could not afford high-profile attorney David Cromwell Johnson. They had little money. Hardly any assets. And Johnson's fee was pricey for two people not working.

Still, Johnson told the press that "the police know where the McCords are staying."

No one else did, however.

Johnson's prudent advice was made clear in an article written by Carol Robinson that day. "They're just trying to get away for a while," the attorney commented, "and I think they should."

With all that was happening around her, faced with a situation she knew to be the result of her own behavior, there was something about Jessica that automatically switched into "how do I get out of this?" mode. Or, more pointedly: "how can I spin this to my favor?"

Take your pick.

When Jessica checked into the hospital to give birth to McKenna in November 1992, she claimed to have almost died. According to one source, Jessica said the hospital had failed to give her an epidural *and* she nearly bled to death. Upon visiting her in the hospital, the source couldn't believe the stories coming out of Jessica's mouth regarding the treatment she had received while in the hospital.

As her friend Candice (pseudonym) sat with Jessica a day after the birth, Jessica carried on about the hospital staff and how bad the service and medical treatment was during her short stay. The staff was brutal, she reported. She had suffered every moment while being in the place.

Jessica is going somewhere with this, Candice thought as she sat and listened.

"I need to use the restroom," Candice said at one point. She had sat for a while, listening to Jessica's diatribe. It was time to step away from her and catch her breath.

"You can't use the bathroom," Jessica said from bed. "Don't go in there."

Curious because of the way Jessica had phrased her words, Candice walked over and pushed the restroom door open.

"When I got there," Candice told me later, "the bathroom floor . . . was covered in blood. I was physically ill from this."

Looking back at the scene, going over those complaints from Jessica, knowing what Jessica had said about suing the hospital, Candice realized Jessica "was only doing all of this so she didn't have to pay for the hospital bill."

* * *

On Wednesday night, February 20, 2002, Jessica had a major problem to confront. She and Jeff were holed up at a friend's house in Alabaster, Alabama, twenty minutes south of Birmingham. Jessica had grown up with the guy. He was a friend of the family.

The HPD had a source inside Jessica's assembly of family and friends calling in the McCords' status whenever possible. This person was close to the action. No sooner had Jeff and Jessica shown up in Alabaster than the HPD got a call.

The HPD and Roger Brown had been waiting on word from ballistics for a match to the bullet found in the McCords' garage against the bullet found in the trunk of Alan's rental car. By late Wednesday night, that report had finally come in.

Arrest warrants for Jeff and Jessica were issued immediately afterward.

At some point Detective Laura Brignac telephoned Naomi, who was taken aback by the accusations surrounding her friend. She had been reading about Jessica in the newspapers. The possibility that Jessica was involved did not override the fact that Alan and his wife (two people Naomi knew and liked very much) were dead. Still, hearing the news, Naomi was now certain Jessica was somehow responsible.

Naomi had been trying to find Jessica for several days. She had given a statement to the Bureau and HPD, inviting them into her home so they could record any phone calls from Jessica. Investigators let Naomi know they were looking for a particular friend of Jessica's in Alabaster, a guy Naomi and her husband had also gone to high school with and knew fairly well. Naomi called the guy and left several messages, asking him to phone the HPD immediately.

He never did.

"Naomi, can we bring Jessica's children by . . . ?" Detective Laura Brignac called and asked that night. The kids were being driven back from Florida, and the HPD needed a friend of the family to look after them while they found grief counselors. There was an indication that Randy Bates, who lived in Birmingham, was going to eventually take the kids and drive them to Georgia.

Naomi said no problem.

That night came and went, and the HPD never showed up with the kids.

The next morning, while Naomi was at work, Jessica called. "You believe that I did this?" Jessica asked pointedly. She needed to know.

Naomi paused. She didn't want to get into it. Not at work. She couldn't record the call, anyway. What if Jessica admitted something important or incriminated herself?

"I would hope you didn't do it, Jess," Naomi said.

"Listen, I need you to put your house up for me for my bond and my legal fees if I am arrested."

There was no pause this time. "I cannot do that, Jess. I already have a second mortgage—"

Jessica interrupted. Said she didn't care. "Just do it."

"I can't get any more money out of this house. It's just not possible."

Jessica turned irrational, Naomi later said. ("She just wasn't getting it.") She did not want to take no for an answer. She did not care about banks and equity and mortgages. Jessica McCord wanted what she wanted—and that was that.

"Are you okay?" Naomi asked, changing the subject.

"I'm mad. . . . I didn't do it!"

Naomi had no idea how to play this. But at some point she decided that she wasn't going to sugarcoat the situation any longer. Enough of playing along like everything was okay and she believed in her friend. Time to expose the elephant in the room.

"Jess, how do you expect me to believe *any* of this when you and I, we had that conversation last week?"

Naomi sat at her desk, waiting for a reply, thinking about what Jessica had told her just about a week prior. It was near Valentine's Day. Naomi called Jessica. "Jess, I need help with this project of mine. Can you do it?" One of Naomi's kids had to say ten words in Spanish. Naomi knew Jessica and Jeff were somewhat fluent in the language. She figured they could help.

"Look," Jessica said, "we're all asleep right now. Can I call you back?"

Naomi took the phone away from her ear: *Asleep?* It was six o'clock in the evening. *What in the hell are they all doing sleeping now?*

Naomi went back to cooking dinner. She wondered what in the world was going on with her friend.

Jessica called back later that night. "Ready?"

After Jessica helped the kid with his homework, Naomi got on the phone and started to talk about things.

"I know you mentioned you had a deposition coming up, Jess. When is it?"

"This Friday."

"Okay . . . so, how are you thinking things are going to go?"

"I'm really concerned about it. Alan's really pushing for custody." This was a different Jessica. She sounded more worried than angry. There was genuine concern in her voice. Perhaps even dread. Definitely defeat. "He's flying in and then he's going to have visitation with the kids as well."

"Oh," Naomi said. "That's good. He should see the kids."

But then the conversation took on a different course. Jessica went from being distant and cerebral, almost sympathetic, to vengeful. She needed to do something. There was no way she could sit back and let Alan beat her.

"We're going to set him up," Jessica said.

"Alan?" Naomi asked. She was shocked. Confused. Such a strange comment. What did Jessica mean by "set him up"? "What are you talking about?"

"Domestic violence . . . we're going to set Alan up for domestic violence charges."

It was clear that Jessica and Jeff had devised some sort of a plan to entice Alan into hitting her or doing something irrational to get himself in trouble. The ignorance was incredible. To think Jessica had been married to the man all those years. There was no way Alan would engage in violence with his ex-wife. He'd had several opportunities to strike back at Jessica while she hit, yelled or pushed him down the stairs and broke his arm. He had never so much as raised a hand.

"Why are you gonna do that, Jess?"

"I need to. My case is not going good."

"Come on."

"He's going to get custody!"

In the midst of cooking dinner, helping her own kids with their homework and doing what normal working mothers and housewives do every weeknight, Naomi thought, *Oh great! This darn story again.* She had heard it all from Jessica before. *"I'm gonna get Alan," etc.* It was common speak whenever Jessica mentioned Alan in the same breath as the child custody matter.

"What are you going to do if Kelley walks up while this is happening?" Naomi asked. She was worried if Jessica lured, provoked and plied Alan with enough

hurtful words, he might finally snap and do something
to Jessica. And if that went down, Jeff and Alan could
get into a fight. Naomi mentioned later that she was
privy to only Jessica's side of the story—that Jessica
had built Alan up into a bully, a deadbeat dad who was
capable of doing something like this. So it was easier
for Naomi to fall for Jessica's lies. Jessica had manipulated her children's god parents as well as everyone
else. Yet, Naomi made a point to say later, "I never believed Alan would ever hurt Jessica."

"Oh," Jessica said, "Kelley'll just kill him."

Hearing this, Naomi obviously had no idea Jessica
actually meant it. *This is a whole bunch of hooey . . . how
many times have I heard this before?* Naomi thought after
Jessica said it.

"I gotta go, Jess. I cannot listen to this."

It was old hat. Naomi had heard Jessica's threats too
many times to take her at her word. "So much so,"
Naomi said later, quite remorsefully, "that I didn't even
mention it to my husband that night."

After Naomi brought up that "Kelley'll just kill him"
conversation, Jessica said, "That's funny . . . you're the
only one who doesn't believe me." She sounded as if
she was disappointed in her friend.

"It's not that I don't believe you, Jess." This was
painful for Naomi. She didn't want her friend to be
crazy *or* a murderer. She had put her trust and faith in
Jessica. She and her husband had tried helping her.
Had given her advice and money and food and support. ("It sounds like we took her side in the divorce,"
Naomi clarified later. "But in trying to stay out of it, we
lost touch with Alan, but [we] did have contact with
him over the years.")

"I didn't do it," Jessica pleaded.

"It's just that I am asking you what happened, and if you were involved," Naomi said. She needed to know. No more lies. Fess up.

Jessica thought about it. Before hanging up, she took a deep breath. Paused. Then gave Naomi a clear warning: "Now you keep your mouth shut about our conversation."

33

A few months after Alan and Terra postponed the wedding, things got worse, just as Alan had predicted. Alan and Jessica were in the midst of an impassioned court battle. Jessica hired a lawyer, Lindsey Allison. On September 13, 1999, a short time before their first scheduled trial date, Frank Head sent Lindsey a letter. He wanted to confirm that the case had been postponed to December 9. The more important reason for the letter, however, detailed how Philip and Joan Bates were now going to be picking the children up for scheduled visitations on the third weekend of October and November. Frank Head pointed out that Jessica needed to be made aware that Alan was going to start calling the kids on Sunday evenings at six o'clock, and Jessica was to make sure they were available for "approximately fifteen minutes of uninterrupted conversation."

Simple stuff that lots of broken families did.

Jessica failed to hold up her end of the agreement. Alan and Terra couldn't believe it. Jessica was openly thumbing her nose at the court. When Alan said something about it, Jessica came up with the idea that if Alan wanted to speak to the children, he would have to buy them a cell phone and pay the cost of service. Otherwise, forget it.

Frank Head sent Lindsey Allison a second letter saying the request by Jessica for Alan to purchase the children a cell phone was unreasonable—Jessica needed to let him talk to his kids. Period.

Jessica said: No cell phone, no contact.

The day before Philip and Joan were scheduled to pick up the kids for that first weekend visitation, Lindsey Allison contacted Frank Head by fax. It was October 12. The fax came in under the heading of *Very Urgent: Ms. Bates has just informed me that her grandmother in Salt Lake City, Utah, has died.*

Jessica claimed she, the children and her parents were traveling to Salt Lake that afternoon and would not return until Sunday. The visitation was off. She hoped Alan would understand. She was going to offer another weekend in its place in order to keep in good standing with the court. The death was unexpected, right? What could she do? Philip and Joan needed to pick a date and get back to Lindsey Allison with it.

Alan said no biggie. It was a bad time. A death in the family. For once, it seemed Jessica had a rational explanation for missing a visitation.

Frank Head wasn't buying it. After a bit of checking, he found out Jessica had, in fact, played them. It was a lie. Her grandmother was alive and well.

The scheduled December court date came . . . and then . . . another postponement and additional excuse on Jessica's part about being ill and in the hospital. In the interim Frank Head drafted another missive to Jessica. It spelled out what was going on and what Alan was preparing to do next. Throughout the fall of 1999—Thanksgiving and Christmas, McKenna's birthday and various other weekends in between—Jessica found a way not to allow Alan to see the children, even once. On top of that, phone calls between the father and his girls were kept to a minimum. Alan talked to them once or twice for a few minutes each time.

Alan called his mother in tears, letting it all out. Jessica was turning his own children against him. He was defenseless. Not even the court seemed to want to hold up visitation orders. She had found a way around the system. What could he do?

In his latest letter Frank Head stipulated that Alan was going to give Jessica one more opportunity to fall in line with the court's ruling and live up to her end of the divorce decree. It was that, or "Alan will have no alternative but to file a contempt petition." Alan wanted "makeup" visitation for the time he had missed. Head encouraged Jessica to "contact him immediately" to set up a new visitation schedule—and this time, well, she had better *stick* to it.

Frank Head waited.

Jessica or her lawyer never replied.

It was time to file contempt charges, Head suggested to Alan.

Alan had thought about it, and he didn't want to do it. But maybe he needed to take things to the next level. Maybe a good kick in the behind by the court would snap Jessica into order. He agreed to the filing.

Jessica was busy herself. She and Jeff applied for a marriage license. Jessica soon found out that Jeff had some money his mother controlled, and she convinced Jeff to push his mother into giving them the money so they could get married and buy their own house in Hoover.

Jeff balked at first, then he started working on his mother.

"It had been a long time since Jeff had any type of contact with his family," a McCord family friend later said. "He just pops in town and visits his grandmother and drops by to see [his mother]. The strange part of this is that Jeff would have never done what follows . . . unless he was harassed to do so. We found out it was to ask his mother for money for a down payment on a house. . . . Bottom line, she gave him money, but it was not the generous amount she had planned."

Jeff's mother, as well as his family and friends, recognized he was being manipulated. "Because after they got the check," that same family friend recalled, "the not responding to calls began [all over] again."

34

The HPD had a solid tip from an inside source: Jeff and Jessica McCord were in Alabaster. So officers staked out the house. On February 21, 2002, as the hazy sun rose over the eastern side of Alabaster's Old Highway 31, the HPD was in position to make the arrests.

Most of the team parked outside the home. One of the investigators called Jessica on her cell phone, explaining that it was best she and Jeff calmly walked outside with their hands raised above their heads. If they did, there would be no problems.

The arrest could go easy, or Jeff and Jessica could make it difficult. Either way, by the end of the morning, Jeff and Jessica McCord were going to be behind bars. There was no one else Jessica could call. No one else she could manipulate. No way she was going to talk her way out of this.

The HPD knew enough about Jessica to assume that few things in her life were ever done without some sort of fuss, problem or, in this case, maybe much worse. The thought was, if she had talked Jeff, an armed and potentially dangerous former cop, into helping her murder her ex-husband and his wife, how hard would it be for her to convince that same man he should run out of the house, guns blazing? Jeff was a fallen police officer. Now he was accused of double murder. He had weapons.

As agreed by phone, Jessica walked out of the house first. Tom McDanal was waiting for her.

"I'm pregnant," Jessica said upon seeing the detective. Apparently, she was hoping the announcement would convince the HPD to show her some sympathy.

Should anyone believe her? The HPD had caught Jessica in so many lies by this point, how could she be trusted?

"At that point," one investigator told me, "we couldn't believe *anything* she said."

The plan was for Detective Laura Brignac to escort Jessica to the county jail. A warrant officer would drive them. Brignac could sit in the front seat, Jessica in the back, so the detective could keep an eye on her suspect and maybe open up a dialogue.

There was going to be media at the jail when they arrived, Brignac explained to the warrant officer.

"Be prepared."

Brignac read Jessica her rights as Jeff was escorted away from the scene without incident. Then Jessica was handcuffed and searched.

"Watch your head," Brignac warned, helping Jessica into the backseat of the cruiser.

Brignac went around and sat down in the front passenger seat.

Jessica and Jeff were formally charged with capital murder. Their lives had just taken a solemn turn. It was a crime punishable by the death penalty. If there was something Jessica wanted to say—or needed to confess—now would be a good time to do it. After the two of them were split up, chances were that one or both would want to make a deal at one time or another. Husbands

and wives often turned on each other. After a bit of
pressure, faced with the reality of life in prison or death
by lethal injection, matrimonial loyalties faded like
memories of romantic sunset walks on the beach. If that
was the case here, Brignac and the other detectives
knew, this was going to be some day. Since Brignac was
a female, maybe Jessica would feel more comfortable.

"Do you want to talk to me?" Brignac asked. They
hadn't left the scene yet. Jessica was in the backseat of
the cruiser. Shifting around. Twisting and turning.
Trying to get her handcuffs in a position that didn't
strain too much or bite into her wrists.

"This is uncomfortable. My wrists hurt."

"You want to talk?"

"Not without an attorney," Jessica said.

Brignac could sense a defensive, rebellious attitude
in her voice, as if Jessica was saying, *You've got nothing!*

"Okay," Brignac said, nodding to the warrant officer.
It was time to move.

Brignac sat down. Jessica mumbled something to
herself. Then: "These cuffs are too tight, come on."

"Hold up," Brignac told the officer. "Don't leave yet."

The detective got out. Walked around. Loosened up
the cuffs a little.

"Better?"

"Could you adjust my bra and blouse?" Jessica asked.
Apparently, her bra was digging into her skin. Her
blouse was hung up on the cuffs.

Brignac fixed the garments.

"This is so uncomfortable," Jessica pleaded.

"Too bad," Brignac said while slamming the door shut.

The media end of the case was of great concern to
Brignac and members of the HPD. Jessica's kids were just
now learning to accept their that dad and Terra were
dead. Did they need to now see their mom being
brought into the jail in handcuffs on television, sneering

and snapping at reporters, turning away from the camera, doing the perp walk?

As they worked their way down the interstate toward the county jail, Brignac unhitched her seat belt and spun around. She wanted to address Jessica, face-to-face. One more shot, the detective figured. Never can tell when a suspect will crack. Most are immediately defiant, a normal human reaction. But after they have some time to think about jail, what they've done and what is ahead, many change their minds. That's when a good, experienced cop can step up the pressure and get what she needs.

"Have you told your kids about the service coming up for their dad and stepmother this weekend?" Brignac asked. Kids were a surefire way to get a suspect to think about the future.

Jessica moved around in her seat. Smiled out of the corner of her mouth. "My kids are none of your business, Detective."

"Oh, okay, then, Mrs. McCord. I take it that they are not going to be attending their dad's service?" There was sarcasm in Brignac's otherwise calm and soothing Southern drawl. She wanted Jessica to understand that by her determination to try and control this situation, she was going to hurt the children more than they had been already.

"Look, my children are none of your damn business!" Jessica said again. More authoritative and direct. "I'll be out'a there in *no* time, Detective—and I'll take care of my kids."

This was a far cry from the same woman a week prior. That same person on the telephone with Joan Bates. Jessica herself later claimed that talking to Joan during those moments when Alan and Terra were considered missing was uncompromising and nerve-wracking. She told Joan: *"Please let me know . . . what's*

*going on when you find out. I would need to tell the kids
something."*

Jessica had plenty of opportunity to talk to her children about what was going on. By this point she hadn't
said a word. Now she was concerned about them?

Brignac knew better. She was speaking to a woman
who had admitted stopping at a fast-food restaurant on
her way home and eating all of the food inside the
family van by herself, down the street from her house,
so she "didn't have to share" with the kids. Jessica
McCord was a selfish, uncaring, conniving, manipulative accused murderer. She was focused on her own
needs. Not what her children deserved or needed.

"In some ways," one source close to the case told me,
"I'm surprised [Jessica] didn't kill the girls, too, so she
could punish everyone. She liked feeling as if she had
some sort of control over *everything*."

Steel bars and concrete walls were no match for this
woman. Nothing was going to stop Jessica from wielding her manipulative ways over her kids. Her reputation preceded itself.

While she had been in jail during Christmas, 2001,
for contempt, and the kids were with Alan and Terra,
Jessica called Alan one night. The kids were acting
normally up until that moment, getting along well
with Alan and Terra. They were all doing their best to
rebuild relationships and become a family unit. For the
kids it was a far different experience from living back
in Hoover with Jessica.

"That was until [the kids] had their phone calls with
Jessica," one source later explained, "and then Terra
and Alan would have to spend the next few days getting
them back out of whatever sort of spell Jessica put them
under."

As they drove, Brignac took a call from her colleague

Tom McDanal, who was already at the jail. "Get ready, there is a lot of media here waiting on you."

Brignac thought about it. By now, the detective had been awake for almost two straight days, working various angles of the case in order to secure the arrest warrants. She was as sleep deprived as the rest of the team—and beginning to feel it.

"Thanks, Tom."

Jessica complained again from the backseat. Her cuffs were too tight. "I'm pregnant," she said. "I'm going to have a baby," She hoped the comment would convince Brignac to cut her some slack.

Hanging up with McDanal, Brignac unbuckled her seat belt and turned around to face Jessica again. The comments—"I'll be out'a there in *no* time," coupled with the constant crying about being pregnant and uncomfortable—grated on the detective's fragile nerves, eating up any energy Brignac had left. Her short fuse had burned out. She was tired. Fed up with Jessica's attitude. The way Jessica spoke to a police officer, showing no respect for the law. Another human being, for that matter. Who did this woman think she was, sitting back there, handcuffed, on her way to face charges for double murder that could result in her death? Who in the heck, Brignac considered, was this woman to sass back at her?

"Look," Brignac said, entirely fed up, "I have some news for you. You're not getting out of jail! And I hope to hell that you *are* pregnant. Because you're going to give birth in jail, and they're going to snatch that baby from you—and you'll *never* see it again."

Brignac turned around. Sat down with a thud without waiting for a response. "It was a horrible thing to say," Brignac recalled later. "But I was very tired."

The warrant officer looked at Brignac, an incredulous crinkle in his brow.

Jessica fumed. "We'll see about that, Detective."

"She was mad as a wet dog. Still real cocky," Brignac remembered.

Pulling into the jail parking lot, the warrant officer was "nervous," Brignac explained. "Here was this media [circus] waiting on us all."

He parked by the back entrance, where prisoners are escorted into the building. Brignac, one hand on the door handle to get out of the car, looked over at the warrant officer and said, "You ready?"

They exited the vehicle. Brignac walked to the back to help Jessica, who was trying to hide her face from photographers as best she could.

As the warrant officer got out, he somehow tripped the car alarm.

Brignac laughed.

Then, as he went to go turn it off with his key ring, he hit the trunk button, instead, popping it open.

Brignac couldn't take it: she broke down. "He was flustered," the detective recalled.

Jessica and Jeff were processed and placed in lockup.

That control over everyone else's life that Jessica had so much centered her days and nights on was now in the hands of the state of Alabama.

PART III

THE NARROW GATE

35

Jessica is a fan of Hollywood. She loves superhero movies, those big blockbuster types with the hundred-million-dollar budgets and young stars flying around in flashy spandex suits, stomping their way through computerized scenery. Something about the good versus evil archetype encompassing those films spoke to Jessica's egotistical pride—and her aggressive, violent nature. An old friend of Jessica's later spoke of what she called a "clichéd" albatross of "good and evil" that hung around Jessica's neck. How it was there from the beginning, when Alan first met her in the late 1980s. The idea of Alan being raised in such a wholesome, good-hearted family, and turning out to be a peaceful, productive human being, represented the "good" in a world of "evil" that Jessica, in many ways, seemed to almost thrive in.

"When we were kids, I could not help but feel a negative energy around Jessica whenever she was near," that friend explained. The description sounded hackneyed, the friend added. "I know it does." But with Jessica came a "dark shadow" hovering over her—a metaphoric cloud, representative of the malice and

impiety present in most everything she did. And as
Alan and Jessica's marriage crumbled and the divorce
and custody battle turned vicious, this malevolent
nature in Jessica's heart rose to the surface.

That "good versus evil" dynamic, always there between them, now took center stage. "I recall clearly
Jessica once telling Alan," that friend concluded,
"'You marry her (Terra) and you'll never see your kids
again.'" This was from the same woman who had, back
in high school, laid eyes on Alan before they hooked
up and said, "I'll get him no matter what . . . and trap
him if I have to."

To Jessica, strength could always overcome weakness. Ultimately the tough survived. Not the virtuous
or lawful. But the most powerful. In Jessica's world
you didn't need good on your side to win. You needed
to outthink your opponent. To be smarter and more
cunning. This self-righteous, win-at-any-cost attitude
Jessica harbored—fighting Alan over the kids because
the thrill of the fight and winning fed her ego—was
going, with any luck, to push Jessica toward a victory
she so desperately needed. Not getting the kids. No.
She could never be comfortable with that. This was
about something else now.

Destroying Alan.

Yes. Watching Alan crash and burn.

In early 2000, Alan filed an "amendment to [his] petition" for custody, stating that a new job would send
him all over the country, traveling with a theater
group. He wanted to see the kids during the week, as
well as on the weekends he was back in town.

A new trial date in the custody matter was set for
April 4, 2000. This was when Jessica and Alan could
work out what had become a plethora of accusations
against each other: from not paying bills to not being
able to see the kids. Jessica turned what appeared to

be a straightforward, amicable divorce five years prior into a mess costing both of them more money than they had. Why couldn't she allow the man to see his kids? It seemed so simple.

Jessica announced she was pregnant. It was Jeff's baby. She called Naomi to tell her the news. She was upset about something Jeff's mother had said. Mrs. McCord was against the idea of Jessica and Jeff getting married.

"She wants me to abort the child," Jessica claimed. "She doesn't want me to marry Kelley."

More lies.

Naomi was stunned. Jessica's life was running at hyper speed all the time. There was always some dilemma, some problem to overcome. Alan was this. Alan was that. He never wanted to see his kids. Now Jeff's mother was coming down on her, trying to ruin her life with Jeff. It was always something, someone.

"Can't you talk to her, Jess?" Naomi said, referring to Jeff's mom.

"I won't let that woman tell me what to do!"

Jessica was not ready to have another baby, apparently— because Jeff drove her to Mississippi, according to several sources, where she got another abortion.

Alan Bates and Frank Head arrived at Shelby County Circuit Court on April 4, 2000. They were there to begin the process of hashing out the details of the divorce decree and visitation. Hopefully, the court could get Jessica in line with her legal obligations. That's all Alan wanted.

The 9:00 A.M. hour came and passed.

Then ten.

Eleven.

Noon.

Jessica was nowhere to be found.

This madness needed to end, Alan and Frank agreed. Alan and Terra had moved to Maryland after Alan had been offered a job in the theater that would put him in one place, as opposed to traveling the country. As stage manager of the Alabama Theatre, just about every touring company that came through Birmingham noticed Alan's skills behind the scenes and offered him a job on the road. Alan was flattered and would have accepted any of the jobs—if he didn't have kids. But his first priority was to his two girls. He wasn't about to leave them.

Jessica had been keeping the kids away from Alan so much by this point that months had gone by without Alan speaking to them. It got to the point where he started saying to his brothers, "Well, why am I here? If I cannot see them, I might as well take one of these offers to see if I can at least develop my career, so I can benefit the children in that way."

Alan did accept a proffered position and traveled with the stage company for one year. Terra met up with him from time to time in certain cities. On the weekends he was supposed to have the children, Alan flew or drove home. But then he stopped that, too, knowing Jessica wasn't going to allow the visits. Then Alan was offered a job in Maryland to manage a company in charge of sending out the touring companies. It was permanent, stable. Terra wanted to continue her studies in Baltimore, so the arrangement worked out for the both of them.

Alan wanted to rectify the situation with Jessica. According to the divorce's final judgment, paragraph four, Alan was entitled to have the kids *eight weeks of summer vacation . . . with at least 30 days advance notice . . . each spring break or school spring holidays from Saturday to Saturday; every Thanksgiving holiday . . . [and] any occasion . . . [that he was] in the Jefferson or Shelby County area. . . .*

Jessica had not complied with any of the court's original orders. The divorce decree was a piece of paper to her. Nothing more. No one, Jessica made it clear to Alan on more than one occasion, was going to make her do anything.

Alan and Frank Head sat in court, patiently waiting for Jessica to show up on April 4, 2000. Jessica's attorney (one of about eight she would have over the course of the custody fight), Lindsey Allison, sat alone, waiting for her client. The court put the case on hold for the morning. Then the bench decided to proceed without Jessica as the noon hour approached.

"I hereby make a motion for continuance," Lindsey Allison offered, doing her best to get Jessica out of a mess she'd created by not showing up.

The judge denied the motion and told the lawyers to get on with it.

After some time Lindsey said she "wanted to make a motion to withdraw as attorney of record in this case."

The judge granted it. Jessica was now without an attorney. After that, the judge made several rulings in Alan's favor. This wasn't the first time the court had heard from Alan's attorney on the matter of Jessica not allowing his client to see his children. The judge, one could gather from reading the record, was fed up with Jessica not following the rule of law. Alan provided written confirmation and documentation to prove he was not being allowed to see the children. There were police reports detailing Jessica's arrest the previous fall for assaulting Alan by pushing him down the stairs and breaking his arm.

None of the evidence was contested.

Alan testified. He brought in witnesses to back up his claims.

The plaintiff being ready in this cause, the ruling stated, *and presenting testimony and evidence in support of the Petition . . . the Court finds the defendant in contempt for numerous instances of failure to comply with the visitation provisions in the Final Judgment of Divorce, and the Court also finds that the visitation provisions should be modified due to the plaintiff's living arrangements in another state. . . .*

Finally justice.

But there was more.

"The defendant," the judge ordered, though Jessica was not present, "is herewith found in contempt, and is ordered to serve ten days in jail for two of several instances wherein the court finds she willfully violated the visitation provisions of the Final Judgment of Divorce. . . ."

Jessica was going to comply with the law or face a penalty.

"The jail time is suspended," the judge continued, "for a period of six months, and this cause is set for a compliance hearing on October 10, 2000, nine A.M., to determine whether the defendant complied with the order herein."

It was a major victory for Alan. It was time for Jessica to live up to her end of the visitations. It had been five years of ridiculous conduct on her part. It needed to end. Right now. Ten days, Alan's attorney knew, could turn into ten months for Jessica if she continued to play games.

Alan and Terra were satisfied. The court heard Alan's plea and acted. All he needed was for his former wife to live up to her obligations. If she didn't, she was going to jail. If she did, great. The judge would suspend the time. Maybe jail—or the threat of it—would scare Jessica into submission? Perhaps she would now understand that the court was no longer taking the passive route.

Several weeks after that no-show court date, Alan wrote Jessica a letter. He and Terra had plans, though he wasn't about to share them with Jessica yet. Instead, he wanted to make her aware, per the court's order, that he was giving her thirty days' notice before taking the girls that summer. He slated June 19 through August 13 as the time frame for which he wanted the girls. He wrote he expected and *appreciated* Jessica's *attention and cooperation with this matter.*

Jessica, surprisingly, complied.

This is great, Alan thought. He and Terra were scheduled to be married on June 24, 2000, a year after that original date had been bungled. If he got the girls on June 19, they'd make the wedding. There seemed to be nothing to keep them away.

Alan contacted Jessica by phone on June 19. She promised the kids were going to be at her mother's house. The plan was for Alan's mother to drive from Atlanta to Birmingham to pick up the kids. She would keep them for a few days. When Alan returned from a business trip, he could pick them up in Atlanta. Alan would never have to see Jessica.

For whatever reason, Kevin and Robert Bates said later, "Alan showed up to pick up the kids." Probably because he hadn't seen them in so long. He didn't want to waste one minute. He had gotten out of the business trip a few days early.

After the wedding at the Alabama Theatre on June 24, the plan was for Alan and Terra to honeymoon for a few days while the girls spent some time with their grandparents. Then Alan and Terra could take them back to Maryland for the summer.

Maybe Jessica had finally seen the light. Perhaps she decided it wasn't worth destroying the kids' lives for her own self-centered benefit.

Jessica affirmed that she was not going to be a nuisance

anymore. The kids had suffered enough. When Alan called to say he was picking up the kids, and not his mother, Jessica explained that she had something to tell him. Something important. Something he'd probably be surprised by. But she wanted to do it in person.

Could be just about anything, knowing that woman.

Alan walked into Jessica's home in Montevallo, a house, incidentally, he had handed over to her as part of the divorce, no questions asked, so his kids could have a stable life and environment to grow up in. There was someone else there, Alan noticed. A barrel-chested man, maybe five foot nine, two hundred pounds. Stocky. Rough around the edges. He had beady blue eyes, very distinctive and unique in color. His hair was cropped short. Buzz cut. He was thirty years old. (Jessica was about to turn twenty-nine on June 25.)

Alan stuck out his hand.

The guy looked like a cop.

"This is Jeff," she said. "My husband."

"Husband?"

Jeff was a Pelham police officer, Jessica explained with a smirk. They had gotten married the previous Saturday, she explained with a beaming glow about her. Her mother knew. A few others. But besides that, Jessica said, she hadn't told many people. Jeff was "shy," she seemed to point out to Alan for no reason. She called him a "loner." Said he didn't like a lot of fuss. "[Jeff] would be very difficult to provoke in any way," Jessica said later. "He avoids confrontations."

As far as Jeff being a police officer, Jessica addressed that in court in a bit more detail, saying, "Police officers, if they are even involved in an assault of any kind, they lose their jobs. They are trained to use other methods than drawing their gun whenever they can. And, you know, I don't know if it's from television or media or what, but people seem to have this impression that, you know, police officers tend to be very controlled and will not just, you know, walk up on you and they're going to draw their gun and things like that. It's not the Wild West, and people think that way."

Jeff Kelley McCord seemed like an all right guy, Alan considered. What divorced father of two girls wouldn't want a police officer—a protector by nature—in the same house with his kids if he wasn't there? This might turn out okay, after all, Alan felt. Maybe this was the reason why Jessica had suddenly turned into a cooperative ex-spouse. She was happy, for once in her life.

Still, it would have been nice beforehand to know that the kids were going to have a stepfather, Alan thought after leaving the house. But that was Jessica— she had to one-up Alan. Now the court would see who was married first, he knew. Jessica also said she and Jeff had purchased a house—but she didn't say where. It was a nice home in a middle-class neighborhood by a lake outside Birmingham. They were moving there soon.

Of course, there was one minor detail she forgot to mention to Alan in all of this. Jessica was going to have Jeff's baby. One friend said it was right after Jessica convinced Jeff to get that money from his mother that she became pregnant again. Before this, Jessica had an abortion for Jeff, perhaps even two.

Alan got the kids into the car. No argument on Jessica's part. Alan and Terra were married on June 24, 2000, with both of Alan's children there by his side. It was a beautiful ceremony, replete with the affection that had been missing from Alan's life with Jessica all those years. Alan had found and married the love of his life. They were the ideal couple, mimicking the plastic model atop the wedding cake.

You can see the radiance in the photographs of their wedding. Terra was pictured talking to guests, Alan in back of her, smiling, as if he had just met the love of his life. He'd probably heard those stories she was telling ten times already, but he still hung on every word. The look in his eyes was magical, respectful, dignified. He loved this woman with every ounce of his soul. Terra had brought such permanence, such unconditional love, into Alan's life. She was the blessing he had been searching for all along. They would rise together in their chosen careers, spend the summers and holidays with Alan's kids, maybe start a family of their own. This wedding, with all of its past difficulties, was behind them. They could begin their lives anew.

And it appeared that even Jessica was now going to accept it.

36

As soon as Jessica and Jeff moved into the house on Myrtlewood Drive in Hoover, Jessica began to create a new plan to keep Alan away from the kids. And Jeff went along, doing whatever he was told.

The only reason there were no problems for Alan during the summer of 2000 was because Alan had kept the kids at his home in Maryland. He and Terra set aside a room for the children. Decorated it. Spent the summer rebuilding relationships Jessica had spent years destroying. It didn't take the kids long to realize Alan loved them, no matter what Jessica had said or drilled into their heads. It was clear in Alan's words, gestures and pure show of affection that his love was genuine, and had been all along.

Alan and Terra dropped the kids off in Birmingham at the end of the summer. Then returned to their lives in Maryland. Alan lost touch with his girls the next day. It was easier for Jessica now that Alan lived nine hundred miles northeast. He couldn't drop by unexpectedly and say he wanted to see the girls. Now, same as she had before, Jessica refused to allow the children to speak with their father on the telephone. More than that, Alan had no idea where, exactly, did Jessica and Jeff lived in Hoover.

Here we go again. . . .

All Jessica had to do was conform with the court's order and she would have saved herself from serving ten days in jail—the sentence she had been given was six months suspended. This was, however, providing she proved to the court she made an effort to live up to her obligations. October 2000 was just around the corner, a time when Jessica and her new lawyer would have to prove she was living under the provisions of the court's ruling.

Frank Head let the court know she wasn't. He also made it clear that Jessica never provided written documentation—a note from her doctor—regarding her "inability to appear for trial" that past April 4, 2000 (her excuse a day later was that she was ill).

Alan and Head showed up in court on October 16, 2000. Jessica's new lawyer was there. But once again, Jessica chose to skip it.

"Your client, is she here?" the judge asked Jessica's lawyer.

"I have not had recent contact with my client, Your Honor, this after diligent efforts."

The judge ordered both sides to get on with the hearing.

By the end of the session, the judge ruled that Jessica had "failed to comply with the Order of the Court entered [in April that year], by failing or refusing to allow [Alan] to speak with his children at least one evening each week on the telephone for up to fifteen minutes of uninterrupted conversation. . . ."

In addition, she hadn't paid Alan's attorney's fees, which she was responsible for.

With that, the judge ordered the contempt charge against Jessica be put into action. Someone needed to find Jessica McCord. She owed the judge ten days in jail.

When she heard, Jessica became infuriated. She called a friend a few days later to vent. She described the "gall" Alan had to demand that she be put in jail. This was all Alan's fault. He did it. He could have stopped it, but he chose to make her suffer.

"I'm going to get him," Jessica told that friend. She repeated a prior threat: "I'm going to set him up for domestic abuse."

Jessica's plan was to provoke Alan into hitting her; then she would run to the police and press charges.

The judge signed off on a writ of arrest and sent deputies to find Jessica and put her in jail.

But then something happened.

"To the best of my recollection," Jessica's mother, Dian Bailey, later said in court, "it was somewhere right in November 2000" when Jeff left Jessica. They split up. "And they might try reconciliation a day or two [later]," Dian added.

Jessica and the kids stayed at Dian's. According to Dian, Alan wasn't the poster child for fathers he had claimed to be in court. "Alan was not consistent in his visitation," Dian told the court, "whether that it be the first or the third, or it might be two hours on a Saturday if he can't make it, or it might be that he would take them out for dinner. . . ."

Further, Dian claimed, Alan had skipped visitations. He'd call and say he would be there, but he would never show up.

After a time Jessica moved back into the house on Myrtlewood Drive, reconciling with Jeff. She wasn't pregnant any longer, she said. Either she had lost the child, lied about being pregnant to begin with, or had another abortion.

During this period Jeff and Jessica didn't claim an

address. Jessica told Alan she and Jeff were buying a house, but Alan didn't know where. The kids, moreover, weren't enrolled in school. It appeared that Jessica, Jeff and the kids had disappeared.

Alan and Terra were horrified by the prospect that Jessica and her new husband—a man Alan didn't know very much about—might have packed up and taken off with Alan's kids. Jessica was now hiding the children from him, more than just denouncing his advances to see and speak with them. But it wasn't only Alan she was running from. Jessica owed the court ten days in jail.

By the end of November, Frank Head filed additional court actions against Jessica regarding her desire not to allow Alan to see the kids during the Thanksgiving holiday, or on McKenna's birthday. Alan was beside himself. Jessica was like a broken record. The same behavior all over again. She refused to follow the court's ruling, even if it meant jail time.

Frank Head asked the court to issue a subpoena to the custodian of records for the Hoover City School System so he could find out where the children's educational records popped up. The idea was that Jessica would have enrolled the children in school somewhere. There had to be a record. It was Alan's belief they were attending Green Valley Elementary, on Old Columbiana Road, about a mile from Jessica's mother's house. Alan knew the kids were being dropped off there at different times.

When the Hoover City School System failed to return a hit on the kids' whereabouts, Frank Head went to the custodian of records for Southminster Day School in Vestavia Hills. Alan heard that maybe the kids were enrolled there. Of course, he called the Pelham PD, but they couldn't give him any information.

By this point Jessica was served several Violation of Previous Orders. All with no response from her. In a December 21, 2000, letter (which he had no idea where to send), Frank Head announced that Alan wanted to see the kids on Christmas, per order of the court.

Christmas came and went, as did the New Year celebration.

Alan never saw or spoke to his kids.

The issue now became, not if Alan Bates would ever see his children again, but where, exactly, was Jessica hiding them.

37

By the end of January 2001, Alan still could not find Jessica or the kids. It consumed him. He was torn over not being able to maintain any type of ongoing relationship with his girls. He feared the worst—that Jessica had taken off, out of the state or the country. Alan and Terra had taken the kids into their Maryland home that previous summer, but after dropping them off a few weeks before school started in August, they had not heard from them since.

Five months. Not a peep.

The stress began to wear on Alan. All that time he had spent with the kids over the previous summer, building up their confidence, was now, undoubtedly, being deprogrammed out of them by Jessica and her twisted lies.

"Look," Kevin Bates said, "she never really had a job, so she never had any money, and when the kids wanted to have things and she couldn't buy them, after having used the child support that Alan gave her every month, she started to tell the kids, 'Oh, your dad is not paying me child support, so we have to eat rice every night.'"

Had it all started again? Jessica telling the children

Alan was a deadbeat dad who didn't want to see them? Alan could only imagine what she might be saying now that she owed jail time to the court.

Jessica knew the more time the kids spent with Alan, the better the chances were that they'd realize he wasn't some sort of one-eyed hideous monster she'd made him out to be. Sooner or later, as the kids grew, they were going to figure out that she had been the liar all along—that is, *if* they continued to see Alan.

On February 8, 2001, the court postponed the Bates/McCord trial until May 15. There had been over a year of postponements by this point. The date gave Alan no repose. He was certain Jessica planned not to show up. How could the woman be jailed, held in contempt or follow the court's ruling—if she had been on the run?

When Alan understood that any hope of a civil (or legal) arrangement was dashed by Jessica's inability to live up to her obligations, it "threw him for a loop," family members said. "At this point," Kevin Bates added, "my brother began to see and realize how much damage her behavior was doing to the children—all for her own gain."

To see his kids being used and abused tore the man apart. He needed to end it—to do something. Alan wanted to reach out to the kids and explain what was going on.

"Alan doesn't get to the point to where he wants to file for custody until very, very late in the game," Robert Bates added. "The court action he took was, simply, to enforce the visitation rights he had in place already."

Jessica knew how to work the system. Alan had believed the system was going to protect him. She was sentenced to jail and she was dodging the court and the sheriff. What else could Alan do?

He was powerless.

In all of this, Terra became Alan's anchor, his best friend. The woman he could turn to and vent his frustrations. She never judged. She stood behind him, and encouraged Alan to do whatever was necessary to see that his children were taken care of. Despite how much money it cost. How long it took. Or where they had to travel to get the job done.

Why? Alan wondered. *Why is Jessica being so difficult?*

Kevin and Robert could see it on Alan's face every time they saw him.

Why?

Jessica was only hurting the kids. It didn't matter who was right, who was wrong. That simple rule whereby whatever divorced parents did affected the children was so true. However Jessica and Alan acted in front of the kids would reflect how the kids turned out as adults. Look at Jessica. Her life was a case study, in and of itself. According to what she had said, her father used her and her siblings as pawns after her parents divorced—and here she was doing the same damn thing.

Jessica later reflected on this period of her life, saying, "I don't recall ever boasting and laughing about denying Alan anything. . . . I wasn't angry at Alan that he was going to see the kids. I thought that would have been nice. . . ." In regard to picking up the children, or telling them Alan was on the way, Jessica said, "You know . . . you have to keep in mind that a lot of times he didn't come. So I don't know that the children put a lot of stock in me saying, 'You're going with your dad for the weekend, or you're leaving with them at such and such time.'" Jessica said there were times when "we were sitting by the door waiting . . . and many times he was not [there]. And, frequently, he wouldn't call, either. So I think it was kind of old hat for the kids for him not to come."

Lies. That is how Alan's family and friends summed up this statement Jessica made in court. There was documentation and anecdotal evidence proving Alan did everything in his power to see and speak to his children. It was Jessica who outright refused to allow him to do either.

Jessica knew Alan's lawyer was not going to let up. The more she pushed, the harder and more forceful Frank Head was going to pull. So Jessica called out to Jeff one night. It was before the new school year started. They were home, according to Jeff. She needed something done.

Jeff ran over. "What is it?"

By this time Jessica knew she was going to have to do some jail time at some point. There was no way to avoid it. That said, the court still had to serve her papers or, by Jessica's view, find her before it could uphold the order.

"Take the mailbox down," Jessica told Jeff.

"What?" Jeff didn't understand. Did she want him to repair it? Was it broken? What the hell was she talking about now?

"Take it down! They cannot serve me if they don't know where we live."

Jessica was "tired" of the letters from Frank Head's office, anyway, she told Jeff. This custody matter and all the paperwork was getting out of hand.

Out of sight, out of mind.

"Okay," Jeff said.

"If the deputies come around here," Jessica concluded, "and they're looking for me, or somebody comes to try and serve papers, you tell them you don't know where I am. You got that?"

Jeff thought about it. "Yes."

38

Naomi got a call on June 26, 2001, a day after Jessica had turned thirty. It was not a happy occasion. "Can you believe he forgot my birthday?" an impatient, agitated Jessica announced.

Naomi had not been over to the Myrtlewood Drive house since Jessica and Jeff had moved in. Naomi worked two jobs. She had a husband and kids to take care of. She was busy tending to her own life. Jessica was high maintenance. She never reached out to say hello, or stopped over to just hang out. There was always a dilemma or a problem when Jessica came knocking. For Naomi, phone calls would have to do right now. She was far too busy to deal with Jessica's instability.

Not too long after this, Jessica said she was pregnant with Jeff's child. She was going to have another baby. Later that summer, while Jessica was "seven or eight months" into the pregnancy, Jessica called Naomi.

It was late at night. The call was unexpected. "I need to stop by and drop a box off," Jessica stated.

"A box?"

"Yes. We're on our way to California and you're on my way."

"No problem, come on over."

Jessica, the kids and Jeff walked into Naomi's house that night. Jeff sat on the couch, Naomi said, "stone-faced. He had this look to him." He didn't talk. Barely moved. No emotion. Flat.

Jessica put the box in the basement. Came back up the stairs and said they were leaving. Naomi knew she was definitely pregnant this time because Jessica looked it.

Off they went.

A few days later, Jessica sent Naomi a postcard letting her know they had arrived in California without a problem.

You know, I'm awfully worried about you, Naomi thought, staring at Jessica's postcard.

"She should not have been on the road at that point in her pregnancy," Naomi recalled later.

Jessica's new attorney managed to convince Frank Head they needed another postponement for the trial. Frank said okay. Still, he needed to get Jeff McCord into his office for a court-ordered deposition, which Jeff, playing the same game as his wife, had been putting off. As of late, Frank Head had not heard from Jeff or Jessica.

Meanwhile, it was the middle of the summer and Alan didn't have his kids. Furthermore, Alan still didn't know which school the kids were attending. Or if Jessica, who had said she was planning on homeschooling them, had acquired her certificate and was teaching them herself.

Maybe it was time, Alan considered, to just sue for full custody? He had talked it over with Terra. His family. Nothing else seemed to be working.

The trial date was postponed again, this time to July 31, 2001.

Alan's blood boiled. He couldn't even get a day in court anymore. Jessica came up with every excuse imaginable, and the court was allowing it.

Because of privacy issues, the trail of red tape to get information from the school system—even though Alan was the father of the girls—turned out to be as long as this postdivorce fight. There was no end to how much the system wasn't working for Alan. Sooner or later, he knew, the authorities would catch up with Jessica, arrest her and cart her off to jail. But what about right now? What about the welfare of the children today? Who was watching them? He had not seen or heard from them in almost a full year.

July came and the court postponed the trial *again*, this time to September 19, 2001. This mess of Jessica's contempt charge had gone on now, well over a year. Alan began to wonder if he would ever see Jessica in a court of law.

On September 28, 2001, Jessica gave birth to Brian (pseudonym), a healthy baby boy. Her and Jeff's first child together. With Jessica in the hospital, postdelivery, Naomi paid her a visit. She wanted to see the new baby. Of course, Naomi had no idea what was going on behind the scenes. She didn't know Jessica and Jeff were basically hiding out. Nor did she have any clue that deputies were looking for her friend. What she did know, however, was only what Jessica had told her—that she was "in and out of court" and there were more court dates coming.

In reality—Jessica hadn't been to court in years.

When Naomi arrived at the hospital, Brian was in the nursery getting several of his shots. Jessica was in bed. She looked beaten and bitter. Not even a visit by her friend had brought a smile. At one time Jessica was a beautiful woman. Long, flowing hair. Clear skin. Great shape. Inspiring attitude. Now she was a thirty-year-old mother of four, countless abortions behind her, fighting a battle with her ex-husband that she could never win in the long run. No career. No schooling to fall back on. Married to a cop she had apparently hooked up with out of necessity.

A train wreck.

"The baby's not here," Jessica told Naomi.

"It's okay," Naomi said. She understood. No problem. Another time. How 'bout the two of them just sit and chat. Like old times.

Jeff was there. As usual, he sat and said nothing. The man just stared and looked at Jessica whenever she barked an order.

Naomi was sitting when Jessica picked up the phone and berated a nurse for no apparent reason. "Get my child in here right now!" Jessica screamed. She wanted the baby in the room so she could show him off to her visitor. *"Now."*

Naomi was embarrassed. "Look, I have all afternoon, Jessica. I can wait. Don't worry about it."

Jessica didn't care. "Bring the baby in here right now!" she kept yelling into the phone.

Jeff never moved. Never said a word. Just another day in the life of Jessica McCord. Flip the page of a magazine and do what she says. Life was so much easier that way.

Georgetown Place is what they call the grounds surrounding three-acre Batson Lake, which is located in Hoover on eight acres of unspoiled landscape. There's playground equipment and plenty of things for the kids to do on the lake grounds. There's a gazebo at the end of a dock, out on the water. In winter months the place is all but deserted. Jessica and Jeff lived down the street from the lake and passed by a certain area of the park whenever they left their house. In fact, their Myrtlewood Drive home was on the same street as the park entrance.

After Jeff nestled the kids into their car seats and left his house on the morning of November 21, 2001, turning right at the north side of the lake, heading toward Dundale Road, he noticed a car get up behind him, he later said.

Odd, this time of the morning, Jeff thought. *Especially here.*

It was obvious the car had been waiting for him to leave.

According to Jeff, the man driving that car was Alan. Fed up with Jessica's refusal to allow him to see his children, Alan had decided it was time to do something about it himself, Jeff said.

"I was not aware of any reason for him to be there," Jeff said later. "We had not received [anything], no phone calls, no certified mail, nothing in the mail, no messages regarding this [visit]. . . ."

How in the world could they?

Anyway, Alan stayed on Jeff's tail, following him closely behind. They traveled into downtown Hoover via the interstate. Then into Green Valley, where Jeff picked up his pace and led Alan into a subdivision before heading into Pelham—where, of course, Jeff had plenty of friends.

Jeff said he was scared. Jessica had primed him with a version of Alan replete with "rage," he said, "anger, domestic violence, whatever." Whether it was true was beside the point. Jeff was under the impression, he later claimed, that it was. "I'm just taking her word for it."

And now here's Alan, following him like some madman.

As Jeff got closer to the Pelham PD, Alan backed off, he said, realizing that Jeff was not going to stop. Confronting the guy in the parking lot of the police department where he worked was probably not the best idea.

Jeff claimed he dropped the kids off at the sitter's after Alan took off. Then he went to work. Grabbed an officer, one of his coworkers, and asked him to fill out a report. He certainly wasn't going to be harassed by Jessica's crazy ex-husband.

39

In between Thanksgiving and Christmas, Alan's lawyer bombarded the court with motions. He also filed several subpoena requests for school records. The court still could not find Jessica or the children. She was either keeping them out of school, home-schooling them, or they had moved far away. The fact alone that Frank Head had done all this work—not to mention that Alan lived nine hundred miles away— was a good indication that Jeff was either lying about Alan following him that day, or—in a paranoid state Jessica had induced—he had convinced himself that a stranger was Alan.

Frank Head filed a motion for a December 11, 2001, hearing date to hash out what was turning into a legal quagmire. The woman was breaking so many different laws. Where was the accountability, and what was the court doing to find her? Thus far, it appeared that the court hadn't done much to serve an arrest warrant.

In turn, the Eighteenth Judicial Circuit Court of Shelby County rubber-stamped two Failure to Abide by Previous Order of the Court orders by Alan and issued another series of arrest warrants.

It did no good.

As it turned out, Jessica had been hanging around Brad Tabor's place during this period of time. Unbeknownst to Brad, she and Jeff and the kids were hiding out. Brad even babysat the kids from time to time. But when Jessica didn't show up on time to drop off the girls, Brad called her. One such day he asked what was going on.

True to her nature, Jessica found a way to blame Alan: "Kelley has the girls," Jessica said breathlessly, "in the car . . . and they're . . . Alan had been following them. He's not bringing them home because he doesn't want Alan to know where we live." She made the implication that Alan was a raging lunatic, looking to cause violence.

A day later, Brad called Jessica to ask what was going on. Why all the fuss about Alan knowing where she lived?

"I'm concerned Alan is going to win custody," Jessica said. She sounded dismayed.

"Really?"

"It's the homeschooling. That's what's going to win it for him." Jessica was never licensed to homeschool the kids. In addition to everything else, she had lied about that, too.

Brad didn't know what to say. Jessica mentioned jail. Brad had no idea things had spiraled so out of control.

"I can't lose the girls, Brad, and the child support. I *need* that money."

Jessica liked to say she and her children had a "close relationship." She could always talk to them, she insisted, about anything. And yet what she claimed to have talked to them about at times bordered on the psychotic and bizarre, considering how young they were.

"And when they were growing up," Jessica admitted, "you know, all along the years, they would ask me things, have questions after watching a TV show about maybe drug usage or premarital sex, which, I mean, I had premarital sex and was not married when I had them. (Not true.) We would have separate conversations about each of these things and about just different types of values that we found to be important." Jessica instilled in her kids, she claimed, not to "have preconceived notions about other people, because you're not that person. You haven't lived their life. You don't know! How road rage is just crazy, because you're driving down a road and you don't know why this person cut you off in a car. You don't know."

She went on to explain why we receive tax refunds "and that you don't have to take that money," she told them, "if you don't want to. . . . That's a choice you make as a member of society. You have to pay your taxes, but you don't have to take extra back."

Did it make sense to share this with ten- and eight-year-old children?

Jessica thought so.

She also described how geometry works and her idea behind Einstein's theory of relativity. "A lot of what we learn is perception . . . and that was what I taught my children. I would want them to continue to understand that things are fluid, things change, and simply because one person says that's an absolute, it may not be. . . ."

Jessica was later diagnosed with borderline personality disorder (BPD). According to the National Institute of Mental Health (NIMH), *[BPD] is a serious mental illness characterized by pervasive instability in moods, interpersonal relationships, self-image, and behavior. This instability often disrupts family and work life, long-term planning, and the individual's sense of self-identity. Originally thought to be at the "borderline" of psychosis, people with BPD suffer from a disorder of emotion regulation.*[1]

This description would serve to illustrate Jessica's behavior inside the next three months, almost as if it were written specifically for her. One of the worst fears a person suffering from BPD can face is the thought that their most sacred possession in life will be taken away.

This, many doctors agree, can cause a person with BPD to spin entirely out of control.

On December 18, 2001, Jeff and Jessica were at their Myrtlewood Drive home with the kids. Jessica knew she was in violation of the law. She'd been keeping the kids away from Alan for well over a year. He had not even spoken to them.

While the McCords were inside, there was some movement outside the house.

Jeff looked out the window. He knew what it was. So did Jessica.

The Jefferson County Sheriff's Office (JCSO), along with an officer from the Hoover PD, was in front of the McCord home. From the bathroom window upstairs, behind the blinds, Jeff watched the two vehicles pull up.

Pulling away from the blinds, Jeff heard the car doors slam.

---

[1] For more information about BPD, including the symptoms to look out for, please see *http://www.nimh.nih.gov/health/publications/borderline-personality-disorder.shtml*. The NIMH is part of the National Institutes of Health (NIH), a component of the U.S. Department of Health and Human Services.

"Can I help you guys?" Jeff asked, meeting them outside in the driveway moments later.

Jessica was upstairs in the master bedroom. According to her, she had just woken up. It was early morning. "We were all still in bed," she recalled, "in pajamas and everything, watching Martha Stewart on TV."

Law enforcement had an arrest warrant. Jessica was being charged with contempt. She was going to jail for not allowing Alan to see his kids—the judge had *warned* her repeatedly.

"I could hear them," Jessica said, "discussing that there was some sort of an order relating to the children and an order for my arrest."

"Some sort of an order," as if she had no idea why they were there.

In fact, Jessica later claimed she had no idea an arrest warrant had been issued for her. She insisted that no one had told her about it.

"Yeah, can I see your documentation?" Jeff asked. The kids were upstairs with their mom, listening. They "became very upset. Very, very upset," Jessica said.

The girls cried, she claimed. Jessica tried calming them. She said she explained what was going on. "Preparing them," she called it. Again, this was after first saying she had no idea why the cops were at her house.

Jeff looked over the paperwork downstairs. It all seemed legit.

Why was he stalling?

"Does this order amount to a search warrant?" Jeff asked. He knew the law.

No answer.

"Well, *does* it?" he asked again.

If it didn't, he said, law enforcement was not allowed into the house to search for Jessica. They would have to wait outside.

Instead, Jeff claimed, the sheriffs walked past him toward the door, one of them asking, "Is she here?"

Jeff opened the door. "Come right in."

"Where is she?"

Jeff looked at the paperwork again.

"We're separated," he said, walking in behind them. He was trying to say that he and Jessica had split up. "She's not here."

Downstairs, undeterred, one of the sheriffs asked Jeff, "Where is she?"

By this point Jessica had told the children that the cops were there to take her away. "Well," one of them said (if you believe Jessica), "just say you're Auntie."

"No, baby," Jessica said, "that's not really going to fly. They are police. That won't work."

"Oh yes, it will, Mommy. Yes, it will."

The kids hugged her.

Downstairs, Jeff looked away after he was asked for a third time if Jessica was home. Then, "I have no idea where she or the girls are, sorry."

There was movement in the house. One of the deputies heard this and headed up the stairs.

He found Jessica in the master bedroom with the kids.

"Are you Jessica Bates McCord?"

"Auntie . . . Auntie . . . Auntie," the kids chanted, according to Jessica.

"That's my aunt," one of the girls said.

"I'm Belinda (pseudonym), Jessica's sister," Jessica said (according to several reports of this incident).

The sheriff was suspicious. It was the way Jessica had answered.

"Why are you here?" the sheriff asked. "Where is Jessica?"

"Um, Jessica left a couple of months ago and we haven't seen her."

"Well, why are you here with the kids? Aren't these Jessica's kids?" The sheriff then asked the children their names, knowing they were Jessica's kids. They had a court order, which had the names of the girls. They were supposed to pick them up, too.

Jessica thought about the question. "Well, Jessica ran off because she caught me in bed with Kelley."

Interesting excuse to give when hiding your identity.

One of the sheriffs called a supervisor to see if someone could dig up a photograph of Jessica and send it over. They also wanted fingerprints so they could verify she wasn't lying.

As they discussed this, Jessica "admitted" who she was to the sheriffs.

After a bit of small talk, Jessica was handcuffed and taken outside. The story she told upstairs, the sheriff later said, "didn't jibe with us."

Inside the sheriff's car, preparing to leave for Shelby County Jail, Jessica broke down. She started bawling. Hyperventilating. She was scared, she claimed.

After crying for a spell, she got angry. Then she snapped out of it and said, "This isn't fair. Somebody's going to pay for this!"

40

Jail was not a place compatible with Jessica McCord's character. The idea that she was in the same room with common criminals that she looked down upon infuriated the woman. When it came time to make telephone calls, it was Jeff who bore the brunt of his wife's anger. She berated him on the telephone in front of other prisoners. Cursed at him. Made unrealistic demands. "And," one fellow inmate later said, "talked to him like he was a five-year-old. . . . You know, *she* gives the orders."

"You need to get off your ass and do whatever it is you can to get me out of here," Jessica snapped during her first call to Jeff. This was before swearing at him and slamming the phone down on its cradle.

She called back a few minutes later. "I'm the one locked up for ten days, and you and my mother are not doing *anything* out there to help me."

Jeff asked how things were going. He was concerned.

"How am I *doing*? How . . . you're responsible for my being here, Kelley."

"Basically," Jeff said later, she made him feel that "I

was responsible for all the problems in her life at that particular time."

Jeff considered that because Jessica was the one sitting in the jail and not him, everything *had* to be his fault. Jessica's constant criticizing was, Jeff said later, all part of the manipulation effort on her part to get what she wanted. "She felt that I should have figured out a better or a different way to have handled the so-called 'problem' (meaning Alan) before it got to the point where she was hauled off to jail."

Jessica was livid. Absolutely furious. She ordered Jeff to call someone and get her out of jail before she went mad. All Jeff could do was listen and wonder what in the world he could do. She had violated an order of the court. Why wasn't she getting that? Sure, Jeff was a cop, but he couldn't do anything for her now. It was ten days. Suck it up.

"Jessica's . . . attitude," a fellow inmate said later, putting it mildly, "was kind of rough."

Jeff had been told over and over by Jessica that Alan was abusive. Jessica explained to him that Alan was stuck on getting back at her and had repeatedly hurt her and the kids. And now the court had the nerve to go and side with him and his new wife. Maybe it *was* Jeff's fault. Maybe he could have done more for his wife. Maybe there was something to what she had suggested a few weeks back—that the only way to get rid of the problem was to tend to it themselves.

As that conversation had progressed, Jessica talked about the idea of losing the children to Alan. She could not allow that to happen. Alan could *never* get custody. That was not an option here.

"I'll do *anything* to keep those kids, Kelley."

She sounded desperate, and Jeff knew what she meant.

"I know . . . I know," he said.

"Kelley, *anything*. I'll do anything to keep those kids. You know that."

She said it "several more times," Jeff later explained.

During Jessica's ten-day stint in jail, Jeff and Dian called Alan and asked if he would allow Jessica to leave the jail for two days—during the Christmas holiday— so she could spend that time with the children. The court wasn't going to allow her out of jail unless Alan signed off on it,

Without hesitation Alan agreed. For him, it had never been about punishing Jessica. It had never been personal. It had always been about the children.

Before leaving jail after her ten-day stint, a fiery Jessica McCord—even after Alan had allowed her the holiday with the kids—turned to a cellmate and let the woman know how she felt about being locked up.

"Somebody is going to pay," Jessica snapped.

PART IV

GONE FOR GOOD

41

Jessica hired a new attorney, David Dorn, as soon as she got out of jail. She handpicked Dorn out of the Yellow Pages and called him. A day later, Jessica sat in Dorn's office. She talked about what she expected out of legal representation. She called the ongoing battle with Alan a "visitation child custody case." Alan was suing for full custody, she explained. This scared Jessica. She saw the children slipping from her grasp. Of course, part of her monthly paycheck left with the kids. There was no way she could allow that to happen.

It was January 8, 2002. Dorn reviewed the case. There was a hearing scheduled for January 14 to discuss what had occurred "prior to then."

Perfect. Dorn could familiarize himself with the case, and the court would bring him up to date on the rest.

Alan was awarded temporary custody of the kids while Jessica was in jail, and he still had them. Terra was overjoyed. Before Alan had left to pick up the children, Terra e-mailed a friend. She explained the situation, noting: *We haven't seen or talked to [the children] in a year and a half (thanks to his ex-wife)*. She explained further that Alan had been granted temporary custody. *It's a sad situation, but hopefully it will all turn out OK.*

During the January 14 court date, Dorn was able to discuss the situation with Alan's lawyer, Frank Head, and Dorn later said, "Bottom line is, Jessica got her children returned to her."

Alan had enrolled the kids in the school system of Maryland. They had gone through three weeks of classes. Jessica, however, proved to the court that she was going to have the children homeschooled properly this time, under the auspices of a licensed homeschooling organization connected to a church near her home.

"I'm on the faculty of a school," Jessica told Dorn, explaining that she was qualified and could teach at Hope Christian School.

Still, the judge wasn't satisfied. It was decided that Jessica would place the children into a more traditional, conventional school system. At least for the remainder of the year. When—and if—she could prove the homeschooling qualifications she claimed to have, and Alan agreed, she could educate them.

Dorn explained to Jessica that the judge was adamant about the visitation schedule—considering her history—being kept. No more fooling around. It was time to heed to the court and allow Alan what was rightfully his.

This riled Jessica.

Alan brought the girls to the courthouse that day. When all was settled, and Jessica begrudgingly decided to honor the judge's orders, the kids were back in her arms.

"Jessica, Alan is going to be taking the girls to lunch," Dorn told his client after court, "so he can say good-bye to them, okay?"

Dorn later said Jessica became "very agitated" by this statement, but she agreed.

Alan took the girls to lunch and then went back to Maryland. He and Jessica were set to face off in court within the next few weeks. The custody hearing was on schedule. They were both set to give depositions in Dorn's office explaining their side of the story. Until then, the girls would stay with their mother.

A few days after that initial court date, Dorn found out Jessica had lied to him. In doing so, Dorn had turned around and had lied—unknowingly—to the judge.

This did not sit well with the experienced, well-liked attorney. So he corrected the record. "[I]t came to my attention," the lawyer later explained, "that the information I had represented to the court about the homeschooling was not true. . . . The children were *not* being educated under . . . the curricula of the homeschooling agency that we had represented, and that Jessica was *not* considered part of the faculty."

She had fabricated every part of the story.

How had Dorn found this out? Alan's lawyer called him and explained that he had checked Jessica's story out, and none of it was true.

After Frank Head called David Dorn, he relayed the information to the court.

The judge called Dorn. "What's the deal?"

Dorn explained.

"Well, I am going to make an order," the judge stated, "that the kids be returned to Mr. Bates immediately."

"I need some time to discuss this with my client, Your Honor."

"Yes . . ."

"Can we schedule an evidentiary hearing?"

Dorn wondered how the matter could be solved like this over the telephone. Frank Head was expected to present evidence in a court of law and prove Jessica was a liar. It was the proper way to go about it.

"The twenty-eighth," the judge suggested.

Ten days.

Alan Bates would be dead by then.

42

It was hard to imagine, but Jessica McCord had won the first round. She lied to the court, the judge and her lawyer, but she had managed to retain custody of the girls.

"What?" was Alan's reaction when he heard. He could not believe it. Neither could his attorney or his family. After all she had done, Jessica had managed to get her way once again.

It was beyond ridiculous.

According to the judge's new order, Jessica could keep the girls *during the pendency of this [investigation, but the] defendant shall not conduct homeschooling of either child absent written consent of plaintiff. It is also ordered during the pendency of this case that both parties shall at all times inform the other of his or her phone number and residential address.*

Alan had heard all this before. They were going around in circles.

Not to fear. During the upcoming trial Frank Head promised he was going to expose every single law that Jessica had broken over the past seven years and show the court the person she truly was. Alan had audiotapes of Jessica raging mad on his voice mail. She sounded belligerent and vicious. He had witnesses. Documentation. There was no doubt: the kids were leaving that court on March 5, 2002, with Alan; he was certain to win.

David Dorn seemed like the type of honest lawyer that Frank Head felt he could deal with in a civilized manner. They were both fighting for their clients' rights. Sure. Yet, they all needed to get along and allow the court to make judgments on facts—not Jessica's version of the events or the lies she told. Dorn seemed like the right lawyer to be able to get that done.

After deciding on the matter of temporary custody, which took place in the judge's chambers, and never made it into the actual courtroom, Head and Dorn decided they both wanted to take depositions from one another's client sooner rather than later. March 5 was right around the corner. The depositions needed to be done quickly.

"Frank, find out when your client can come back from [Maryland] to Birmingham and call me."

"I will," Frank Head said.

A day or so later, Head called Dorn and rattled off a few dates.

"February fifteenth sounds good to me," Dorn agreed.

"Okay. Since Alan's flying in from Washington, he'd like to have the kids for that weekend."

Dorn approached Jessica with the idea. Her reaction was the norm: steam from her ears. Or, as Dorn later put it, "Not positive. You know, agitation."

On February 8, 2002, Frank Head confirmed the date of the depositions to take place at Dorn's downtown Birmingham office, first thing Friday morning, February 15.

Seven days away.

As we discussed, Frank Head wrote in the letter to Dorn, *Alan would like to get the children for the weekend. . . .* Alan could pick them up that Friday after the deposition and return them to Jessica on Sunday night.

On the bottom of the letter, Head wrote a short note to Alan, whom he CC'd. He gave Alan the address to Dorn's office and telephone number, should he arrive that Friday morning in Birmingham and be delayed at the airport for any reason. If he was going to be late for the deposition, he should call.

Alan was looking forward to sitting down and speaking his mind on the entire matter. Laying it all out.

This was it for Alan Bates. Game day. As soon as those depositions were done, he could pick up the kids, head off to Marietta, Georgia, for the weekend and meet up with family and friends. After that, all he had to do was wait until his day in court.

Finally the system was falling back into favor with the truth.

43

As far back as the spring of 2001, Jessica had suggested to Jeff that violence was likely the only way to settle her dispute with Alan. There was no other way. Alan was going to win in court.

"Let's kill him," Jessica said one day (according to Jeff).

Officer Jeff McCord had shrugged it off as the frustrated gesture of a woman who hated her ex-husband. How many scorned ex-wives, full of fury, had sat around with friends, sipping cheap wine during happy hour, and then blurted out, *I wish he were dead*?

In mid-February 2002, after a meeting with David Dorn at his office downtown, Jeff and Jessica returned home and picked up that "let's kill him" conversation once again. Jessica turned to Jeff and, according to what Jeff later claimed, said, "We should just kill him."

They were in the living room. Alone. The kids were gone. Probably over at Jessica's mother's house.

Jeff looked at his wife. She sounded serious this time. Like she actually meant it. He was startled by this.

Alan and the custody matter was the focus of the McCord marriage. From the moment it appeared that Alan was going, by Jessica's count, "to get his way," life inside the McCord household centered around how Jessica was going to get Alan back—and how Jeff was going to help her.

Jeff didn't put too much thought into the suggestion of killing Alan. "I figured she was blowing off steam," he said later, "just ticked off . . . standard divorce stuff." Jeff added that he never had any reason to "think she'd even consider following through with anything. So I didn't pay any, *any* real attention."

Then she said it again a few days later. This time over the telephone. "In my opinion, Kelley, Alan needs to be killed."

"What?" Jeff had forgotten about those prior suggestions.

"Different people—'friends'—have suggested," Jessica continued, "everything from the only way to get rid of this problem is to put a bullet in his head, to something needs to happen to him. . . ."

Jeff was taken aback by this recent proposal. Jessica sounded matter-of-fact, as if murder was an option she was now actually considering. She wasn't just "blowing off steam" anymore, Jeff could tell. The woman was talking—and apparently had been talking to others—about killing Alan.

Jeff recalled, in his circuitous, hard-to-follow way of dismissing his involvement, "Her reason at that time, she really didn't specify reasons, other than the prior history of domestic abuse [she claimed], just in her, according to her, the type of person he was, how he . . . how badly or however he mistreated [the children], how controlling he was, so forth and so on."

Jessica had made all of that up. Alan was none of those things. There was no record of Alan ever being abusive toward Jessica or the kids.

The idea of losing the children to Alan didn't jibe with what David Dorn later said. Describing this same time period and the tone of Jessica's demeanor then, Dorn reported that he had been telling his client he was fairly confident she would be able to retain permanent custody of the children, as far as he was concerned. "All throughout the process, you know," Dorn testified in court later, "it was my professional opinion we were going to win. . . . There was never a time when I told her [that] we were going to lose."

But Jessica went home and played it off on Jeff differently. She made it appear as though she was under the enormous amount of pressure of losing the children—and she couldn't allow an abusive maniac to raise her kids. She had told Jeff that both of her wrists had been broken by Alan and that he had once cracked her sternum. She showed him the scars, Jeff said.

Looking at them, Jeff responded, "Oh, my goodness." He believed every word. "From watching the way she was able to pick up things," Jeff said later, and the way she had to handle anything heavy, her wrists didn't have the same strength as most people. "At least what I've seen in my experience."

And so it was that display of weakness, apparently, that had led Jeff to believe that Alan had hurt her wrists.

Jessica described two separate incidents where she claimed Alan had put her in the hospital.

Jeff was curious, his cop instinct creeping up on him. "Did you file a police report? Did you have him prosecuted?" Jeff also wondered why the judge in the custody matter wasn't persuaded by any of this.

"Look, at the time this happened [the mid-1990s]," Jessica said after Jeff questioned her, "when I called the Shelby County Sheriff's [Office] for assistance, when a deputy showed up, his attitude was 'Well, you know, you're not dead. . . . You know there's nothing I can do. He's married to you.'"

And so, with Jessica's continued references to the children being forced by the court to go live with an abusive father, Jeff McCord began to think about protecting his wife and her children any way that he could. The question gnawing at him as deposition day approached, however, became: how was he going to step in and defend them?

44

The thought of getting rid of Alan consumed Jessica. It was now a focal point rather than a passing joke. In Jessica's mind, the court would see the facts of the case. She couldn't escape from the past: jail, hiding the kids from Alan, assaulting him, keeping the kids out of school, all the lies.

Despite what her attorney was saying, it all added up to a loss. The only way to avoid putting the kids through the hell that awaited them with Alan and Terra, Jessica kept nagging Jeff, was to take Alan out of the picture.

"To her," Jeff commented later, the kids being taken away to live with Alan "meant 'gone for good.' The kids would be out of her life entirely. She would *never* be able to get them back." Jessica was convinced, Jeff believed, that "Alan and his family would do everything in their power to see that she had little, if any, contact with them."

Payback. A taste of what Alan had endured for seven years. Such a turn of the tables terrified Jessica. So she made up her mind: she was no longer going to allow the court to decide the fate of her children.

During the first week of February 2002, Jessica called Naomi. They had not spoken in some time. Naomi could hear the rage in Jessica's voice coming out of the telephone. "She was livid."

"Can you believe it?" Jessica said. "Can you *believe* he had me put in jail?" Here it was well over a month since she had been released and Jessica was still stewing about it.

"How are you doing?" Naomi wanted to know. It was the first she'd heard that Jessica had gone to jail.

"I cannot believe that he allowed me to stay in jail over Christmas. . . ."

Naomi had no idea Jessica was lying about this. She didn't know what to say. How to react.

"Alan's incredible," Jessica said before they hung up.

As deposition day neared, Jessica was back to not allowing Alan to talk to his children.

Alan was patient. He felt the court was going to work for him this time around. It was a matter of waiting for that March 5 trial date and following the court's orders up until then. He'd waited years. What was another few weeks?

Jessica approached Jeff once again with the idea that the best way to deal with Alan was to have him killed or to do it themselves. Something had to be done. March was right around the corner.

"She said the only way to do it," Jeff said later, "the only way to handle it, was to kill him, or have him killed. . . ."

After another meeting with her attorney, Jessica came home, and she was fuming. Jeff wasn't home when she walked in. So she called Naomi.

"He's trying to get custody of the girls," Jessica said.

She knew how to change her demeanor to suit the situation. She needed sympathy from Naomi.

"Just let him see the girls, Jess."

"He has no rights. He doesn't *know* the girls. There's no *way* he is going to get those girls from me."

"How are you going to go about it?" Naomi wondered.

Jessica laughed. "He is not seeing those kids."

"He has visitation rights, Jess. Just let him see the kids. You should let him have the kids so he knows what it's like to have them full-time."

Jessica explained how she and Alan were set to give depositions in a matter of days. "At the time," Naomi recalled, "you couldn't hear the desperation in her voice, but all I could hear was anger."

"She was very adamant," Jeff added, "about what was the only option [left]."

Jessica approached Jeff the next morning. This time with a plan. Entice Alan out onto the interstate and run him off the road. It would be easy. His death would be ruled an accident, or tied to an incident of road rage.

Brush your hands off, walk away with the children. No court.

When Jessica mentioned this idea, "I figured she was just pissed off," Jeff said, "because of the way the court [was going]." Jeff still didn't want to believe she was being real. He took her seriously, and then he didn't.

It needed to happen that night, Jessica insisted. Alan was in town. She knew where he was staying. All they had to do was follow him and make sure he didn't make it to his destination.

"I have to work tonight," Jeff said. His shift started in a few hours.

When they got home later that day, Jeff said he "made a point of getting ready as quickly as I could, and with [our youngest child] being at the house, he

couldn't be left, obviously he couldn't be left by himself."
Jessica would never take the kids with her to do it, Jeff
believed.

So the plan to run Alan off the road was thwarted.

Jeff left for work, forgot about it, and Jessica stayed
home.

Jessica sat and thought about it. She was going to be
grilled hard by Alan's attorney during the deposition.
Fingers would be pointed in her face, the spotlight
would shine on her behavior. He was going to ask
tough questions she'd have to come up with answers
for, on the spot.

"We need to do this," Jessica said to Jeff that night
when he returned home from his shift.

Here we go again. . . .

Jeff knew by now what she meant. Something,
though, told him not to face it directly. *Is she actually
serious?* he repeatedly wondered.

Some days she sounded as if it were all a joke;
others, she was as serious as Jeff had ever heard her.

"He's going to get the girls otherwise, Kelley," Jessica said.

"Relax. We'll do what we need to do."

"There's no other way to take care of this."

Jeff thought about it at work the next night. Was she
really going to do this? He decided to confront Jessica about how serious she was regarding actually
going through with it. No more talk. No more threats.

The next morning Jeff didn't have to say anything.
Jessica brought it up. They were in the den. Then upstairs in the master bedroom.

"Well, we need to do this," Jessica suggested.

"All right," Jeff agreed, calling his wife on it. "If you

can come up with a doable plan, we'll, you know, see what can happen."

Alan Bates didn't know it, but his life had come down to two people discussing his death as if it were part of a proposal to build an addition onto the house. The rest of the man's life had been distilled down to a police officer telling his wife: "We'll, you know, see what can happen."

Jeff later admitted that although Jessica kept pushing him and insisting that someone kill Alan, something told him she would never go through with it. No matter what she said.

The day progressed. "It needs to be done," Jessica said again. She wasn't letting up.

"Okay!"

"We really need to do this."

The deposition was here, Jessica reminded Jeff.

Jeff recalled later: "I don't know if this is true or not, but she was looking at potentially more time . . . from Shelby County for . . . contempt."

Not true.

Jessica told Jeff that she was going back to jail if Alan got the kids. She'd apparently hoped it would somehow convince him that killing was the only answer left.

Then Jessica came out and explained what type of plan she had been thinking about: "There's not going to be a better day."

Better day than what? Jeff wondered.

She explained.

He thought about it. She was right. The day of the deposition, February 15. "In her mind," Jeff recalled, "the fifteenth was the opportune or the best time to do it."

"Friday," Jessica said.

Jeff nodded. He worked that day. The night shift. If he was going to help, he needed the night off.

Jeff and Jessica came up with a solution together.

Jeff got hold of a fellow officer, a friend of his. Jeff asked him if he could switch days off. It was a deal that gave Jeff both Friday and the entire weekend to himself.

Perfect, Jessica knew.

They would need the extra time to clean up all the blood.

45

As he began to consider the idea of killing Alan, playing the deadly scene over in his head like a movie, Jeff McCord realized several problems with his wife's plan—which was now a carefully thought-out sketch she had explained to Jeff in full on Valentine's Day, fewer than twenty-four hours before the deposition.

"Alan is supposed to be at the house at six or six-thirty," Jeff said to Jessica after she explained what to do.

"Right," Jessica said. She didn't see the problem.

"Okay, what do we do then?"

If they killed Alan and he failed to return home to Terra and his parents—or wherever he was going after picking up the kids—what would happen? The last place Alan was supposed to be was at Jeff and Jessica's picking up the kids. They would be instant suspects, Jeff pointed out.

"We burn the body and torch his car," Jessica suggested, as if she were an old pro at committing homicides.

"All of which, obviously from my background," Jeff recalled later, "I know is a pretty good way to do away with evidence, and really do away with a lot of *trace* evidence, and a good way to mess up some crime-scene stuff."

An officer of the law explaining how to cover up a murder by referring to it as "a good way to mess up some crime-scene stuff."

Apparently, the murder plan now made sense to Jeff. Jessica had thought this thing through quite methodically.

Jeff wanted to make sure that their plan was infallible. They shouldn't take chances. They were too close to the victim. As a cop, Jeff said, he knew the center of the bull's-eye when investigating a murder was the place all cops started: family, friends, acquaintances (especially those having problems with the deceased).

It wasn't rocket science.

Jeff then asked Jessica several questions, playing devil's advocate, testing her.

"Okay, if you're going . . . if you're going to torch the car and burn the [body], how are you going to do it?"

Jessica looked at him. "It's not definite," she said. Jessica was still tossing other ideas around. The bottom line, she made clear, was that they had to get rid of the body. The way in which they did that was beside the point. The fact of the matter was: no body, no case.

"Leaving [the body] in the trunk and ditching the car," Jeff pointed out, "is not a good idea, Jess."

She thought about that.

"Near this time," Jeff explained later, they spent a considerable amount of time "fine-tuning" and "hacking out" a final plan to kill Alan.

"Alan shows up. . . . We get him in the house. Shoot him. Do whatever. Load the body up. Cart things off. And dispose of it wherever it is going to be disposed of."

"Torch the car," Jeff said to Jessica in response to that comment, reminding her how important it was to burn the evidence. "That's *got* to be part of it."

Jessica was not convinced burning the car was going to be necessary.

"I brought fire up, you know, as a viable option," Jeff said later. "I don't know if she finally decided if that was the best way to do it or not."

As for who would do the actual shooting, Jeff was under the impression all along that Jessica wanted him to be the triggerman. He was a cop. He had taken target practice. It seemed practical.

"I figured she would do . . . some of it, given that over time she'd fiddled around with some of my weapons."

They slept well that night. The next morning, as Jessica got ready to leave for the deposition, they picked up the conversation. Jessica came up with a new idea, Jeff said. She told him that he should probably ditch his SUV somewhere. "So when Alan shows up, he won't know you're here."

Made sense, Jeff surmised. Then he reminded Jessica that the space in the driveway would be helpful. "The way my driveway was set up," he said later, "if both vehicles are there, you don't have enough room to move another vehicle up close to the house to do whatever it is you're going to do with it."

After killing Alan, Jeff noted, they needed to get him out of the house as soon as possible. Pull his car up to the back porch so they could put him in the trunk.

"Yes," Jessica agreed.

With the commitment to get rid of Jeff's SUV out of the way, they focused on where to torch Alan's car with his body and the evidence.

"Mississippi?" Jeff suggested.

"No. Gulf Coast of Florida!"

What the heck, Jeff said he thought at that moment, *the woman likes the Gulf Coast.*

"I think Georgia was finally settled on," Jeff recalled,

"because that was the known direction [Alan] was supposed to have been traveling, which, our thinking at the time, would have played into whatever story could have or might have been concocted."

All of this—the car burned up and Alan shot—fit with what Jessica and Jeff believed authorities would think was a carjacking-gone-wrong scenario. That, or an old-fashioned robbery. Jeff was under the impression, given what Jessica had told him, that Alan had made some "other people" really mad and had been "screwing around," she said, "with other people's [wives]." So law enforcement might think one of those jealous husbands had capped Alan and torched his car.

What about an alibi? Jeff brought up next. What were they going to come up with to protect themselves when cops came knocking? The number one problem was time, Jeff explained.

"How do we account for our time, Jess?"

They put their heads together.

"The movies," she said excitedly.

"Yeah!"

"Southside." There was a movie theater there. They could go and sit in on a movie. Jessica had always wanted to go to a strip club and watch Jeff's reaction as he checked out the girls, she said. They could do that afterward.

"The PlayLate Club," Jessica said. It was on Second Avenue in downtown Birmingham. Not far from the movie house.

From there they could go somewhere romantic. Take a walk. Waste some time. Then head over to the Home Depot when it opened and pick up some supplies to clean up the mess, which would fall in line with the remodeling project they had going on in the house, anyway.

"That's it."

So, as Jessica left for the deposition, a murder plan was in play. When Alan showed up to pick up the kids, he would walk up to the front door and see a sign directing him to the back. If Terra was with him, they'd deal with it. Jessica would invite him into the house under a ruse. The kids were not going to be home. They'd be up the street at Jessica's mother's. Jessica said she had a good idea regarding how to convince Alan to walk into a house he had never been allowed in before then.

Once inside, Jeff would surprise him.

Jessica could sit and watch her problem disappear with a few bright flashes.

46

Terra had a major paper due on Friday, February 15, 2002. It was part of the master's program she had been working on at Goucher. So she got up early.

While Alan was getting ready, Terra faxed the paper over to Dr. Victoria Young's office.

"Terra had hope in her voice," Dr. Young said later. Young had spoken to Terra the previous afternoon about the paper. Terra mentioned the deposition. She said she was traveling to Alabama with Alan. She sounded upbeat. Positive. She felt good about how the case had progressed. It was, Young said, as if Alan and Terra had finally gotten the court to listen to them. The system was finally functioning the way it should have been from day one. Terra was comfortable with saying she felt the outcome would be in their favor.

Terra's father, Tom Klugh, left his house early in the morning to go out and get his seasonal potato and onion seedlings at the local feed store in Georgia, near his home. He wanted to set them in the ground that day. He planned on buying a cell phone later on that afternoon, his first. He even promised to call Terra after the purchase.

Alan and Terra's flight went as scheduled. They landed in Birmingham on time. Then they made it to the deposition downtown without a hitch. As Jessica had thought, they didn't arrive the night before.

It was going to take all day, Frank Head told Alan. Prepare for a full day's worth of, well, answering uncomfortable questions about the past seven years.

In Hoover, the mother of one of the girls' friends stopped by to pick up Sam and McKenna and cart them off to school. The girls were scheduled to go from school (late that afternoon) to Jessica's mother's house. Brian and Sara would head to day care until Jessica's mother got out of work and could pick them up. With the day (and night) off, Jeff was at home when the girls' ride to school showed up.

The plan Jessica and Jeff had finalized included Jessica and Jeff saying that Alan, "as usual," had not picked up the kids per a scheduled visitation pickup time at 6:00 P.M. So the children had to be dropped off at Jessica's mother's house. Jessica said she was even going to tell her mother that Alan didn't show up. Ask her to watch the kids that night so she and Jeff could celebrate a belated Valentine's Day. She would pick them up in the morning.

This would open up that window of opportunity to commit murder.

The plan appeared infallible.

David Dorn had advised Jessica to settle her case out of court if she could. He didn't like to see his clients go to trial. Trials never turned out the way either party wanted. It was always better to come to some sort of amicable agreement pretrial.

Jessica said no way. She wanted to see this to the end.

The depositions started at 9:42 A.M., according to the court reporter hired to record what was said.

Jessica went first. She sat. Frank Head asked questions. Standard divorce stuff that lawyers go through all the time.

There was a break late in the morning, somewhere near ten-thirty. Jessica called Jeff. There was a slight, little problem with their plan, she whispered into the phone.

"What's wrong?" Jeff asked.

"Just for your information," Jessica reported, "Terra's here."

Jeff went silent. Even though they had discussed what to do if Terra showed up with Alan, they thought for certain she was staying in Maryland.

"We'll just have to do them both," Jeff recalled Jessica telling him a few nights earlier as this contingency arose during a conversation.

"Okay," Jeff said over the phone that morning, "that's a complication."

They didn't discuss it on the telephone specifically, Jeff said later, but there was an agreement clearly implicit between the two of them: Terra Bates was not going to stand in the way of their plans.

"We're going to have to kill her, too," Jeff explained later, going back to that telephone conversation, describing what he was thinking after getting the news Terra was there, too. "I guess it was just assumed. It wasn't mentioned. I don't recall it being mentioned. . . . Basically, if you're going to do one, you've got to do the other one if they're there together."

Collateral damage.

Most interesting, there was never a moment after their murder strategy had been outlined where Jessica or Jeff backed down and considered abandoning the plan. It would have to be adjusted. Certainly. Any good plan would be. But they were going through with what was now double murder, come hell or high water, and no one was going to stand in their way.

For Jeff, the only deal breaker, he admitted later, was if Alan's parents showed up with him. Jeff said he would have never gone through with it if that had happened.

"I don't know what Jessica would have done."

During a lunch break, at 12:06 P.M., Frank Head and David Dorn took off together to eat and talk things through. They went right around the corner to a local place, Tony's Terrific Hot Dogs. It was a familiar hot spot that Alan and Terra had actually eaten at routinely when they worked at the nearby Alabama Theatre.

As the group began to separate for lunch, Alan told Head, "I'm going to get Terra"—she was in the office waiting room—"and go get some lunch."

"Be back by one," Head said.

Alan smiled.

Jessica ate alone upstairs in Dorn's office. There was a long conference table where the depositions were held. Jessica sat and began eating her lunch there.

Kelly McCloskey, the court reporter Dorn had hired to type the deposition, planned on using the lunch break to get a jump on proofing the record. "Can I work on these transcripts over lunch, Mr. Dorn?" McCloskey asked the attorney before he left.

"Sure."

As McCloskey went through her work, Jessica stepped out to go to the restroom. She looked calm. Confident. Like things were going her way.

When Jessica returned, McCloskey was on the phone with her firm, finding out what her next assignment was. There were some conflicts, McCloskey said later in court, and she was in contact with her office to try to work things out.

Jessica looked on, watching McCloskey talk on the

phone, waiting for the opportunity to say something. It was obvious Jessica wanted to talk. McCloskey had work to do, however. She didn't have time for idle conversation.

"My husband's a police officer in Pelham," Jessica said after McCloskey hung up with her boss.

"Really?"

"He's been a cop for some time. . . . We live in Hoover."

Jessica carried on. Did not stop talking. McCloskey was getting a bit impatient with her, when, McCloskey said later, "Jessica just blurted it out."

"It wouldn't take much for [my husband] to shoot somebody," Jessica explained to the court reporter.

How strange it was for Jessica to say such a thing. McCloskey was startled by this, adding later, "And I just automatically took it to be justifiable homicide that she was speaking of."

McCloskey didn't answer. She gave Jessica a quick roll-your-eyes stare, then continued with her work.

Jessica, though, did not stop. "I don't understand why Alan is fighting so hard for [Samantha, the oldest daughter]—she's not even his child. But, of course, he doesn't actually know that yet." There was a sarcastic tone to her voice. She was making fun of Alan, even though he wasn't around. To a stranger, no less.

Jessica then talked about how Alan used to hit her when they were married.

"She did mention an incident where he had her arrested, and said that he had—she had attempted to hit him or assault him in some way," but that it was actually Alan who had hit her.

McCloskey wanted off the subject of Jessica and Alan's life. She was a court reporter, not a therapist.

It was 1:00 P.M.

Finally lunch was over.

47

During his side of the deposition, Alan discussed a day when he believed Jessica was hiding the children at her sister's house in Florida. David Dorn was disturbed by this—that Alan could make such an allegation without any proof. There were other things said throughout the day, but the case would be in a judge's hands in a matter of weeks.

Alan felt confident as he and Terra got ready to leave Dorn's office. Things had gone well. When it came down to it, Jessica was not a good liar. It was so clear that she was making things up, it was almost embarrassing to have to sit and listen. But there it was: all out in the open now.

It was a little after 3:00 P.M. as everyone met in Dorn's office. Alan mentioned that since they had finished so early, would it be possible for him and Terra to pick up the girls sooner? It would be nice to get a jump on traffic and get out of Birmingham before five o'clock.

Jessica snapped: "No! Won't work. The girls have some things going on after school, extracurricular activities, and won't be home."

So it was back to the original agreement. Alan said he'd be at the Myrtlewood Drive house at 6:00 P.M. sharp. He wanted the kids ready to go.

Frank Head asked Alan if he was all set.

Alan said he was.

They agreed to talk the following week.

Jessica stayed with David Dorn as everyone left. Kelly McCloskey packed her things. She heard an exchange between Dorn and Jessica. Dorn was sitting down, going through some paperwork. Jessica had a "bragging" tone to her voice, as though she had gotten one over on Alan. "That time," Jessica told Dorn, "when Alan was looking for the girls at my sister's . . . [we] all knew where the kids were." She laughed. The reference was to a particular portion of the deposition that had visibly angered Alan. Alan was certain Jessica had been lying to him—and here was Jessica now laughing about it, saying he was right. "My sister had instructions from me," she continued, "to tell Alan the girls *weren't* there."

"What?" Dorn said. He stopped what he was doing. Stood. He was upset. "Perturbed" was how Kelley McCloskey later put it.

"I cannot believe my client would do something like that," Dorn reportedly said to Jessica. "You were in contempt of court. You should have *never* done that."

"Boastfully" was the word Dorn later used to describe Jessica's demeanor during this same scene. She was ecstatic over the fact that she had lied to Alan and had easily gotten away with it.

Jessica didn't react to Dorn's frustration. She just stood there.

"You mean you and your family," Dorn said, disgusted, "did not have the common decency to let this man see his children?"

* * *

Jessica walked in the door at 4:30 P.M.

Jeff was waiting.

They had ninety minutes to get things prepared for Alan and Terra, who were grabbing a quick bite to eat downtown.

The problem was getting Alan and Terra into the backyard so they would walk in the back door. That was key to the plan going off without a hitch.

"The den," Jeff explained, "here in the den."

It was the perfect murder room. There was a couch. Jessica could offer them a seat. Jeff could walk up and take several quick *pops*. It would be over.

The room was adjacent to the garage. "Back of the house," Jeff said later, explaining how he and Jessica went about preparing the house for the murders. "It's the standard entrance. Trees, shrubs, whatever—behind the house. No windows facing either of the neighbors or facing the street."

Jeff had written a note on a piece of cardboard earlier that day and had placed it on the front door: WE'RE HAVING SOME PROBLEMS . . . PLEASE COME AROUND TO THE BACK DOOR.

Jeff took out his weapon, a .44-caliber Beretta. He had purchased it from another officer while working for the Birmingham PD. As Jessica watched, he made sure it was "readily available and loaded." He planned to strip the weapon after the murders. He and Jessica could then spread those pieces out along the interstate.

Jeff's duty weapon as a cop was a standard-issue Glock. *This Beretta will throw a little confusion into the crime,* Jeff thought. *They'll know I carry the Glock. . . . It'll confuse them.*

It was decided Jessica was going to answer the door. She would make initial contact with Terra and Alan.

"I was," Jeff said later, "actually under the impression that she was scared of Alan. . . . My being there was meant as a surprise. I believed she was afraid that if Alan had the opportunity, he might do something to her."

Jessica made it clear to her better half: "You will be in the den when they come to the door."

Jeff nodded his head. He understood.

48

Right on time, 6:00 P.M., Alan and Terra pulled up in front of the McCord home. Alan drove a Grand Am he had picked up from the Avis terminal that morning. Jessica and Jeff were inside the house, upstairs, waiting, looking out the window. They had a new plan. It didn't involve the sign on the front door anymore.

Jessica spied Alan's car. Then she ran outside to greet them.

Alan wanted to park on the street. Not ever being allowed in the house before today, he looked quizzically at the house, until he saw Jessica in the driveway waving at him. She was motioning for Alan to pull into the driveway.

Park here.

Jeff sat on a stool in the den, eight feet away from the couch Terra and Alan were going to be told to sit on. He had his Beretta tucked inside his waistband. By now, Jeff and Jessica had come up with what they believed was a foolproof plan to get Terra and Alan to sit on the couch. It couldn't miss. There was no way Alan would refuse when Jessica told him what was going on. Jessica knew how to address Alan's sensibilities. Using

the kids as a ploy was the key. He'd fall for it without
a second thought.

Terra walked in first. She looked bright and chip-
per, maybe even a little curious. This hospitality was
so unlike Jessica. She had never wanted Alan inside
her home before. Why now? Why had she changed
her mind?

Alan walked toward the door while eyeing the dog.
"He barks. . . . He might bite," Jessica warned.

The dog went nuts. "Come on," Alan said. He was in
fear of the dog. *What is this? What's going on? Get that
damn dog to calm down.*

"Don't be afraid, Alan," Jessica said. "Come on in."
Jessica walked in last, behind Alan and Terra.

Entering the den, Jessica told Alan and Terra to
have a seat on the couch. Why? "The girls are upstairs.
They've been preparing a play for you." She smiled.
Alan seemed a bit confused until Jessica mentioned
the play. The girls were always putting on plays and
puppet shows and pretending. Alan was all about the
theater. "They want to show it to you quickly before
y'all leave, okay?" Jessica added.

Jessica walked up the stairs toward the bedrooms
to make it look good. The kids were supposedly waiting there.

"Okay," Alan said. He sat down. Terra sat on the
other side of the couch. "Fine, fine."

Not even two minutes later, Jessica returned. Alan
and Terra were sitting together, facing Jessica, who now
stood in front of them. There was an uncomfortable
moment of silence and staring.

"The girls have been sick," Jessica said.

"Really?" Alan responded.

"They don't need to be out in this weather."

"Well, we need to get going."

"What do you plan on doing this weekend?"

"Don't know."

"Sam's been having problems with math. Philip might be able to help him, being an engineer, you know."

"Yeah," Alan said.

This was strange: Alan and his ex-wife in her den talking about the kids like normal human beings.

Jeff finally spoke up. "Maybe it's something Sam can pursue, you know, mathematics. What, Alan, with your expertise in physics as far as weights and balances from your theater experience."

"Where are the girls?"

"Oh, they're still getting ready for the play," Jessica said. "They'll be down soon."

Jeff stood. He had been sitting on the hearth area of the brick fireplace inside the den. Terra was directly opposite from where Jeff now stood in front of her. Alan moved away from Terra for no apparent reason and sat at the other end of the couch.

Without a word Jeff reached around to the back of his waistband, pulled out his Beretta and shot Terra near her head.

"I can't remember if I double-tapped her," Jeff said later. Meaning, "You know, obviously, two rounds in the same mass."

Terra fell forward. Dropped to the floor.

Of course, startled and shocked by this, Alan went to stand.

Jeff pointed his weapon at Alan as he moved and fired at him twice.

Both shots hit Alan.

He tried to get up on his feet, according to Jeff, while saying, "You fuckhead."

So Jeff shot him again, a third time, saying, "You're the fuckhead!"

"I put a round in him and he stumbles to the floor," Jeff explained later.

After disabling Alan from doing anything, something Jeff said he had learned from being a police officer, he put two more rounds into Terra, to make sure she was dead.

Terra had not said a word. Or moved.

"The way you're taught, if you've got multiple targets you—you know—at least try to wound one, move to the other, ideally, you know, if you double-tap, fine. Put one down and then move to the other."

The words of a trained killer.

Jeff described killing two human beings as methodical and calculating. It was as if he was talking about someone else, or a movie he had seen. He made it sound so common, so unrealistic. However, what was also clear from his description of that day was that Jeff McCord knew exactly what he was doing. The only consolation one can speculate from all of this is knowing that Terra, at least, had presumably no idea what was happening. She didn't have to suffer the horror of thinking about dying.

"I don't think she had time to assess the threat," Jeff explained, "or recognize, *Oh, damn, something's about to happen.*"

Murder was now a *something*.

While Jeff killed Jessica's ex-husband and his wife, Jessica sat on the second step of the stairs in front of them, watching, looking on as if it was some sort of staged play. She was calm and collected. It was as if every wish Jessica had was coming true in front of her eyes.

She might have even enjoyed it.

"Go move the car," Jeff ordered.

Jessica snapped out of the moment and jumped up. Walked over to Alan's body and rummaged through his coat, looking for his car keys.

"Where are the keys?"

They needed to bring Alan's car up to the back door so they could load the bodies into the trunk as planned.

Jeff walked over. Checked to see if Alan and Terra were still alive. There was blood now soaking into the carpet, like spilled juice. There were tiny spots of blood on the coffee table. The couch, too.

"Visual assessment," Jeff said later, describing his next move as if he were an army medic out on the battlefield communicating via walkie-talkie. "No signs of breathing." The ability Jeff had to detach himself emotionally from the telling of this horrific event was truly frightening. Here was a guy describing how he had murdered two innocent people in cold blood, and he spoke of it as though he was being questioned as part of an exam. No compassion or remorse whatsoever was present in Jeff's demeanor.

Just facts, one after the next.

Jeff reached down and checked Terra's and Alan's carotid artery—neck—pulses, as he coldly put it later, to "make sure."

Confident they were both dead, Jeff went around the room, knelt down and picked up all the shell casings. In his head he kept repeating how many shots he had fired—*six rounds . . . six . . . six*—and he knew he needed to find that number of casings.

After pocketing the casing shells, Jeff broke the gun apart. Then he began to think about what else needed to be done.

Yet in all of it, Jeff was wrong. The coroner later reported finding eight wounds.

49

Late that same afternoon, Tom Klugh was in Georgia, getting ready to head out to the local mall and purchase his first cell phone. He finished placing the onions and potatoes into the ground. Showered. Then he headed out the door. Tom had fought the temptation to upgrade to the technical side of life long enough. Terra was gadget-savvy and connected electronically, like most everyone else Tom knew. So he figured the best way to communicate with his only daughter was to give in and buy a cell phone.

When Tom got home, one of his friends called the house. The guy wanted to go out and get something to eat and have a few beers. They'd meet up with additional friends at the bar.

"Why not?" Tom said.

He arrived back home, somewhere near 6:30 P.M., and started fussing with his new phone. Terra was going to be happy about the purchase, Tom knew. The first person he wanted to call on the new phone was the one person he had, essentially, bought it for.

Terra's number rang several times. Then her voice mail picked up.

By now, it was near seven o'clock. "Hey, sweetie," Tom said into Terra's voice mail, "just want to let you know I got a cell phone today with a plan that allows me to call you anytime I want to. I love you!"

Tom would often tell Terra, "You know, you're my favorite daughter."

She'd sass back: "But, Dad, I'm your *only* daughter."

They'd share the perfect laugh.

When Tom didn't hear from Terra that night, he went to bed believing that she and Alan had picked up the girls and driven to Marietta. They were probably dog tired. They could all connect the following morning. Maybe even get together.

50

The scramble was on in Hoover to clean up the Myrtlewood Drive crime scene. There wasn't a lot of time. Maybe six hours. Seven, tops. People were expecting Alan, Terra and the kids. Maybe Jessica and Jeff had the night and early morning. But by tomorrow afternoon law enforcement was going to no doubt be calling, asking questions. Trying to locate Mr. and Mrs. Alan Bates.

Alan's rental car was pulled up to the gate in back of the house. Jeff found two old blankets and a set of outdated drapes they were going to toss in the garage.

"Help me," he said.

Together they wrapped both bodies.

Terra was the lightest. They picked her up first. Jeff grabbed her shoulders, Jessica her feet, as if carrying a stretcher.

They did the same with Alan's body.

Jessica next went into the kitchen. She picked up the telephone. They had already heard Terra's phone ring as they were cleaning up, but, of course, they didn't answer it. That was Tom calling his daughter.

In the kitchen Jessica dialed Alan's cell phone

number. Voice mail picked up. "Hey," Jessica said, "where are you guys? We're waiting for you. The girls are here." It was a lie, obviously. "We're all waiting for you. Where are you?" Then, with a sarcastic, cynical tone, "It's real *nice* of you not to call."

Jessica and Jeff grabbed some glass cleaner from underneath the sink and a roll of paper towels. They needed to wipe down the rental car after ditching it and setting it on fire.

"Lighter fluid," one of them suggested.

Jeff went out to the garage. They didn't have any. He picked up a gas can.

"No," Jessica said.

Right. It'd be better to stop somewhere along the way and get a few gallons of gas. Buy a new can. Ditch it somewhere along the way.

There was a lot left to be done inside the house. They needed to get rid of the bodies first. Then they could head back to the house to begin the cleanup.

Jeff said he'd drive Alan's rental. He got behind the wheel. Jessica jumped inside the family van after locking the house.

They looked at each other.

Time to move.

Jessica had the Bateses' cell phones with her. She planned on making a few calls along the way to set up a ruse that Alan and Terra had been using their phones, communicating with each other.

The plan was to hit the road and drive "somewhere over the Georgia border." First, though, they'd have to drive into town and purchase those movie tickets.

Jessica suggested stopping at a local strip mall. She had a problem, according to what Jeff later said. She had been fidgeting with Terra's cell phone to see if she could get into the voice mail to hear that message someone had left. In doing that, Jessica thought she had somehow recorded "incriminating evidence" against them as she randomly pushed buttons. She had panicked. She wanted to stop at the Galleria, a local cell phone kiosk, she told Jeff, to ask for help.

"Okay."

Jessica asked the guy behind the counter, "How do I erase voice mail on this thing? Can you help me? How do I listen to it?"

The guy didn't know.

Jessica turned to Jeff, who was standing there with her, looking around. "Let's go," she said.

From there, still in Hoover, they drove to a pay phone in the CVS parking lot nearby. Jessica needed to call her mother and set that part of their alibi in motion.

"Do it," Jeff said.

Her stepfather answered. Jessica said, "Is it okay if the kids are left with you for the rest of the night?" She said something about Alan blowing them off and they wanted to make a night of it alone, without the kids.

The kids were already there. "Sure," Albert said.

It had not occurred to Jessica, however, that she had just called Alan's cell phone and left a message saying that the kids were with her.

After the call Jessica led the way. They hopped onto the I-459, heading up to the I-20 and into Georgia.

After about ninety minutes of driving, Jessica signaled Jeff to pull over.

They were heading into Anniston, Alabama, directly east of Hoover, approximately twenty-five miles from the Georgia border. "We made the stop in Anniston," Jeff explained later, "and got something to eat at the SUBWAY."

After a quick bite they cut up Alan and Terra's credit cards, along with "whatever else from . . . both their wallets or purses."

"Atlanta?" Jeff queried to his now-manic wife.

She shrugged yes. "I made some phone calls."

Jeff was confused.

Phone calls? What did she mean by "phone calls"?

"From their phones to make it appear as if they had car trouble."

Jeff tossed several pieces of the gun along the side of the road as they headed out of Anniston back onto the main road.

Outside Atlanta they stopped to purchase a gallon of gasoline and a new gas can. After passing through Atlanta, still heading east on I-20, Jessica pulled over at a rest stop.

"We need to wipe the car down."

"Right," Jeff said.

They went to work, Jeff explained. They both wiped the "interior of the car. . . . Wiped down the door handles, wiped down anything anybody might have touched." Before leaving, Jeff walked into the information center at the rest area and bought some lighter fluid and a cigarette lighter.

"[We] got back on the road and started driving," Jeff said later. "For whatever reason, she finds Rutledge, Georgia."

Jeff never mentioned why, if they had planned on torching the vehicle, they were so concerned about wiping it down.

By now, it was somewhere near 2:00 A.M. The road Jessica had turned onto in Rutledge was secluded. Dark as motor oil.

Perfect.

Jeff didn't like it so much. He took the lead, drove around and in front of Jessica. He wanted to find a place farther into the forest, away from people and homes. "I went down a couple of side roads," he recalled. "Somehow we turned onto . . . where the car was left."

Hawkins Academy Road.

"Initially we tried to leave it, or thought about leaving it, across the road from where it was finally left . . . but it would have been very noticeable. . . ."

They got out of their vehicles. Stood together. Looked around.

Jeff "doused" the car with gasoline. Then he opened the trunk and poured some of the gas over the two people he had murdered.

After that, he flicked the lighter, took several steps back.

As he described what happened next, Jeff used the word "kerflooey."

Nothing happened.

Inside the McCord family van, Jessica had several paper towels she had used to wipe the rental vehicle down. She grabbed a few sheets. Ran over to the car. Lit one of the paper towels and gave it to Jeff.

He tossed it inside an open window.

Kerflooey!

Still, nothing happened. It wasn't like a Hollywood movie. No big mushroom cloud of smoke below an atomic flame. None. Jeff actually "singed his fingertips a couple of times" while trying to get the car to ignite.

Laughing while later describing this part of the night (yes, laughing . . .), Jeff McCord said he had trouble "trying to get everything lit."

Jessica became frustrated. She stomped about. "Come on . . . come on, Kelley!"

Jeff threw up his hands. "You do it, then."

Jessica grabbed the paper towel.

She must have tossed it in the right place, because as soon as Jessica flipped the lit paper towel into the car—*poof*—a loud suction sound preceded what was that immense fireball explosion they had been expecting all along.

"'Course that could have had something to do with the air and the fumes by that time," Jeff surmised later.

The car was now ablaze. Engulfed in bright flames. The heat was incredible. It pushed Jeff and his wife backward.

They ran for the van. Jessica got behind the wheel and took off out of there as fast as she could.

"It's done," she said happily, driving away. "You've done something great for the girls, you know that, Kelley."

Jeff felt proud, he later said.

Yes, proud.

Jessica had managed to make the guy feel good about murder.

"You've done something great for me, too," she added.

"At that time," Jeff recalled later, "I was taking song and verse, her version on how badly Alan had treated her and how bad he was to the kids. And had actually seen . . . some of that verified by them. 'Them' meaning the girls. . . ."

Jeff never explained what, exactly, he was referring to here.

As they drove away, flames to their backs, black smoke, melting plastic, burning flesh—and child custody matters—were all behind them. As they sped away from the scene like two Hollywood killers, Jeff said he had one last thought.

What is done is done. . . . Nothing I can do to reverse it now.

51

By 3:00 A.M., February 16, 2002, according to Jeff McCord's version of the murders, he and his wife were on their way back to Hoover, desperate to begin cleaning up what was the initial crime scene back at home.

On their way through Atlanta, Jeff and Jessica stopped at a convenience store. Jeff got out of the car and put the gas can on the sidewalk.

Jessica walked over and wiped it down.

Then Jeff tossed the lighters out the window. They landed in a ravine on the opposite side of the sidewalk.

The first place Jeff and Jessica drove to when they got back in town was Home Depot. They were first in line, standing by the entrance before the place was open.

Ten minutes after they were allowed in, all they bought was a razor blade of some sort—"that looked a lot like a pizza cutter," Jeff explained—to cut carpeting and some heavy black plastic.

Entering their Myrtlewood Drive house, Jessica took a look around. Things appeared different now that they weren't scrambling to get two bodies out of the house. She looked at the sofa: bullet holes through the backrest; blood was on the leather. The carpet was also saturated with blood. The place was a mess. It would take forever to get rid of all the evidence, put in new carpeting, patch holes in the walls, toss the couch.

What were they going to do?

Jessica walked around. Jeff knew that look. He was familiar with it. Her wheels were spinning.

"Let's just burn everything," Jessica blurted out.

Another fire?

They could, Jessica suggested, light the side of the house on fire where the murders had been committed. Burn that evidence up, too. It had worked back in Georgia; at least she believed it did.

"No way," Jeff said. Not a good idea. "Let's just see if we can think of a different way to do this."

52

Early Saturday morning, Naomi, her husband and the kids got up and decided to take off. A trip out of town. Spend the day together. They didn't get many chances to have family time, but when they did, Naomi and her husband made the best of it.

Getting home later that evening, somewhere near six o'clock, Naomi plopped down on the couch. She was exhausted. As the kids got settled, Naomi surfed through the vast variety of cable channels on television, not paying too much attention.

When she hit the local news, she left it on.

"Two bodies found inside the trunk of a burned-up car in Georgia. . . ."

Naomi didn't think anything of the report and went to bed.

The next day Naomi turned on the news again. There was that same story. This time, though, the newscaster announced the names of the victims.

"Alan and Terra Bates."

"She did it!" Naomi screamed.

"What are you talking about?" her husband asked, walking into the room.

Naomi pointed to the television.

Her husband realized what was going on. He knew she was talking about Jessica.

"Jessica killed them," Naomi verified as her husband stood there, astonished by this news.

Naomi went into the kitchen and called the Hoover PD.

"Sorry, ma'am, all of our officers are out"—they were at the McCord home, in fact, serving that first search warrant—"at this time. You'll have to call back tomorrow morning."

Naomi spent an hour calling around, trying to get ahold of Alan's parents. She had no idea where they lived. Finally she called Cecil Whitmire, Alan's old boss from the Alabama Theatre.

"They live in Atlanta," Whitmire said.

"Thanks."

Naomi talked it over with her husband the next morning and decided she needed to call the police and explain everything she knew. The time for loyalty was gone. In Naomi's mind Jessica was a double murderer.

Detective Laura Brignac called Naomi later that morning. "Look, we're in the middle of an investigation," the detective said, "I cannot really talk to you right now about this."

Naomi said she had information to share. "I want to meet with you."

"I cannot meet with you right now, sorry," Brignac said.

"Okay . . . but can I at least tell you why I have called you?"

Brignac thought about it. "Sure."

Naomi went through as much as she could as quickly as she could get it out.

Silence.

Then, "I'll be at your house in an hour," Brignac said.

PART V

THE BRINK OF ETERNITY

53

Jessica and Jeff McCord were tight-lipped and unified after capital charges for felony murder were filed on February 22, 2002. Neither was ready to throw the other under a bus, just yet. Jessica wouldn't talk at all. Jeff babbled in circles. Now it was up to prosecutor Roger Brown to make sure all the evidence the Hoover PD had collected, while working in tandem with the Bureau, would serve to convince a jury that the McCords were guilty as charged.

The Edgewood Presbyterian Church in Birmingham was buzzing with talk after Jessica's arrest. Many relatives from her mother's side were members of the church. The pastor, Sid Burgess, focused much of his Sunday, February 24, sermon on "fellow parish member" Jessica Inez Callis Bates McCord.

The title of the sermon spoke to the church's reaction to the charges against its member: "Still 'Open-Hearted,' Still 'Open-Minded.'"

There was going to be no judging going on inside the walls of Edgewood. Jessica was going to be given the benefit of the doubt.

"Right here, right now," Burgess preached from

the pulpit that morning, "this congregation has been rocked on its very foundation. . . ."

Burgess then explained how murder charges had been brought "against one of our own." He called Jessica a "third-generation member." He spoke of the "headlines" in the newspapers and the "highlights" on television. He mentioned how Jessica's family had been pillars inside the Edgewood church community for "almost sixty years." He asked parishioners, after listing all the health problems Jessica's family had endured throughout the years, to be there, as the church itself would be, for Jessica, Dian and Inez, Jessica's grandmother. The "embarrassment, the pain and agony, now the anguish of a daughter and granddaughter charged with a capital offense, we, their brothers and sisters," he shouted, pumping his fist, "must also share."

The pastor next poeticized how Jesus had taken up His cross. Then asked those who believed in Him to stand by His side, follow and do the same for Inez, Dian and Jessica.

Unity.

Jessica's church family was a devoted group of Christians—no doubt about it. Pastor Burgess spoke of how, during the week leading up to that Sunday's service, he thought perhaps he could "duck" out of talking about the case "up here in the pulpit." But after seeing the effect the news had on church members during the week, crying for Jessica's "innocent children," coming together and "openly weeping" for Dian, Inez and Jessica, there was no way he could deny his flock his shoulder. So he decided to take the difficult path and confront the issue head-on.

"How can a pastor not at least try to address such heartfelt pain?"

"Open-Minded, Open-Hearted" was this church's slogan. Local television cameras showed file shots of the building during the nightly news—and there was that recognizable bumper sticker from the church with that so-familiar slogan plastered on the back of Jessica's vehicle as it was towed away by the police.

By the end of his impassioned and compassionate sermon, Burgess said that while the "larger community" was prepared to "give up on Jessica McCord," God was not. Even if she was to be ultimately found guilty, he explained, "we know God has a history of redeeming murderers."

Ending the sermon, he compared Jessica to Saul on the road to Damascus, and recalled how Jesus was able to convince this onetime Christian basher and nonbeliever to drop everything and follow Him.

54

The first the public heard regarding details of the crimes came during a probable cause hearing, on Thursday, April 4, 2002. There was one witness on hand to lay out the state's case against Jeff and Jessica McCord—Detective Sergeant Tom McDanal.

During the hearing McDanal called Albert Bailey a "suspect" who had not been charged yet. The theory was that Albert had helped Jessica and Jeff cover up their crimes by willfully and willingly dumping evidence.

The murders were a family affair, apparently.

Jessica's court-appointed attorneys argued vehemently against the treatment their client had received since charges were filed. They even hinted at the notion that one possible defense might be police misconduct, citing the notion that the Hoover PD did not have probable cause to search the McCord home. They also suggested that "Jeff McCord's position as a police officer influenced Hoover investigators."

"Someone made the McCords a suspect even before there was a body found," one of Jessica's defense attorneys said. Then, at one point, Tom McDanal was asked, "Was there acrimony between your department and his department? Did the Hoover Police Department have any problems with a police officer from another department living in your jurisdiction?"

"No," McDanal said in his terse, matter-of-fact demeanor. It was preposterous to think that police officers would go after another cop like that, especially with two people dead and an investigatory clock ticking. Moreover, the bodies of Terra and Alan Bates had been recovered almost first thing that morning.

The attorney asked about other suspects—why, for example, had the Hoover PD failed to explore other leads?

"It was pretty obvious we were on the right track," McDanal said.

Judge R. O. Hughes ultimately agreed with the prosecution; there was sufficient evidence to send the case to a grand jury.

After that, the notion of Jessica's health came up. After all, she was pregnant again. She had not been lying about that little detail. By now, she was starting to show. Neither she nor Jeff had a history of violent crime convictions (save for that little attack on Alan that had caused him a broken arm). Her attorneys wanted to see them both out on bond. It was only fair.

"She is at a great risk of losing the baby," her lawyer explained.

Roger Brown argued against this, making his point quite clearly, if not candidly. "This is a potential death penalty case. [These were] vicious, brutal killings. These are dangerous people and they need to stay in jail."

The judge considered both arguments.

"Bond denied."

55

It did not take long for Jessica to cause problems from behind bars. In an almost relentless manner, she sent Judge R. O. Hughes letters. Long, tedious, accusatory and—well, in the end—pathetic diatribes describing the conditions of her imprisonment and the fact that her court-appointed attorneys were acting *extremely unethical,* she wrote. Jessica demanded that her legal team be replaced: *I cannot work with them.* She accused them of asking her to *commit perjury [and] injure another client of theirs.*

As they headed toward the end of 2002, it appeared that Jessica and Jeff were going to be tried together the following year, 2003. The Hoover PD was still working on Jeff. Roger Brown's crack investigative team was trying to break the fallen cop, hoping he might cut a deal. Then the focus could be put exclusively on Jessica.

Jessica was not going to back down. She was in this for the long haul. She told anyone who would listen that she was innocent. She was going to prove it when she had her day in court.

Pregnant, Jessica was scheduled to give birth in the neighborhood of mid-to-late September. She and Jeff's case was transferred to Judge Virginia Vinson's Tenth Judicial Circuit Court in downtown Birmingham. Vinson, a stunning middle-aged woman with short brown hair and a charming smile, was fairly new to the chamber. She had been a Criminal Division judge since January 2001. A graduate from Samford University and the Birmingham School of Law, Vinson had nineteen years in private practice behind her as half of Wilkinson & Vinson before taking on the thankless job of criminal court judge. If there was one thing about Judge Vinson everyone could agree on, it was her tenacity to run a tight ship, and not to allow cases to fall on the conveyor belt of postponement. She kept her attorneys on schedule and focused on moving their cases forward. In learning that Jessica was in the final trimester of her fifth pregnancy, Vinson issued an order to keep the double-murder suspect's court appearances to a minimum until after she had the baby. There was no need to put any additional stress—other than what she was going through already—on the accused murderer and mother-to-be.

After getting word of the judge's decision from family members, Jessica became irate. She was appalled that her case was being held up. The idea that she could not argue for bond in Vinson's courtroom before having the baby brought tears to her eyes, she said in letters. It wasn't fair. She needed to be home with her husband, preparing for the birth. The prosecution had not proven a thing! What about being considered innocent before being proven guilty?

On the night of September 25, 2002, five days past her due date, Jessica wrote the judge a long letter, describing her feelings. It turned into what was a ten-page, single-spaced missive, replete with accusations and speculations, random thoughts and a complete firsthand account of Jessica's opinion of prison life.

Jessica wrote that she'd had her hopes set high that she was going to make bond, now that a criminal judge was behind the gavel. Maybe a criminal judge, if no one else, would see how she and Jeff needed to be together, not only to give birth to the child, but to begin to build a credible defense. *Obviously,* Jessica wrote, *waiting means that my husband and I will be separated for the birth.* . . . She said she wouldn't have any support if that were the case. It appeared that Detective Laura Brignac's wish—that Jessica would give birth alone, and the child would be quickly taken from her arms—was about to come true. And it was clear that Jessica was scared to death of that happening. She wrote how she was *terrified to give birth alone.*

After she had the child, Jessica wrote to Judge Vinson, within forty-eight hours, *I will be forced to leave my newborn.* There would be no bonding or breast-feeding. She talked about how she'd had a history of postpartum problems and medical difficulties: *I have nearly bled to death.* . . . She begged for bond, *Please give it to us now.*

As the letter continued, Jessica spoke of how the last seven months had been hell on her and Jeff *because of the accusation.* She wrote she *deserved a chance.* But she realized that in the real world you were guilty before you were able to prove innocence. She called herself a *decent human being.* Then she promised she would, when given the opportunity in a court of law, prove her innocence as well as her husband's. Still, with all that said, if the court took away the moment of birth between a husband and his wife, such a special time, it was something—a memory—she and Jeff could never recover.

Lost forever.

For another half a page, Jessica ranted about how the system was designed in favor of the prosecution. As much as she understood the reasons behind it, she was

only asking for a chance to spend that mother-child
connection time before trial with her newborn. She
had been on bed rest, in isolation, in the medical block
of the jail since August 18. She wrote she had been *as-
saulted, threatened, harassed*. None of the deputies inside
the jail, she wrote, would help her. Instead of making
out a complaint, she wrote, they laughed in her face,
saying, *"Get over it."*

There was never any evidence presented to support
these accusations. On top of that, this would become a
common battle cry of Jessica's: that the prison system,
correctional officers and anybody else working for the
legal system were out to get her; that conditions inside
the prison were unbearable; and that the prison monitored everything Jessica did, said and wrote.

Indeed, prison life was no vacation from life.

On another page Jessica gave an evaluation of the
psych ward she had been once placed in. It was full
of—you guessed it—mental patients. She wrote how
many of them *urinate and defecate everywhere except in the
toilet*. When the women menstruate, she added, *blood
is everywhere*. They brought one woman into the ward
who had complained of having ants and maggots in
her cell bed. She was placed next to Jessica: *She was
bitten by the ants, yet nobody did anything. . . .*

Hell on earth.

Nobody had explained to Jessica, obviously, that less
was more—because for the next five pages of the
letter, all she did was accuse doctors and guards, inmates and the justice system as a whole, of being out
to punish her. She made claims of doctors watching
her bleed and not helping, of cellmates preventing her
from buzzing the nurse, of guards not allowing her to
take showers or to use the bathroom. She had no TV,
no radio, no contact with the outside world. The
emotional stress was crippling. Yet, there was one

thing that hurt more than anything else, she revealed:
Albert Bailey, her stepfather, had died back on June
25 (Jessica's thirty-first birthday) from a reported
heart attack, and *I was denied a family grieving visit . . .
my grandfather passed away [last] April and I couldn't go to
his funeral.* She hadn't seen her kids in months. She
wasn't being allowed to write to Jeff. She was fed
poorly. Many of the food servers in the jail were *HIV
positive and have hepatitis,* she lamented. Inmates were
required to wash their undergarments in the sinks and
toilets inside their cells if they wanted them cleaned.
She quoted an article from *American Baby* magazine
describing how breast-fed babies were more unlikely
to get ear infections. Then she broke off into a rant
about the scores of diseases she and her newborn
could get inside the prison. She promised the judge
she'd meet any conditions asked of her by the court
if the judge let her out on bond. Psych exams, she
wrote, *to demonstrate my mental state and lack of hostility.*
She said she'd check in daily with the powers that be.
She wasn't running. She just wanted to be with her
newborn, husband and children.

I am a good person. . . . I am innocent, she wrote, but
not before begging one last time for *a chance.*

The judge took everything Jessica said seriously.
Thought about it. Then she kept the court's order and
denied Jessica McCord bond.

Jessica had her baby. Not long after the delivery, the
infant was taken from her and placed with family members. Jessica was now the jailed mother of five. Christmas, 2002, came, and New Year's Eve chimed in with a
bang as word came down that Jeff McCord was getting
a separate trial. Inside Jeff's camp the discussion centered
on the possibility of him taking a deal to avoid any

chance of facing a jury that held his life in its hands.
Jeff's trial was scheduled for April, but Jessica would
face a judge and jury first.

As Jeff contemplated his future, Jessica got busy
doing the only thing she really knew how to do at this
point: scribing more missives to Judge Vinson. This,
mind you, as it was announced that Jessica's trial was
set to begin as early as February 12, 2003—almost a
year to the day that she had allegedly masterminded
and, with Jeff, carried out a plot to murder Alan and
Terra.

This recent letter was shorter than those preceding
it. Once again Jessica wanted Judge Vinson to know
that she was not happy with her counsel. She demanded that the court appoint her new attorneys. She
said her lawyers were not devoting enough time to
preparing her case.

I find this to be intolerable, she wrote. She wanted an
immediate hearing to rectify the problem. She said she had
written every week since she was indicted late the previous year, and she was certain that the jail personnel
was tampering with her mail.

The same old story. A broken freakin' record.

By the end of the one-page letter, however, Jessica
made a grave mistake—that is, if she was ever hoping
to reach the judge on a personal level.

She blamed her legal woes on Judge Vinson. Jessica
claimed that by the judge's denial of her bond, Vinson
had forced her to compromise her defense. Jessica
wrote that the *prosecution [was taking any] action [neces-
sary], legal or illegal, to manipulate [her] conviction.* A fair
trial, in Jessica's humble opinion, was now going to be
impossible.

The court sent Jessica a form to fill out requesting
new counsel. It was An Explanation of Your Complaint. It made the inmate state his or her case in writing,

certifying that the words on the page were correct—
and that he or she would be willing to sign a statement
under oath. Jessica had her formal complaint nota-
rized on January 8, 2003. Attached to it was a five-page
explanation by Jessica of all the problems she'd allegedly had while incarcerated. It was a toned-down
version of her previous diatribes to the judge.

A day later, Jessica sent a second letter "to whom it
may concern," this time trying to verify receipt of the
complaint. Again she talked about her mail being tam-
pered with and—in not so many words—how the entire
prison system was out to get her. She also mentioned
the idea that she wanted to file multiple complaints.

The loss of control Jessica had in her life—being confined to jail and unable to find out what was going on
or to call people and tell them off and to manipulate
those in her life—was eating her up inside. You can
sense it in the pages of her letters. The desperation.
The lack of ability to let go. The impossibility to manage
her own impulse to reach out and attack people. Jessica
McCord could not shut up, do her time and wait for
her chance to speak in court. She had to get her hands
wet. As she had done with Alan all those years, she believed she could influence the court system enough to
play by her rules. She obviously thought that by writing the letters, filing complaints, making erroneous
accusations against anyone not on her side, she would
one day see freedom—that someone would listen and
understand and fight for her cause. She wrote letters to
a judge of the court, asking question after question, expecting, somehow, that in the simple act of asking, the
allegations alone would free her. There was never one
bit of remorse, accountability or sorrow for the deaths
of Alan and Terra, regardless if she was responsible
or not. She never once mentioned the fact that her
children were now without a father. The letters focused

entirely on her own needs. Symptoms of narcissistic personality disorder bled from every stroke of her pen. Jessica failed to recognize or understand—or maybe thought she was beyond reproach to face double-murder charges—that two people had been viciously mowed down with a hail of bullets, and the evidence—all of it—pointed to her and her husband.

56

By the end of January, Jessica got her sister involved in a new letter-writing campaign. This time the missives were sent to John Wiley, her attorney. The main thrust of the content focused on Wiley not doing exactly what Jessica McCord wanted. His integrity and honor were attacked. His concern for all his clients put under scrutiny. His ability to do his job severely strangled by the accusations and wild speculations of an alleged murderer. The guy had not said a word in open court and he was already being branded some sort of failure who clocked in and out of his professional life as though the freedom of his clients didn't matter.

By February 9, 2003, Jessica had apparently settled her differences with John Wiley. On that Sunday, Wiley released a statement to the Associated Press citing his uncertainty as to whether Jessica was going to take the stand in her own defense. With Jessica's trial days away, Wiley got busy getting ready. Jessica would have to put her dream of freedom on the back burner for now. No matter what she said, whom she wrote or complained to, Jessica McCord was scheduled to face a jury of her peers on matters that could put her on death row.

Roger Brown would not comment on his case.

Both sides agreed, however, that Jeff McCord was not expected to testify against his wife. His trial was still on the docket for an April gavel slap.

According to an Associated Press article, John Wiley released a statement saying prosecutors *lack[ed] conclusive evidence tying the couple to the murders,* adding, *We're very hopeful we can show the jury how the state is unable to prove her guilty without a reasonable doubt.* Wiley claimed to be confident of his client's innocence.

If nothing else, Jessica had an advocate in John Wiley—someone willing to fight for her alleged virtue, even if she had previously attacked the man's credibility.

57

Jessica's trial began at 8:53 A.M., Tuesday, February 11, 2003. It was a partly cloudy day. The temperature was forty-one degrees. The wind, barely noticeable, blew gingerly south-to-southwest at 3.5 miles per hour. Room 375 of the Mel Bailey Criminal Justice Center in downtown Birmingham, on Richard Arrington, Jr. Boulevard North, buzzed with talk of this high-profile double-murder case. Three men and eleven women were chosen to sit and hear Jessica's case. Jefferson County chief district attorney Roger Brown, who had been as quiet as a CIA agent, had given the press no indication where he was headed with his case, other than calling the murders of Alan and Terra "vicious and brutal."

Brown had his boxing gloves on. He was ready for the opening bell. His witnesses lined up behind him.

The veteran prosecutor had a deep, serious vocal tone, but it simultaneously came across as clear, sincere and unlabored. In the courtroom was where Brown felt most comfortable. Early on, Brown had decided to try the case himself and not hand it off to one of his attorneys. He was there to represent Alan, Terra

and their families. He was there to see that justice
would be served. And he was also there to extend a
hand of virtue and morality to the jury in the hopes
that they understood the severity of these inhuman,
savage murders. Lest no one forget, if you believe
Brown's version of his case, these murders were calcu-
lated, premeditated and carried out with an evil re-
course that was rarely seen.

Brown first gave a narrative of what he called "that
weekend." Of course, he was referring to the evening
when Alan and Terra were murdered. How much Alan
had looked forward to giving his deposition and ending
a battle with Jessica to see his kids. Brown built up the
suspense of Alan and Terra walking into Jessica's
lawyer's office and then leaving with smiles on their
faces. He said Alan was confident the depositions had
gone well—maybe even his way. Then Brown told the
jury how Alan and Terra had stopped and ate at a
nearby hot dog shop. How they drove to Hoover, probably discussing how great it was going to be to see the
kids again, then slowly, as if they knew something was
wrong, approached the McCord house in the rental car.

"So, Alan and Terra, who had never been allowed in
this house before," Brown said in a thunderous roar,
"turned back down . . . the driveway, probably hand in
hand, toward the fence that led to the back . . . completely unaware that, step-by-step, they walked closer
to the brink of eternity in those last few minutes of
their very too-short lives."

The prosecutor waited a beat. Allowed the gravity of
those words to sink in.

"How did we come to this?" Brown asked before em-
barking on what was a long, violent and emotionally
tormented history between Alan and Jessica. All the
fighting on Jessica's part. All the visitations Alan never
had with his kids. All the chaos "that woman over

there"—pointing, raising his voice—had caused Alan
Bates to endure throughout his adult life.

Something the media hadn't discovered, a suggestion by Brown that was never made public, came out
of the experienced prosecutor's mouth as he approached the motive portion of his opening. He was
talking about that particular lightbulb moment for
Jessica.

"And while she was in jail [during that Christmas
contempt charge in 2001] . . . she read the book *The
Murderers*. Told her inmate friends there [in jail] she
would do anything, *anything*, to keep her kids."

The Murderers, by W.E.B. Griffin, is a fictional explo-
ration of corruption inside law enforcement. The plot
involves the wife of a Philadelphia cop, who leaves her
husband for another cop, after reporting his "dirty"
tactics. The book is a Lifetime Television version of a
team of murderers you'd least likely expect: cops.
Roger Brown's aim was to point out the fact that Jessica McCord was talking about how much better her
life would be if Alan was gone, and also reading books
for ideas on how to get away with murder.

"So she began to hatch this plot while in the Shelby
County Jail," Brown said, "because she not only was
going to make his life miserable, she was going to end
it! 'Things would be a lot better if he was just dead,'
she said [to an inmate]."

Kaboom . . . there it was: the meat and potatoes of
Brown's case.

From that point on, Brown went through the murder,
step-by-step. Then the cleanup. The coverup. The lies
Jessica and Jeff told and the missteps they took as they
tried explaining their way out of what the evidence had
actually pointed to.

Brown's opening was short, only about fifteen minutes. Brown was all about getting to the heart of the

matter—and here, in this case, Brown was certain that the evidence and his list of witnesses would speak to that. He didn't need to add anything to the truth. From Brown's point of view, the more sugarcoating you frosted on the facts, the less impact they would ultimately have.

John Wiley was a bit more reserved. He kept his opening even shorter, simply standing and explaining to the jury that his client would be freed by that evidence Brown had so haphazardly tossed around.

"Now, look here," Wiley said, standing. "This is the time of the trial when the lawyers stand up and say what they expect the evidence to be. What lawyers say in a trial is *not* evidence, and Judge Vinson will tell you that later on."

Wiley said that there would be a "great *lack* of evidence of Ms. McCord's guilt in this case." He went through what he thought was Brown's weakest points: no murder weapon, no true motive, no smoking gun pointing to his client.

Many squinted their eyes at some of what the lawyer said: *No motive?* Was he talking about the same case?

"Under the law, Ms. McCord is presumed to be not guilty, and that is evidence in this case and must be considered by you along with all of the other evidence in this case."

That all sounded good. But Roger Brown and his investigators, the cops who had shown up in solidarity with the Bates and Klugh families, knew that what Wiley was suggesting was absolutely absurd. The accused were judged on the way they acted in court. The things they said. Their facial expressions. Whether they testified, or chose not to testify. Their lack of remorse. The way they whispered to their attorneys.

Smiled with family and friends. And, perhaps most important of all, hearsay and the media. It didn't matter what a lawyer stood and said, Wiley was right about that. What mattered more than anything—when push came to shove—was how a juror felt about a witness, a piece of evidence, a suggestion by an attorney. As unbalanced and unfair as this might sound, a defendant *was* judged the moment she sat down—maybe even before—whether she committed the crime or not.

Prisons, after all, are not only full of guilty people.

Wiley used the word "doubt" in his final few sentences three times, throwing it out there, hoping the jury would grab hold of any part of it.

"The evidence and the lack of evidence," Wiley closed, "goes in concert with the presumption of innocence."

Brown called Philip Bates. Alan's father talked about raising his children, moving the family, and that night he and Joan went through hell realizing that Alan and Terra, never late or no-shows, had disappeared. He told the jury how he called rental car agencies and that Avis told him to phone the GBI.

And that was when his heart sank. "I knew."

Wiley kept Philip focused on the time frame of that night, which would come up again and again during this trial. Philip was clear—Alan and Terra were supposed to pick the kids up at 6:00 P.M. and start heading to Georgia immediately.

Next witness.

Tom Klugh gave the jury memories of his daughter, accentuating the high note of how much she and Alan had loved each other. Then he talked about buying

that new cell phone, calling his daughter and leaving
Terra a voice mail she never heard.

"Thank you, Tom," Brown said. "I believe that's all
I have."

John Wiley did not stand. "No questions, Your
Honor."

Tom Klugh walked out of the courtroom, head
bowed, shoulders slumped.

Brown had a representative from Avis prove to the
jury that Alan had indeed rented the car his body was
found in.

As Brown rolled his eyes, Wiley asked the Avis rep
questions that seemed to be ridiculously unimportant.
That witness was off the stand within fifteen minutes.

After a lunch break Alan's longtime attorney, Frank
Head, sat. At first, Head went through the extended
explanation of the child custody matter at the center
of the feud Jessica seemed to have with Alan. Head was
clear and concise with his answers. There was no one
in the room who knew the story of Jessica versus Alan
better than Frank Head. He was obviously broken up
by the deaths of Alan and Terra, unable to understand
that a woman who did not want her ex-husband to see
his children would go to such deadly lengths.

Written on Head's face, and on the face of just about
every witness Brown presented during this opening
day, was the same, unanswerable question: *why?*

These murders—perhaps more than others—seemed
too darn senseless.

As Head talked his way through the afternoon under
Brown's direct examination, one theme became clear:
Jessica McCord had done everything in her power to

keep the children away from Alan Bates. But the true
denouement to that story was that she had done it all
for no apparent reason. Even when the court demanded she allow the children to see their father, Jessica disappeared, wouldn't allow it. Took down her
mailbox. Didn't answer her phone. Asked friends and
family to lie for her. Hid at the homes of those same
people. She took the kids out of school. Became violent
and threatened Alan repeatedly. The truth was there—
the evidence—in the letters Head had written to Jessica
and her attorneys. In the testimonials Alan had given.
In the transcripts of the days in court Jessica refused
to show up for. It was all *there*. In. Fact. Perfectly laid out
for anyone to sit down and see. The truth—Frank Head
made clear to Jessica's jury—was undeniable.

Jessica sat with a stoic bearing about her, her demeanor mostly unchanged, as each witness came in
and put another nail in the door to her freedom. She
could do nothing about any of it. She wore glasses and
appeared skinnier than normal. The obvious wear and
tear of life in prison, not seeing her newborn, and
preparing for trial, had worn her down.

What became a hot-button issue as Frank Head answered
questions—both on direct and cross-examination—
was that Head had brought out the fact that Jessica
McCord had lied so much to so many different people,
it was impossible to trust *anything* she said. The woman
had even lied about things she didn't need to, like the
duration of a supposed separation she and Jeff had endured during the fall of 2001.

There just seemed to be no end to the lies she told.

As testimony wrapped up on the first day with
Pamela Merkel Sayle, the girls' dance instructor, the
jury heard again—this time from a neutral witness

who really had no stake in the outcome of the trial—
that Jessica had a terrible grievance against Alan. She
was consistently angry with him. And this attitude of
Jessica's, so hostile and nasty, only increased after Alan
met Terra, Sayle suggested with her testimony.

"She made comments . . . that if he ever tried to get
the girls, he would regret it," Sayle told the jurors.

58

Day two picked up where the previous day had left off. Roger Brown built his case, brick by brick, each witness adding his or her blow to Jessica's constant plea of innocence. Critics of Brown, however, might be quick to point out that if hatred toward an ex-spouse was motive for murder, coupled with things we said in the heat of anger and under our breath, we would not be able to build enough courthouses to prosecute the accused.

As Brown moved his case forward, he made that hatred Jessica had for Alan, which Brown believed had turned into a thirst for revenge and murder, the center point around which every witness pivoted. By the end of the day, Brown would send nineteen witnesses to the stand. Among them, few could describe that hatred in more depth and detail than Naomi Patterson, Jessica's longtime friend.

Naomi was nervous, of course. But she was also there to tell the truth, as far as she knew it. She wasn't looking for vengeance, as Jessica had implied by the look on her face when Naomi raised her right hand and sat down.

Naomi had been there since the beginning; she could offer the jury a complete portrait of Jessica and Alan's married life before all the trouble started. She could show jurors how much Alan loved his pregnant young girlfriend and wanted to do the right thing by marrying her. And again, how Jessica, after she and Alan divorced, routinely abandoned her kids.

"Y'all were pretty close?" Brown asked.

"Yes."

"After they divorced, did you continue to visit with her, to see her?"

"Yes, sir."

Several questions later, "Did you have discussions with her . . . from time to time, about her living with this man [Brad Tabor] in his apartment, and her children being over there at her mother's house?"

"Yes, sir. She knew that I didn't approve of it."

Brown was smooth in the way he was able to work in various facts surrounding—or leading up to—the point of no return he felt Jessica had ended up at. As she appeared more and more slighted, each man Jessica dated post-Alan saw through her greedy, malicious way of shunning her ex-husband. It was obvious in the way Jessica had pushed the brunt of her troubles on Alan: she blamed him for everything.

Yet the bomb Naomi dropped exploded after Brown asked her to talk about a conversation she'd had with Jessica not long before Alan and Terra were murdered.

"Did she say anything about Alan coming to the house [on February fifteenth] to pick up the children?"

"Yes, sir, she did."

"What did she tell you . . . ?"

Naomi spoke with a likable earnestness. It was hard not to believe what she said. Her credibility was spotless.

"It got to the point," Naomi began, "in the conversation, that she stated to me that when Alan came to the house to get the children, she was going to set him up for domestic violence and that she was going to— Kelley was going to hide the car so that Alan would feel that she was home alone with the children, and she was going to provoke him for the domestic violence so that it would help her in her court case."

The courtroom let out a collective sigh as Naomi told her story. It wasn't a stretch for most—including the jurors—to take a leap from setting Alan up for domestic violence to murder. If she was capable of planning and carrying out one, why not the other?

"And did she say what was then supposed to happen?"

Naomi paused. Cleared her throat. "And she also stated"—this was harder than she thought—"that if Alan were to touch her, that Kelley would *kill* him."

After a few more questions, Brown handed Naomi over to John Wiley, who seemed eager to question the young mother.

"Well . . . you knew Alan, too, didn't you?"

"Yes, sir. I did."

"And you went to high school with him, too, didn't you?"

"Yes, sir."

"And y'all had been friends for many years?" Wiley's inflection implied that there was something wrong with all of this. Or that he was perhaps leading up to a zinger of a punch line.

"Yes, sir."

"But more recently, y'all hadn't been as close as y'all had been before, right?"

"That's correct."

"And, in fact, you've never even been to the Myrtle-wood Drive house, have you?"

"No, sir."

"You never even visited there?"

"No, sir."

"So you and Jessica were not nearly as close friends as you once were?"

"We were fading, yes."

Brown looked at his coprosecutor, Laura Hodge, wondering where Wiley was going. Brown and Hodge had spent months preparing for trial, searching through documents, putting together witnesses, making sure they understood the custody case inside and out. They had spoken to Naomi themselves. What was Wiley's strategy here? His questioning seemed to build up to nothing. Sure, Jessica and Naomi weren't regularly having beers together anymore, attending Bible class or having tea and meeting at the park with their kids. But Naomi and Jessica had talked on the phone enough to be considered very close friends. Naomi was, after all, a sounding board for Jessica, who regularly called to dump her ex-hubby baggage on Naomi.

After a few more questions, Wiley broke a golden rule most defense attorneys will say you never, ever consider doing—unless you're sure the case has slipped from your hands: attack the victim.

As casual as if he were asking about a shopping trip, Wiley said, "Okay, now, you know Alan used to beat her up when they were married, don't you?"

A loud gasp filled the courtroom. Courtroom spectators looked at one another with shock. Had the man any evidence of such an accusation? Was he stomping on the grave of a dead man, who was unable to defend himself?

"No, sir."

"She's told you that, though, hasn't she?"

"Not until recently."

This was where Jessica was headed with her defense. She thought she had covered her tracks by telling

Naomi that she'd had some important secret to
admit—all that time she and Alan were together, Alan
had been violent with her.

"Alan was the *last* person on earth who could have
ever done such a thing," Naomi said later, clearing
up any confusion as to where she stood on the matter.

Jessica's former attorney, David Dorn, testified later
on that same afternoon. The problem for Jessica was
that Dorn was an honest man who told the truth—and
the truth was what began to hurt Jessica the most as
each witness came forward and exposed another
mean-spirited, hurtful, threatening remark or threat
on her part toward Alan. No one was immune to Jessica's arrogance and malicious mind-set. She spared
no one around her the eruption of her wrath, most of
which was focused on Alan. All because, Brown and
Laura Hodge proved with each witness, Alan wanted
his ex-wife to hold up her end of the divorce decree.

Jessica believed the rules did not apply to her, and
each one of the state's witnesses agreed.

By the end of the second day, Brown had shown the
jury graphic photographs of what was left of the badly
charred bodies of Alan and Terra. This as a slew of law
enforcement witnesses took the stand to talk about
what they hoped truly mattered in a court of law: hard
evidence.

Brown and Hodge were determined to keep their case
on a taut leash and not allow it to get out of hand with experts carrying on and on for hours. Juries tired easily
from sitting all day. Attention spans became frayed. Attitudes easily touched off by a witness rambling on about
this strand of DNA and that mitochondrial definition of

blood. Brown didn't want to alienate the jury by boring
them with unneeded forensic nonsense, trying to make
his case out to be some sort of hour-long television show
that it was not. He had his experts explain the evidence
in simple terms that the jury could wrap their minds
around without too much added noise.

One of the state's most impressive—if not substantial—
pieces of evidence, Brown and Hodge knew going in,
was the information the state had acquired from Terra's
and Alan's cell phones. Jessica would have been better
off leaving the phones alone, but she had to play with
them. And that, the prosecution felt, was going to now
come back to haunt her.

Brett Trimble sat. Brett was the custodian of records
for Spring Communications Company. Here was one
of those unbiased witnesses Hodge had brought in to
talk about data. Pure, unadulterated information.
Brett wasn't sitting in for either side. The guy was
there to talk about the information he had taken from
cell phone records. This sort of evidence was ironclad.
People lie. Cops sometimes leave things out for their
own biased reasons. Friends can have an agenda. But
records—documentation like this—speak to a truth
no one can taint.

It is what it is, as they say.

Brett went through and described how he had
looked at Alan's and Terra's cell phone numbers and
matched them up to cell towers during that particular
period of time the prosecution was interested in—
between Friday night, at approximately six o'clock,
and the next morning, very early. He did a search for
"activations and locations."

When you make a call on your cell phone, the signal
hits the closest tower in the area where you make that

call. That transfer of electronic information produces a record. A hit. The company who owns the tower knows which numbers are using which towers, where and at what times.

Brett called it a "cell site." (Some may want to refer to it as one more addition to the Big Brother family.)

As you drive in your car, for example, away from, say, tower one, and come closer to tower two, your cell phone picks up that second tower site. From the time you start the call, Brett explained to the jury, until the phone call concludes, no matter where you drive or walk, each tower records all your moves.

Bad news for Jessica McCord.

Hodge showed Brett photographs of several cell towers, which covered a range, or radius, of about three miles, Brett said.

After the witness viewed several photographs, Hodge asked Brett to explain how those recordings—of the cell towers—are made.

"Well," Brett said, "a call is made and it is entered into our computer system. Our computer system looks for the subscriber and locates it, and it is sent through the tower in to the customer."

"So the subscriber and customer are the same thing?"

"That's correct, yes."

"How is a tower going to know where your cell phone is?"

"Well, towers are constantly in contact. They ping your cell phone."

"What do you mean by 'ping'?"

"Well, they send tiny bits of information to update your time and your date."

"Is this like a sort of signal in a way?"

"Yes."

Jessica was getting antsy in her chair. This information was adding up to a curtain-raiser of some sort, and

there was no way that what was behind it was going to
work in her favor.

Technology, a lifesaver. Computers are always looking over our shoulders. Recording everything we do.
In this case that electronic information was proving to
be one of the most powerful pieces of evidence Laura
Hodge and Roger Brown had presented. If Alan and
Terra were dead at six-thirty on that night, who could
have been using their cell phones?

Only their killers.

Hodge asked a series of questions that walked jurors
through a few phone calls made on Alan's cell phone
on the night of his murder. One was made at 5:57 P.M.,
the other at 6:14 P.M. Both calls pinged the same tower,
Rocky Ridge Road at Patton Chapel, which is in
Hoover, near Route 31.

"At Rocky Ridge Road," Hodge queried, ". . . at five
fifty-seven, we've got the north side. But then at six-
fifteen, we're moving to the southeast side. Is that correct?"

"That's correct," Brett said. The phone calls were
made from different locations, Hodge had Brett point
out. More than that, the 6:14 call, Brett explained
after being asked, was made from Alan's phone to
Terra's phone.

"Do your records also show a phone call made from
Alan's phone at eight-thirteen [P.M.] on Friday, February fifteenth?"

"Yes."

Hodge asked what number Alan's phone called.

Alan's phone again called Terra's phone.

"Did a cell tower receive a signal from Alan's phone?"

"Yes."

"Which tower was that?"

It was that same tower, Brett testified.

As they went back and forth, Hodge brought out
the fact that at 8:58 P.M. Terra's phone called its voice

mail system and then called Alan's cell phone again. The tower that recorded those calls was located on Jackson Trace Road, in Lincoln, Alabama, a good forty miles east of Hoover/Birmingham. Thus, the calls were being made by someone traveling east, toward Georgia. That second call, in fact, ended, Hodge pointed out on a map she set up for the jury, in Easta-boga, Alabama, even farther east.

It seemed like compelling evidence—that is, if Hodge and Brown could prove who was using the phones. Because at this point all the evidence showed was that two people were communicating with each other via the Bateses' phones and checking their voice mail.

After all, those people could have been Terra and Alan. No expert had testified to a time of death.

59

During a break for lunch on Thursday, Brown indicated that he was likely going to wrap up his case by day's end. He was confident in the few witnesses he and Hodge had left. If you're Roger Brown, you want to end a trial for double murder on a high note. As a prosecutor, you want the jury to have all the information it needs without clogging up the case with unnecessary odds and ends. "Thank God," Brown told me later, "this type of crime is no rare. It's so nonsensical. Ludicrous. One of the stupidest things I have ever seen in my career. All over a child custody battle. Jessica McCord didn't give a *flip* about her kids. She used them to torture Alan Bates."

The trial had gone as Brown had anticipated. "Look," he added, "I know people expect it to sound like some mystic stuff, but trial preparation and following through is not. After you do it five hundred times, you don't really think about what you do. It's kind of instinctual. The Hoover PD and the GBI did a great, terrific job."

* * *

As day two moved into late afternoon, Roger Brown and Laura Hodge had Hoover PD detectives Peyton Zanzour and Rod Glover carry what *Birmingham News* reporter Carol Robinson, inside the courtroom covering every nuance of the case, called "the star in the courtroom." But it was not one of Brown and Hodge's witnesses. Instead, the detectives placed that black leather sofa in front of the jury. The one Albert Bailey had transported around town a day after the murders, only to drop it off in back of a warehouse building next to a Dumpster. The prosecution had the sofa brought into the room to show the jury how it had been stripped of its backing.

This was the couch, Brown insisted, that Alan and Terra sat on as they were shot to death. The backing had been taken off, obviously, because it had bullet holes and blood. Looking at the couch, one could easily figure there would be no other reason to strip it like it had been, other than to hide something. Why would you strip a couch halfway and then discard it? That wasn't rational behavior.

To explain the sofa, among other details of the case that had been uncovered, Brown called GBI agent Kimberly Williams.

Williams pointed out from the stand that yes, the couch tested positive for blood. But no, it was not Alan's or Terra's DNA profile. Still, what the lab had found instead of blood was perhaps much more telling: a certain common household chemical.

On cross-examination John Wiley tried to poke holes in the fact that Jessica and Jeff gave Agent Williams and Investigator Sheron Vance different times for dropping the kids off at Jessica's mother's house on the night of the murders. But he got nowhere. Then he started in on the couch and how Williams had drawn conclusions—speculations—about it.

In response to Williams not answering the way Wiley had perhaps wanted, Brown asked Williams on redirect, "Mr. Wiley asked you about this [sofa] being luminoled and revealing the presence of blood. What else did that luminol reveal? Did it reveal the presence of bleach?"

"Yes, sir," Williams answered.

"Where it had been wiped?"

"What appeared to be that, yes."

Brown played a smart game. Trial lawyers liked to ask questions that they knew the answers to, not those they didn't. John Wiley, it seemed, pulled things out of midair to try and trip up the witnesses. In Wiley's defense, however, one would have to assume that his biggest problem in defending Jessica was that he had a pathological liar for a client.

Brown and Hodge next brought in their expert on ballistics, Ed Moran. Moran explained the details surrounding what was a compelling photograph of two bullets—one found in the trunk of Alan's rental car, and the other found inside of the McCords' garage—side by side. As one looked at the photo, it was not hard to tell with a naked, untrained eye that they had identical tool markings. And that, Moran explained, meant those projectiles had been fired from the same gun barrel. Now, how could a bullet fired from a weapon in the McCord home, and a bullet fired from the same barrel found underneath Alan's body, have been fired by anybody else besides Jessica and Jeff McCord? Save for a setup, there was no other explanation.

* * *

After Moran left the stand, Brown recalled Hoover detective Peyton Zanzour, who answered one question to clear the record.

"Mr. Zanzour, I apologize," Brown said, "I neglected to ask earlier. This location of Myrtlewood Drive, the house of the defendant and her husband, Jeff McCord, is that located in the Birmingham Division of Jefferson County, Alabama?"

"Yes, sir."

"That's all. Thank you."

"I don't have any questions," John Wiley said.

"You can step down," Judge Vinson told Zanzour.

Brown stood. Whispered something to Hodge. Then: "May it please the court," he said, "the state rests."

"All right. Ladies and gentlemen," Vinson said, "this has timed out very well for our afternoon break. And always at this point in a trial, there are things I have to take up with the attorneys. So we'll let you have your afternoon break."

Wiley made an immediate motion for verdict of acquittal. It was based on, he said, "The state's failure to make out a prima facie case of capital murder, just for the insufficiency of the evidence and, in particular, for the state's failure to prove during its case that the two bodies are these of Alan and Terra Bates."

The reach—it was worth a shot.

"I'll overrule your motion," the judge said politely.

Court adjourned at 3:45 P.M.

60

On Valentine's Day, a Friday, both sides were back in the packed courtroom by 9:00 A.M. Roger Brown and Laura Hodge knew from speaking to Judge Vinson and John Wiley in chambers the previous afternoon that this day was going to be one of the more memorable of the trial. The gallery was a bit stirred, waiting and wondering if Jessica was going to take the stand, or would she roll the dice and keep her mouth shut. Those who knew Jessica were certain that she would demand to have the last word. There was not a situation in her life where Jessica had not given her two cents, and then some. If nothing else, she was relentless when it came to letting people know how she felt and what she thought.

After the morning gavel the judge took care of a few preliminary matters. Then John Wiley stood and, with a sense of reluctance in his voice, said, "The defense calls Jessica McCord."

She stood. Walked to the stand like a peacock. Everyone watched. Here was the star of the show, raising her right hand, preparing to tell her side of this terrible tragedy.

There was a certain smugness to Jessica she couldn't hide. It was in the way she carried herself. How she smiled out of the corner of her mouth. The way she looked at people and seemingly said, *How dare y'all not believe me.*

All Jessica had said since her arrest was that she needed her day in court to explain her innocence. Then everyone would see that she'd had nothing to do with killing Alan and his lovely wife. Well, here was that chance.

Wiley walked Jessica through her family life.

The children.

Home.

Marriages.

She seemed nervous, Wiley pointed out. Though Jessica hardly showed it once she found her groove.

"I'm sorry," she said after Wiley told her to relax.

As Jessica talked about meeting and marrying Alan, she expressed a version of the marriage that few had heard. She claimed she and Alan were "incompatible" on every level, especially in the bedroom, at church and at the political polls—seemingly three deal breakers in the fine print of a romance contract.

Then the attack on Alan's fathering skills began. Jessica talked about how bad a father Alan was for not wanting to see his children or maintain any sort of regular visitation schedule with them. She gave the impression that after the divorce Alan was more interested in his work than his kids.

This raised eyebrows. But not in the way, perhaps, that Jessica might have wanted.

As she got comfortable, it was clear that Jessica McCord was not going to give brief, succinct answers to the questions her lawyer asked. Rather, she launched into tedious criticisms of Alan, his attorney and the way Alan had handled the custody matter from day one.

Bash the dead guy.

It got to a point where—taking into consideration all of the evidence the state had presented already—one had to wonder if Jessica was talking about the same person. The same life. Or even the same trial. For example, Jessica accused Frank Head of "not seeing" her in court on several of those occasions he had claimed she failed to show up for a custody hearing.

Many wondered if she was actually being serious when she said this. It was either that, or Frank Head must have been wearing a blindfold.

She even went so far as to blame Alan for the continued court postponements, saying he was always away on tour with the theater group.

To anyone who knew the history, Jessica's answers were pathetic and so transparent that it was hard not to laugh out loud in open court.

"When did you first learn," Wiley asked, "that the judge had held you in contempt of court and issued a warrant for your arrest?"

Jessica repeated the question.

"Yes," Wiley affirmed.

"I did not learn that until I was arrested."

So Jessica was theoretically asking everyone to believe that for over one year she'd had no idea an arrest warrant had been issued in her name. For twelve months she did not realize she was being held in contempt of court. Would a jury believe this, or resent the idea that Jessica felt she could get away with such an outright lie? After all, this same statement was coming from a woman whose husband was a cop at the time!

Several questions later, Wiley asked Jessica about the arrest. How she remembered that day. "And you heard testimony," he concluded his question, "that you pretended to be your sister?"

For the record the witnesses included sheriffs, cops and attorneys.

Still, according to Jessica, they had it all wrong. "I heard that," she said, "yes."

"And you don't—that's not exactly what happened, is it?"

Jessica said no.

Wiley asked her to explain.

"Yeah, the day that they came, it was very early in the morning that day. We were all still in bed, you know, in pajamas and everything, watching Martha Stewart on TV." One big, happy American family, in other words. Enjoying themselves as they woke up. Some were surprised Jessica had not tossed in a story about breakfast in bed to put a nice bow on it all. "And my husband heard some knocking and went around. I was using the restroom. And I could hear them discussing that there was some sort of an order relating to the children and an order for my arrest." When she told the sheriff she was her sister, Jessica asked the jury to believe, it was more or less in a mocking fashion. She was joking. She claimed she told the children what was about to happen—that she was going to jail—and they became emotional, crying and bawling, begging her to say she was their auntie. So, to humor the kids and save them from the immediate impact of their mom being taken away in handcuffs, Jessica said she told the sheriff she was her sister. But that the sheriffs knew she was joking around.

No one bothered to point out that Jessica had just got done saying she had no idea there was an arrest warrant issued on her behalf—therefore, how could she possibly tell the children there was an order for her arrest if she didn't know it yet?

It was all just a misunderstanding, Wiley suggested

with his questioning. A way to divert the children's attention for a moment so the impact of the arrest wouldn't be so bad on them.

"As a matter of fact," Jessica told the jury with a straight face, "I'm an extremely sarcastic person, and I tend to use it at inappropriate times."

"Did it ever occur to you that you could pass yourself off as your sister with these police officers?"

"Good Lord, no," Jessica said, a slight smile, her phony Southern belle demeanor sounding forced. "They're experienced police officers. If somebody could pull something like that on them, they need to go back to the academy."

As Brown and Hodge looked on, shaking their heads in disgust, the jury gave indications in their movements that they had seen through Jessica's narcissistic, self-indulgent lies. She had made no mention of the fact that the sheriff who had arrested her had called into the department for fingerprints and a photograph, and they waited for ten to fifteen minutes in the house before Jessica finally admitted she *wasn't* her sister.

Wiley asked Jessica to explain the previous day's testimony from a woman Jessica had spent some time in jail with during that ten-day stint during Christmas, 2001.

"Did you ever have a conversation . . . about how you could kill your [ex-]husband and get away with it?"

"No," Jessica said. She sounded flippant. It was as if this, too, was another misunderstanding. The woman had taken what was a joke and turned it around on her. "The longest conversation I had with [that witness] was about when the Pelham PD arrested her and how angry she was about it." The insinuation was that since Jeff McCord was a Pelham police officer,

the witness was getting back at Jessica any way she
could. "Everybody down there (in the jail) knew that
my husband was a Pelham police officer. Several of the
girls had been arrested by Pelham, and I had a picture
of my husband there. They all knew who he was."

Over and over, Jessica bashed Alan whenever the
chance arose. At one point she talked about how Alan
would come to town but not visit with the children.
"[B]ecause he was too busy." She never mentioned
that Alan could not find her or the kids—that she had
hid out from him. Jessica said Alan had lied during
the deposition, claiming that he had been denied visitation. The fact was, she said, she had never denied
him anything.

Clearly, Jessica had an answer for every situation that
went against her, and even some that didn't. The
reason for the bullet found in the garage was simple,
Jessica explained. Jeff had misfired his gun in the
house. After a complete search, however, neither she
nor Jeff could find the bullet. She claimed all that talk
about her saying she wanted Alan killed was a misin-
terpretation of the facts. Didn't matter that three
witnesses—none of whom knew each other—had
testified that Jessica had said Alan would pay for what
he was doing and needed to be killed. What she had
actually said, Jessica tried convincing the jury, was
that Jeff was a police officer, and most people had the
impression that cops are "very, very aggressive" people,
"when, in fact, police officers tend to be very controlled and will not just, you know, walk up on you and
they're going to draw their gun and things like that. It's
not the Wild West and people think like that."

Her answers did not always match the questions.

For a time she played herself off as the caring ex-
wife, never once saying anything bad about Alan. She
certainly never "boasted and laughed about denying"

him what was rightfully his. Witnesses had testified the previous day that Jessica ridiculed and taunted Alan as they left the deposition that Friday afternoon, telling him he would never see the kids again.

"I wasn't angry at Alan that he was going to see the kids" that weekend of his death, she said. "I thought it would have been *nice* if his parents had come to town to visit with everyone here. . . ."

"And the children," Wiley asked, "were aware that he was going to take [them that weekend of his death]?"

"You know," Jessica said, "I told them. You have to keep in mind that a lot of [the] time, he didn't come."

"What do you mean?"

"So I don't know that the children put a lot of stock in me saying, 'You're going with your dad for the weekend. You're leaving with them at such and such a time.'"

"You mean there were times after the divorce when his visitation time would come and he wouldn't appear to collect the kids?" Wiley sounded shocked by this. Alan had been portrayed during the state's portion of the case as a loving father who was being denied visitation.

"Right," Jessica said without missing a beat. "Again, you know, first and third [weekends] for the longest period of time until April 2000, he had first and third [weekends]. And first and thirds, six o'clock, we're sitting by the door, waiting, you know."

"And he's not there?"

"Many times, he was not. And frequently he wouldn't call, either. So, you know, I think it was just kind of old hat for the kids [to expect] him to *not* come."

Many sat and considered how easy it was for Jessica to sit in that chair and lie. How commonplace it was for her to attack a dead man. The documentation, she must have forgotten, would tell a different story. There was page after page of affidavits, signed by Alan, resolved by judges, describing the polar opposite to what she was now trying to pimp. Yet the most laughable part of her testimony, said one source in the courtroom, was that as Jessica sat and told her tales with a straight face, she was "probably believing half of the lies herself." She was so vain that she actually believed the jury was going to buy it all.

For a woman facing the death penalty, that could be a fatal oversight.

Jessica agreed that Alan was scheduled to pick the children up that night at her house on Myrtlewood Drive. That fact was never in dispute.

Wiley asked Jessica what she did after leaving David Dorn's office on deposition day, February 15, 2002.

"I drove back toward Hoover," she said. "I went to Chick-fil-A and got something to eat, and I kind of tooled around the subdivision eating it in the car so I didn't have to share. And then I went home." She got home around "four-thirtyish."

According to her version, from that point on, she and Jeff collected the children (from day care and a friend's house), then got them ready for Alan at her mom's. As she and Jeff went about doing that, they considered going out that night for a belated Valentine's Day celebration. It was near six o'clock when she realized that they were all at her mother's, and Alan was on his way over to her house.

"So what, if anything, did you do then?"

"Well, let's see . . . I kept getting ready."

"What was your plan? I mean, the arrangement was for Alan to pick up the kids at Myrtlewood. Yet the kids were all at your mom's?"

Roger Brown and Laura Hodge were whispering

things to each other. Brown was writing viciously on a
notepad in front of him.

"Right."

"What was your plan about that?"

"Well, I had their bags packed there. I just, you know,
put some clothes into a backpack of theirs. And in the
event that he went to Mom's home, Mom said she was
going to put some stuff together, too, just so, you know,
there was no conflict if he came there first. The kids
were all playing, you know, and stuff. So it's possible, if
he had driven by, he would have seen them there and
stopped there first. But my plan had been, *'Here's the
bag, go get the kids, see you later, see you Sunday.'"*

"You know" seemed to be one of those phrases Jessica leaned on as she figured things out in her mind
while in the middle of speaking.

"So, did Alan ever come by your house?"

"Not when I was there, he didn't."

"How long did you stay at your house?"

It was 6:30, she said, perhaps 6:40 P.M.

"And then what did you do?"

"Well, before I left, when I left, or what?"

"Well, did you leave the house?"

"Yes, I did leave the house. We went by Mom's."

"You say 'we'?"

"My husband and I. And I stuck my head in the
door and said, 'Is everybody okay? What's going on?'
And, you know, [Alan's kids] were still there, and I
think they were watching Nickelodeon or something
like that. . . ."

Wiley decided to play devil's advocate. Maybe to in-
terject, one could only speculate, a bit of authenticity
into the conversation. Jessica's testimony was confusing. She sounded casual and removed. She came across
as cold and unfeeling. It was as if she was sickened by

the idea that no one believed her at face value and she had to explain herself.

"A lot of us are going—well, let me withdraw that." Wiley paused. Thought about it. "How could you have been so flippant and unconcerned about the fact that there was an *arrangement* for Alan to come and pick up the kids at six o'clock and, yet, Alan hadn't done so?"

Wiley was right. Jessica had given the jury a confusing scenario that seemed to cover her tracks—no matter what she was asked later. She was at her mom's. Then at home. She was back at her mom's. Then on the road.

Many times juries will consider the parts of the story you leave out as evidence, too. As they would figure out soon enough, neither Jessica nor Wiley had mentioned that Jessica called Alan on his cell phone from her home—a fact telephone records proved—during this time period.

Answering Wiley's question regarding the arrangement, Jessica took the opportunity to stomp on Alan's memory some more.

"Because it happened so frequently. I mean," she repeated just in case no one had heard her the first time, "it happened so frequently. You know, I cannot take you through all of the years we were divorced, but it did happen frequently. . . ."

Wiley moved on to Terra.

"We got along," Jessica said. "We got along *very* well. Our big thing was that I cared about my kids, and *she* cared about my kids. And anybody who cares about my kids, I'm going to try to get along with. And she was very diplomatic and tried really hard to, you know, whatever conflict Alan and I had, to not let that really, you know, get all over the kids. She was real concerned about my kids."

And then, as if she had rehearsed talking about this

portion of the night in preparation for a Broadway role, Jessica told her version of the remainder of the evening and the next morning.

Movies. *The Lord of the Rings.*

She and Jeff didn't like it, so they went to the bathroom and snuck into *Black Hawk Down.*

Didn't like that, so they left the theater.

"I went back to my mom's to see—I was hungry. We had not, you know, eaten that evening. And went back to Mom's to see if she would be up for keeping the kids any longer. Thought maybe we could kind of nudge her into it, since it was so late."

Although she had a cell phone, Jessica testified that she called her mother from a pay phone near the movie theater earlier that night.

When Wiley asked what time she returned to her mother's, she had no trouble recalling that it was "midnightish."

She said they left her mother's house and went to Southside, the southern half of Birmingham's downtown district. "We parked and walked . . . and, you know, just talking. I had spent a lot of my teenage years down on Southside, hanging out, and telling [Jeff] all about that. And he wanted to go to a strip club."

Since she had never been inside a topless bar, Jessica said what the heck. Let's do it. Why not?

They ended up, according to her testimony, at the PlayLate Club, somewhere near two to two-thirty that next morning, February 16.

They stayed an hour. "It was not my cup of tea."

The problem with this story, jurors figured out easily enough, was that the bouncer at PlayLate, a man who had testified during the state's portion of the case, was a former cop who knew Jeff McCord. And that former cop said he would have recognized Jeff if

he had walked into the club—*especially* if Jeff was with
a woman, seeing that it was not every night females
frequented the PlayLate.

The rest of the early morning, Jessica testified, was
a hodgepodge of lies she had a tough time keeping
straight. She explained how, tired and beaten down by
being up all night, walking hand in hand with Jeff,
like two young lovers, they went over to the Home
Depot as the sun came up. They looked at carpet sam-
ples. She said she wanted the house to look good for
"the March court date" with Alan. The state was going
to be coming into her house to check things out.
Their dog, a black Lab, had ruined the carpet. It "was
really nasty and it needed to be replaced."

They didn't buy anything, however, Jessica said,
except for a carpet "trim knife."

Then came her excuse for removing the backing on
the leather sofa. She and Jeff wanted to reupholster
the couch. The backing had cigarette burns on it. She
said the dog had chewed up the seat cushions. The
mattress, which police never recovered, had been
tossed out in back of the yard. They decided to dispose of the sofa after tearing off the backing and realizing it wasn't worth fixing.

Of course, they replaced the wallpaper in the den
because Jeff had mistakenly shot the television out
one night, Jessica testified, and then shot at the wall
while practicing "night firing" he had to qualify for at
the Pelham PD.

So Jeff had practiced his skills with a gun inside the
house?

"I was furious with him."

As the morning break came, Jessica had given answers to just about every question the state posed. Her
testimony was designed to chisel away at the state's
case, and she went through, one by one, each piece of

evidence, providing an alternative explanation. For those in the gallery who might have believed Jessica, as she implied that the charges were based on conjecture and circumstantial evidence, you'd have to leave the courtroom thinking, *Is this not the unluckiest woman in the world?*

61

After a short morning break, John Wiley got his client back on track. There was a clear indication Jessica was almost finished. She had spent nearly three hours on the stand already. Had her direct examination been productive? Had she accomplished putting reasonable doubt into the minds of the jurors?

"When she was being questioned by her attorney," Carol Robinson later told me, "her demeanor was almost laughable. It *was* laughable. She was trying to come off as prim and proper, very Pollyannaish—and it just wasn't working. No one in the courtroom was buying it, and the jury wasn't, either."

Jessica testified about how distressed she was after talking to Philip Bates on February 16 and learning of Alan's disappearance. She mentioned how ill-tempered and disgraceful she perceived the Hoover PD to be when they arrived to serve the first search warrant. She gave the jury the impression that the HPD had ransacked her house, which was, she admitted, a mess, anyway.

Jessica talked about the early-morning hours of Saturday, February 16. How she and Jeff hung around the house. This was a slippery slope for Wiley. On that Saturday, Jessica had been questioned by Kimberly Williams and Sheron Vance. She had to watch what she told the jury about this.

In turn, the best way to deal with the situation, Wiley apparently had decided, was to avoid it completely.

Not long after the lunch break, Wiley introduced several photographs of Jessica with her children. Roger Brown objected. The photos, Brown implied, bore no relevance to the case. They had been introduced to present Jessica as a maternal type. She was trying to show the jury she was a loving, doting mother.

The judge said they'd discuss it during lunch recess.

"Thank you," Brown said.

"Jessica," Wiley asked, "did you kill Alan Bates?"

"No, I didn't."

"Did you kill Terra Bates?"

"No, I didn't."

"Thank you."

Roger Brown had held his tongue long enough. Now Brown stood and, with a measured tone, said, "You told us just before lunch that when the police asked about searching your car and your husband's SUV, you volunteered it. . . . Is that what you said?"

"They did."

"I didn't *ask* you that," Brown said. And this was where Jessica was going to run into trouble: On direct she could dance around the issues and answer questions at will; here, on cross, she would have to answer Brown's questions frankly. Brown was not going to allow scripted answers that served Jessica's agenda.

"Isn't that what you said?" Brown asked.

"Yes."

"You didn't have anything to hide?" he posed.

"No."

"You were going to be very cooperative with police, right?"

"I allowed them to look through my vehicles, yes," Jessica agreed.

"Sure, because you *didn't* have anything to hide, right?"

"I allowed them to look through my vehicles because they asked."

"Did you have something to hide?" Brown questioned.

"No."

For the next few minutes, they went at it: back and forth. Jessica said she did this. Brown said no, you did that.

"That's not true," Brown said.

"Yes, it is," Jessica replied.

"No, it's not."

"*Yes,* it is."

Brown had an easy way about him. His colleagues showed him the respect he deserved. Definitely a trial lawyer's lawyer. "Roger is fun to watch in a courtroom," Carol Robinson said later, "and always has been. He is an incredibly strong presence and just inspires confidence. He is intimidating. . . . He's always sort of reminded me of Harrison Ford. He's not flamboyant, just steady, dry and sarcastic. A force to be reckoned with, if you will."

Jessica skated on the questions she didn't want to answer and talked in circles around those she did. It was not hard to tell she was afraid to answer certain questions, for fear of getting caught in a lie. She had told so many untruths it was difficult to keep track. Brown knew this—and started to chip away at it.

The fact that Jessica had allowed police to search her vehicles, Brown pointed out, yet she would not allow them to search her house without a warrant, spoke volumes as to where her loyalties were in the investigation. This told police she knew something. Her ex-husband and his wife were missing—murdered. Jessica claimed not to have had anything to do with it. Yet, all that aside, she was unwilling to do everything in her power to help.

Sure it made her an immediate suspect. Why wouldn't it?

Brown asked, "So [you made] a telephone call . . . at what time? Six-forty?"

"Six-thirty to six-forty, something like that."

"So you said, 'Thanks for coming by'?"

"I said, 'Thanks a lot for'—I think I said, 'Thanks a lot for not showing up.'"

"Oh, okay. And you also said, 'I don't know what the hell's going on, Alan, but we're here waiting for you,' didn't you?"

Jessica studied Roger Brown like the opponent he was. Her facial expression told the room what she was thinking: *Where are you going with this?*

"Yes," she finally answered.

"Well, that was a lie, wasn't it?" Brown said.

"Kelley and I were there."

"He wasn't picking you up for visitation."

"Kelley and I meant 'we.'"

"Oh, I see," Brown said. "But the fact of the matter, Mrs. McCord, is that Alan and Terra's lifeless, dead, bullet-riddled bodies were down on that couch in your den, and you made this call to set up some kind of an alibi?"

"No!"

"'We're waiting for you and we have movie plans. We need to go. I wish you would hurry up.' Isn't that what you said?"

"I don't remember the exact words."

"Well," Brown said, poise and experience oozing from each word, "there certainly wouldn't be any reason for you to sit around and wait. That wasn't interfering with your movie plans, was it?"

"I'm sorry, could you restate that?"

Brown repeated the question.

"*What* wasn't interfering with my movie plans?" Jessica made it sound as if she was confused.

"Alan's not coming by."

"We had to wait on Alan because that was where he was supposed to come."

"You told us this morning that sometimes he would come there, and he would always go to both places."

Which was it?

The exchange was heated and accusatory. Brown knew she was lying. He asked Jessica about that phone call she made to her mother from the pay phone near the theater. Jessica claimed to "step out" of the movie while it was playing, leaving Jeff by himself, so she could go around the corner and call her mother.

Brown made her pinpoint an exact location.

She did.

The smart prosecutor then pointed out that the pay phone Jessica made the call from was "two miles" from the movie theater.

Two miles.

"And you went down there," Brown said, recalling a statement Jessica gave during her direct testimony, "because you needed to get some Pepto-Bismol?"

"I had an upset stomach all day."

"So the drugstore that is approximately a hundred yards from the movie theater in the same shopping center . . . that was too inconvenient?" Sarcasm bled from Brown's inflection.

"What drugstore is that?"

"I don't remember the name of it. . . . You didn't go there?"

Jessica was caught in a bit of a sticky situation. Brown made it clear there was also a grocery store nearby, which she could have walked to in minutes. Someone with a stomachache would not likely go to the farthest store away to seek a quick remedy like Pepto. But Jessica had testified that she walked past a grocery store and drove two miles to a pharmacy.

Logically speaking, it made no sense.

"Then you went back to the movie with your Pepto-Bismol?"

"I went back to the movie theater, yes."

"And they let you in without a ticket?"

"Who says I didn't have a ticket?" Jessica sassed back.

"The ticket stubs were in your husband's wallet." She herself had testified to this fact.

But Jessica had an answer for that, too. "They were in his wallet later."

"Well, how did they get from you to his wallet?"

"I'm sorry?"

Brown repeated the question.

"I assume at some point I gave them to him."

"Oh, so you took them so that you could get back in?"

For the next few minutes, the prosecutor and the defendant sparred, going back and forth on the same points: the strip club, times, where they went after the movie, the ticket stubs. They discussed the front door at the house. Brown wondered why they never replaced it.

Jessica said they couldn't afford it.

The problem Brown had with the door was that if it was not working on the Friday night Alan was supposed to pick up the kids, and they had gone to the trouble of leaving that note on the door, why did she walk out the front door several times that Saturday and Sunday? She had just admitted they couldn't afford to fix it.

"We did go out the front door, yes."

"So, obviously, this blanket (covering the door) and this sign and all of this problem with the front door was down by then, wasn't it?"

"No."

Brown moved on to the Contempt of Court Arrest Warrant. He suggested that Jessica had called three different people—two of them lawyers—to find out if there was a warrant out for her arrest; yet she testified that she had no idea the warrant existed.

"You talked about [killing Alan] so much," Brown said near the end of his cross-examination, "that when you were about to get out [of jail after the ten-day sentence, one of the inmates] said to you, 'You're going to kill that man, aren't you?'"

"[She] hardly spoke to me while I was there. No, she didn't say that to me."

"And your response was to laugh, wasn't it?"

"Again, I just said she didn't make the statement to me!"

"So [she] didn't say that, either?"

"[She] said she hated police officers and their wives and hoped they all die. [She] did not make the statement to me."

Brown asked about another inmate whom Jessica had supposedly said the same thing to.

"I don't know who [she] is," Jessica answered.

Brown went through Jessica's previous statements regarding her not allowing Alan visitation based mostly on the fact that scheduling was sometimes off. It had nothing to do with her denying him an opportunity to see his kids.

If that was the case, Brown suggested, why wasn't Jessica more upset over the contempt charge? Why not show up in court to fight it? Why ignore it and then serve time in jail without kicking and screaming? "And knowing that there was absolutely no basis for that, you were outraged," Brown asked rhetorically, phrasing it more as a statement, though.

"No," she said, "'outraged' is not the right word."

"Well, we'll use yours then. What is it?"

"I was upset."

"Upset? Angry?"

"Not at that point, no."

"No?"

"Not at that point," Jessica answered.

"Just upset?"

"I was upset."

"Upset emotionally so that you cried?" Brown posited.

"Oh, I'm sure I did."

"Upset so that you vented your anger? Did you scream and yell?"

"You mean upon finding out?" Jessica countered.

"Yes."

"Did I stand there and scream and yell?"

"Yes."

"I don't believe so, no," Jessica answered.

"What did you say?"

"I don't recall the exact moment I found out. You know, I—"

"Now, Mrs. McCord," Brown said, interrupting, "you have portrayed yourself all morning to these ladies and gentlemen as being a very cooperative and nice Martha Stewart–type mother who was doing everything you reasonably could to allow Alan to visit with his children. Now, all of a sudden, here comes a piece of paper with all of these lies in there that says you're denying his visitation rights. *That* didn't make you mad?"

Jessica had no response. She kept dancing around

the issue, and looked worse for it. She was so non-compliant and arrogant in her replies that Brown actually snapped back at one point: "Alan made phone call after phone call after phone call to you to try to arrange visitation, and you uniformly ignored his messages, *didn't* you?"

"Phone calls to where?"

"To you!" Brown responded.

"Again, where?"

"I'll ask the questions, Mrs. McCord. It doesn't matter *where*. Did he make a phone call to you to try to arrange visitation?"

"At what time?" Jessica asked.

The judge had heard enough. She leaned over and said, "Mrs. McCord, just answer the question."

"He has in the past called me regarding visitation . . . ," she finally agreed.

Brown brought up the point of the missing mailbox.

"It kept getting knocked over," Jessica said. "There didn't seem to be much point. We were running behind on bills because if they cannot deliver the mail, your bills are late. So [Jeff] got a PO box and the mail wasn't late." It just happened they did this when Alan and the court were looking for Jessica.

Then they discussed schooling for the kids. Jessica said she took the kids out of school—not to hide them, but because she had been "unhappy with the Hoover schools for quite some time."

"Pathetic" was the word that came to mind when those in the courtroom later recalled Jessica's answers. She seemed to have an excuse for everything. Her answers were beyond transparent and reprehensible.

Brown took a few deep breaths. He realized the best way to attack the lies Jessica spewed was to use her own words.

"You didn't have any problem with Terra?"

Jessica hesitated. "Not"—she started to say, then thought better of it and stopped midsentence before changing direction—". . . we never had a fight, no." The phrasing of her answer was obvious. It left things open-ended. Brown had some ammo in the chamber, though. The look on Jessica's face spoke to how sure of it she was.

"Well," Brown said, "how about explaining the incident when you went storming into the Alabama Theatre and said to Alan, 'If you think you and that *slut*, Terra, are going to get my kids, it will be over my dead body!' Tell the ladies and gentlemen of the jury about that occasion."

Jessica shifted in her seat. "I have absolutely no idea what you're talking about or who told you that, that was said. I don't know what you're talking about."

"So you deny ever doing that?"

"I don't remember ever making that statement to anybody."

"Well, do you deny calling Terra a slut?" Brown queried.

"I don't think I've ever called her a slut."

"You don't think?"

"I don't think I have."

"Well, you don't think you have. Is that the best answer you can give me on that? You don't *think* you have. Okay. That's fine," Brown stated.

"I answered you at least twice!"

"Yes, you certainly have. . . ."

After touching briefly on the various men Jessica had been with, in between Alan and Jeff, Jessica calling them all liars, Brown asked what she and Jeff bought at Home Depot that morning. She testified to purchasing a carpet knife.

"You bought some heavy plastic, didn't you?" he

asked. The Hoover PD believed they had used it to wrap up the bodies.

"No," she said. "I bought a carpet knife. As a matter of fact, I think I offered the receipt to the police."

Brown said, "Oh, you did, sure."

"I think I did."

"You did! Because they already had the records, didn't they? They already had the records where you had bought some sheet plastic, and then you realized you had forgot something and then went back and got that knife!" Brown asserted.

"I didn't buy sheet plastic that morning and—"

"Did your husband buy it?"

"Not that I am aware of, no."

They next discussed the fact that Jessica could not deny that she and Jeff made a dump run that Saturday morning. So Jessica's response to it was that they had made the trip to toss out some old toys. She claimed the call from Philip Bates about Alan being missing had upset her. But Brown was quick to make the connection that "rather than waiting there [at the house] for a phone call to hear anything, you took broken toys . . . to the dump, thirty miles away from your house."

There was a dump site within a few miles, Brown let the jury know. Yet she and Jeff, Jessica testified, drove to a dump more than a half hour away.

"I waited for quite a while," she said.

"Ma'am, is that true?"

"I waited for quite a while," Jessica responded again.

"Ma'am?"

Finally, "A while later, yes, I went."

Brown mentioned the bullet found in the garage. He wanted to know what Jessica thought about that little piece of damning evidence.

"What is your explanation for how it got there? Did the police plant it? Is that what you're saying?"

"I don't know how it got there. I don't have an answer for that. I don't know," Jessica replied.

Brown introduced State's Exhibit Number 94. He showed the photograph to Jessica. "Do you recognize that?"

Jessica played stupid, mumbling more than answering. "Do you mind if I look at it to see what—I recognize the author, but I don't recognize the—I'm reading the summary on the back of the book. I don't necessarily remember this particular book, but I recognize the author."

"You don't recognize it? So, is this another 'I don't think I read it,' or 'I don't remember it,' or 'I don't know'?"

The photograph was of W.E.B. Griffin's *The Murderers*. It was taken from inside the McCord home. It was a brilliant move on Brown's part. He wanted the jury to understand that Jessica might have gotten the idea from that book to murder Alan and cover it up.

Brown asked several more questions over a fifteen-minute blitz, for which Jessica would not answer with any type of accountability, no matter how insignificant or irrelevant to the case the question turned out to be. Finally, accusing Jessica of being a flat-out liar, Brown leaned down and whispered something into Laura Hodge's ear.

Then: "No further questions, Your Honor."

Mopping the floor came to the minds of most in the courtroom.

Wiley cleared a few things up over redirect and sat back down.

Jessica was released from the witness stand.

62

Since day one of the trial, the courtroom had been packed. There was a certain "energy" in the room, as one person later described it. It wasn't "somber," or terribly sad, "though there were definitely times that were more solemn than others." Still, the subtle tone simmering in the background hummed with the feeling that everyone was present because two people had been brutally murdered. It was sometimes easy to forget there were victims—the dead. Trials become about suspects. Victims often get lost in the shuffle of testimony and evidence. Kevin and Robert Bates, as well as friends of the Bates and Klugh families, were there to remind everyone that victims should never be forgotten.

Even though Jessica had finished testifying, the day was far from over. The accused double murderer had spent upward of four hours in the witness-box. As she sat down at the table, with her family—including a brother dressed in his U.S. Navy uniform—there in the front row to support her, Jessica had to feel somewhat wounded. At times she had been impatient and argumentative with Roger Brown. At others, well, she sounded desperate and unwilling to tell the truth in spite of implicating herself. This was not going to sit well with the jury.

As Jessica settled in her chair, her mother, Dian Bailey, stood and walked toward the witness stand. What would soon prove to be an important part of the trial—something most everyone would overlook as a mere formality—Dian raised her right hand and swore to tell the truth.

"The whole truth and nothing but . . ."

Dian spoke in a low monotone. She was not comfortable in the witness stand, testifying at her daughter's murder trial. What mother would be?

After Wiley had Dian talk about where she worked inside the court system of collecting money from deadbeat dads, she talked about Jessica moving into her house after Jessica and Alan had divorced. The point of it was to clarify that Alan's kids—all of Jessica's kids, for that matter—were frequent guests at the Bailey household.

The next several questions focused on how Dian and her late husband, Albert, had made a second home for Jessica's kids. They had clothes for the children at their house. There was a bedroom "denominated" (Dian's word) specifically as the children's.

Some sat and wondered where this line of questioning was leading. But that was made clear when Wiley asked, "Had there ever been times, to your knowledge, that Alan was scheduled to pick up the girls for visitation and failed to do so?"

"Yes."

"Few or many times?"

"There would be a lot of times that you would find out he wasn't coming, yes."

Another round of slapping a dead man across the face was under way.

"Would it be safe to say that it got to the point where no one was surprised that he didn't show up?"

"Yeah. For me, yes."

As she continued, Dian painted a gloomy and stressful picture of her life at the time Jessica and Alan were fighting for custody, saying, "My father was—we put him in a nursing home on Valentine's Day, the day before [the deposition]. My mother was at home ill with pneumonia."

Dian testified that she got home from work on Friday, February 15, 2002, at "five-thirty [P.M.] or so. . . . My husband and grandchildren were [there]." She said she understood Alan was going to pick the kids up at Jessica's Myrtlewood Drive home that evening. But Alan had picked up the kids at her house in the past "many times." He would also come by her house to "look for them."

Wiley asked if Jessica came by that evening.

"Yes."

"Did she tell you what she was doing or intending to do, or anything?"

"Yes."

"What did she say?"

"She was going to go to dinner and a movie [with Jeff]."

Wiley asked about a phone call Dian had received from Jessica later that night. She said it was somewhere near eight o'clock (during the movie, when Jessica said she had stepped out for the Pepto-Bismol).

"She wanted to remind me to give [the youngest] his medicine."

"Later on that night, did you have a conversation with Jessica?"

"Yes," Dian answered.

"And do you know about what time that was?"

"It was after twelve-thirty."

"And how do you know that?"

"Because I had just given [the youngest] his bottle. Just finished giving [him] his evening bottle."

"And what was the gist of—was that a telephone conversation?"

Dian did not hesitate: "No. She came to the house and she was going to pick up the kids. And I told her, I said, 'The kids are asleep—let them stay here.'"

Roger Brown whispered something to Laura Hodge. What Dian had just testified to was in stark contrast with the state's findings. Dian was saying, in effect, that Jessica had stopped by the house *after* midnight. Brown and Hodge knew that was impossible if Jessica and Jeff were in Georgia, driving to Rutledge to dump the bodies and to torch Alan's car. Either Dian Bailey had just committed perjury, or Jeff and Jessica *were not* responsible for the murders of Alan and Terra.

"Do you know whether or not her husband was with her?" Wiley asked.

"Yes, he was. He was in the car."

Brown wrote something down on the legal pad in front of him.

"Would it be unusual for Jessica to ask you to let the kids just stay over like that?"

"Oh no, no."

"Would it be safe to say, really, your house was just like a second home for those kids?"

"Definitely a second home for the kids."

"That's all I have, Your Honor."

Roger Brown didn't waste any time. "More like a *first* home, Mrs. Bailey?" the prosecutor said, standing, looking down at his legal pad.

"I'm sorry?" Dian asked.

"It was more like a first home, *wasn't* it?"

"Yes, it was."

Two questions later, "The evening Mr. Wiley asked you about when you said she came by your house or, excuse me, called you on the phone, I'm not sure which it was, and told you her plans were to go to dinner and a movie."

"Right," Dian answered.

"Was that on the telephone or at your house?"

"That was at my house."

"What time was it?"

"I want to say it was sometime after six-thirty or so."

"Sometime after six-thirty?"

"Yeah."

After Dian said she believed Jeff and Jessica were driving the family van during that six-thirty visit, Brown asked what vehicle they were driving when they returned to the house early the next morning, at or around twelve-thirty.

"I didn't get up and look."

"You didn't notice when they came inside?"

"No."

Through extensive questioning, Brown made a point to the jury that while Jessica was hiding out from Alan and the court, Alan's lawyer, Frank Head, had hired someone to serve Dian with an order to take a deposition, but Dian had lied to that man when he came to her door. She told him she was someone else. Then one day when the same man came upon her while she was outside at work, smoking a cigarette, she ran inside the building to avoid him.

"In fact," Brown added, "he followed you into the building and tried to engage you in conversation, and you went into a secure employee area where he couldn't come back there, right? Is that true?"

"Yes, it is."

Brown wanted to keep his cross brief. Hit Jessica's mother with the facts and let her fall on her sword.

"Finally, Mrs. Bailey, do you recall in the spring of 2002, I invited you by subpoena to come to the grand jury and tell the grand jury what you knew about the situation, didn't I?"

"Yes."

"And you did come to the grand jury, didn't you?"

"Yes," Dian replied.

"And when you came in there, when I began to ask you questions, you invoked your right against self-incrimination, didn't you?"

"Yes."

"And refused to answer my questions?" Brown asked.

"Yes."

"Thank you. That's all."

Wiley concluded his case with one more witness, bringing the grand total to three. Brown called a few rebuttal witnesses. It was late in the day. After Brown had rested his case, and Wiley waved his hand indicating he was also finished, the judge said it had been a long day. It was a good time to end proceedings. But everyone was expected back in court the following morning—a Saturday—by nine.

The judge gave the jury its familiar warning regarding discussing the case among themselves. After all, each side still had closing arguments left to give.

63

First thing Saturday morning, a year to the day Alan and Terra were murdered, Roger Brown, looking confident and prepared, began his closing by paying homage to the jury. He said there was no way he could drive a forklift, work as an engineer, "manage" homes or be a nurse—all jobs held by the jurors—and yet, "Any one of you," Brown said humbly, "can come down here and do what I'm about to do—argue this case on behalf of the state of Alabama, and Alan and Terra."

Brown talked about the obvious: every murder was senseless. He spoke of the questions one might have when confronted with such horror: namely, why?

"What did they ever do to *her*?" Brown asked, pointing to Jessica. He went through the visitation and custody matters in brief, not spending too much time rehashing what his witnesses had testified to already. Just about every point Brown made hit on target to rebut what Jessica had said on the witness stand.

"It's all about *her*," Brown said in a loud voice.

He talked about how Jessica and Jeff got rid of the couch because it was likely covered with blood and

bullet holes. Finally, just ten minutes later, Brown
challenged Jessica's defense team to "get up here and
tell you what is a plausible, reasonable theory consistent with her innocence on these facts."

Brown was done.

Bill Neumann had been part of Jessica's defense
team from the beginning of the trial. Yet Neumann
had been invisible. Now he stood and made a point to
note his absence in the case. "I know you haven't
heard my voice," Neumann said, "since about Monday,
and . . . I guess you were wondering if I had a voice
left." He explained how he had caught a cold that was
"getting progressively worse."

It took Neumann some time to get his thoughts in
order. He apologized for anything "inappropriate" he
might say in defense of Jessica—especially those
things that the jury might consider an insult "to the
memory of Alan and Terra Bates." But it was his and
John Wiley's duty as officers of the court to defend
their client's rights. Part of such a defense, apparently,
was going to include a walk over the graves of these
two murdered people.

Regarding all of the fighting that went on between
Alan and Jessica, Neumann said, there was one constant. "Do you remember what the attorneys said?
That [Alan and Jessica] were moving toward an agreement . . . and she was going to likely keep custody."

He disputed those witnesses who claimed Jessica
had said she'd kill Alan before she let him have the
kids. He talked about those witnesses' arrest records.
Their drug habits. He mentioned the lack of forensic
evidence the state had, not giving a clear indication
as to why Terra's blood might have been found on
the McCord coffee table—seeing that Jessica herself

testified that neither Alan nor Terra had ever been inside her house and had even failed to show up on the night in question.

From there, Neumann beat the drum of circumstantial evidence and how one might think twice about convicting someone on it alone.

"It's circumstances, and that's all it is. There are many explanations for a set of circumstances. . . ."

Indeed, there were—and Brown had done a great job of pointing them out.

He then moved on to the bullet, which he believed to be the definitive piece of evidence of the state's case. There was only one way to attack its credibility.

"But what [the scientist] said also was that the projectile was markedly deformed." Setting that trap, Neumann explained that ballistics, in his opinion, was not the same as DNA. "Not quite at the same level as what you perhaps had some expectations of before you walked in here."

For the next ten minutes, Neumann talked about speculative matters: Where was all the blood? he asked. If Alan and Terra were murdered inside the McCord home, why wasn't there more blood? Then he called the murders an "elaborate scheme" the Hoover PD fit into a box wrapped around Jeff and Jessica. He said Jeff could have very well fired his gun in the house. But then gave no explanation as to how a matching bullet ended up underneath Alan's body in the trunk of his rental car—that is, other than saying ballistic experts were wrong.

Did the fact that Jessica left the movies and went to a store two miles away make her a murderer?

Of course not.

What about presuming a suspect innocent? Where was the benefit of the doubt? In a facetious tone, mocking Brown's assumptions, Neumann added, "You know,

Mrs. McCord's mother must be lying about Jessica coming by the house around, I believe she said, twelve-thirty. She must be lying about talking to her on the phone . . . and if she's lying, Mrs. McCord is guilty of murder. They want you to take a lot of *little* things and, just for the lack of a better expression, make a mountain out of a molehill. . . ."

Neumann and Wiley did not have a lot to work with. In defending Jessica, their hands were not tied behind their backs, but practically severed. Jessica had not given her attorneys any tangible, clear explanation for the evidence against her. On top of that, she came across as arrogant and even taunting on the witness stand. It was a hard sell to come out and claim that she was telling the truth. But what else could Neumann and Wiley do? They had to fight.

"Circumstances, circumstances, circumstances. How good is it? Well, that's for you to decide."

Neumann went on for another ten minutes, repeating himself many times, then apologizing for repeating himself. Finally, "There's so much at stake here. We're talking about a lady who's got five beautiful children who—well, I appreciate it, ladies and gentlemen. I'll leave the rest of whatever I've missed to Mr. Wiley. . . ."

With that, Neumann passed the torch to his partner. It was quite common in Alabama courtrooms that when two or more lawyers defended a client, both gave closing arguments.

Wiley talked about the idea that it was a capital murder case and a woman's life was at stake. He tried to play on the sensibilities of twelve men and women playing God with a person's life. He cleared up the notion that it was the judge's decision to sentence Jessica—if she was found guilty—to life without parole, or death. The jury was simply there to make recommendations in these matters.

"So, in your deliberations, you've absolutely got to think about your guilty verdict. You are *killing* Jessica McCord, just as surely as if you pulled that switch and electrocuted her, or if you open a little valve and let the lethal fluid into her veins. You have *got* to know that if you find her guilty in this case, you are *executing* Jessica McCord. You are *causing* her death."

Silence.

Wiley was playing the guilt card in more ways than one.

The experienced lawyer carried on, beating the same drum Neumann had just completed, trying to bolster the argument Neumann had made about blood, DNA, ballistics. It sounded as winded and as weak as it did the first time around—only now the jury was tired of hearing it again.

And then Wiley mentioned Dian. "She's telling the truth!" he shouted. "She saw Jessica and Kelley McCord there at twelve-thirty at her house! And because of that fact"—he paused a moment—"they couldn't have been over in Georgia burning that car between one and two [in the morning]."

Exactly what Roger Brown and Laura Hodge had been saying all along.

Wiley continued for another fifteen minutes.

Then Brown got up and gave a rebuttal.

Brown made a great point—he said if the jury was to believe what Wiley and Neumann had argued during their closings, that would mean, simply put, that "everyone is a liar."

Cops.

Doctors.

Scientists.

Every single expert the state presented.

They were the liars and—yes!—Jessica McCord and her mother were the truth tellers.

64

It didn't take long. By 4:45 P.M., Saturday, February 15, 2003, after just two-and-a-half hours of deliberations, the jury foreman indicated that a unanimous decision had been reached.

Jessica sat still as a leaf. No emotion whatsoever.

When polled, each member of the jury stood and answered "guilty."

After a bit of movement amid the whispers in the courtroom, Judge Virginia Vinson explained that everyone was going to be returning on Monday morning, at which time the defense would argue for life; the state for death.

Before any of that, however, the jury would hear testimony as part of the death penalty phase. Then they could deliberate once again and make a recommendation to the judge for life or death. Would Jessica be executed for her crimes, or be sent to prison for the remainder of her natural life? Either way, the outcome was not something Jessica was going to accept without a fight.

Wiley asked the judge if Jessica could have a moment with her family before being taken to jail.

The judge did not hesitate.

"No."

Perhaps she wasn't in the mood to be granting a double murderer any conveniences.

Dian Bailey was on the verge of breaking down when Jessica, being escorted out of the courtroom by two guards, mouthed, "It's okay." Life or death was her future, but . . . it's okay?

Members of the Bates and Klugh families cried. There was no jubilation or pending celebration in learning that what you had known all along—but had held out the slightest bit of hope was not true—was now a fact.

Jessica McCord had murdered Alan and Terra.

If anything, it was time to commemorate two lives lost and think about how the family members were going to address the one person responsible for those deaths.

Two days later, on the morning of February 17, 2003, Jessica was marshaled back into the courtroom. This time, however, she did not wear a slick blue suit coat, white shirt and black shoes with flashy buckles. She was now dressed in an Alabama Corrections Department jumper.

Dian Bailey took the stand first. Jessica's mother told stories of Jessica being beaten as a child by her natural father, George Callis. Much of the animosity between Callis and Dian postdivorce, Dian suggested, was centered around visitation rights. The implication was that none of what Jessica had done could be considered her fault alone, simply because it had happened to her as a child. She had been hardwired.

In many ways, this was true. Yet, on the other side of the argument, how many kids out in the world had undergone the same abusive treatment and *did not* grow up to be double murderers?

Jessica testified next. She talked about her children. How much they needed her. Especially her four-month-old. She didn't allow the young children to visit her in prison. Not because jail was not the right place for a child to see his or her mother, or the environment was not conducive to rearing children, but, Jessica said, because "there's germs and stuff in jail."

Jessica talked about high school and her grades. She said she had gone to a "school for the gifted." It was, in some ways, sad to hear that a woman with so much promise as a high-school student had gotten pregnant, dropped out and then led a life of constant struggling. Jessica wanted it all, but in her mind a wonderful husband, a house and child weren't enough. And when Alan decided to leave the marriage, well, she couldn't take it.

She snapped.

Jessica's tone was more subdued, now that she had been convicted. At times she drifted off into stories of sitting, talking to her children, explaining life to them.

When Roger Brown cross-examined Jessica, he focused on her and Alan's first child—the pregnancy that led to their marriage.

"You told Kelly McCloskey (the court reporter during the deposition) . . . 'I don't know why he even wants [Samantha]. She's not his.' Is that what you said?"

"I didn't say that to her exactly, no. And as I just stated, he is her father on her birth certificate."

"But he's not her father biologically?"

"No, he's not. Not to my knowledge, he's not."

"So you became pregnant by someone else?"

"I became pregnant and, unfortunately, the time is in question, yes."

"So you lied to Alan about him—"

But Jessica wouldn't allow Brown to finish. "No."

"—him impregnating you?"

"Absolutely not! Never. Alan was at [college] when that happened, and his entire family knows it."

The bottom line here was that the Bates marriage was based on a lie; Alan had married Jessica out of responsibility to a child that wasn't his.

Philip Bates, who had learned recently that he had prostate cancer, sat on the stand next. Brown questioned him about the children and their "monstrously different" attitudes whenever they came from Dian Bailey's house. It took about two days, Philip figured, after Jessica had them, before the Bates family could get the children back into "a routine."

Brown asked Philip if he ever asked Alan about Samantha being his child.

"On two occasions," Philip said, "I specifically remember asking him, was he sure it was his child, and he just shrugged it off. 'Oh, Dad, sure it is.'"

Jessica was still lying. Here she was facing her mortality, and yet still not ready to be remorseful or come to grips with the fact that she could be sentenced to death.

Both sides gave closing arguments, each, of course, standing on his side of the death penalty.

The judge told the jury what it needed to do.

The jurors returned ninety minutes later.

Life without parole was the recommendation. The vote, however, had said something about Jessica Bates McCord: seven for life, five for death. There were five human beings on that jury who believed Jessica should die for her crimes.

The judge wasn't prepared to render her sentence just yet, though. She needed to study the evidence and read through the testimony given that day. She had to make a conscious decision based on the jury's advice.

Word was that Jeff McCord, understanding that one jury had seen through Jessica's lies already, wasn't willing to roll the dice any longer. He was now itching to cut a deal.

The more compelling news, however, had little to do with Jeff or Jessica directly. Behind closed doors Roger Brown and Laura Hodge were preparing cases against two people connected to the McCords in relation to Alan's and Terra's murders—both of whom were about to be indicted.

65

It wasn't necessarily closure the families wanted. Just truth. The Bateses needed to know what happened. They felt Jeff McCord could give that to them. Roger Brown waited until after Jessica's trial, because he didn't want one case to meddle or cause problems with the other. But Jessica had been found guilty, the jury recommending life. It was time to go to Jeff and see if he wanted to talk.

Now or never.

The state offered Jeff two consecutive life terms in trade for the truth. All of it. Step-by-step, what happened? When? Where? How?

Jeff thought about it. Jessica's jury had spoken loud and clear. Why would a second jury believe him?

Jeff called his attorneys.

"I'll take it."

66

Hoover PD detective sergeant Tom McDanal asked everyone in the room if they were ready.

Head nods and "okays" followed.

"Testing, one, two, three, four . . . five," McDanal said aloud, adjusting the tape recorder.

It was 9:20 A.M., on April 15, 2003.

From there, Roger Brown took over. They sat inside the jury room adjacent to Judge Virginia Vinson's courtroom. Laura Hodge sat next to Brown; McDanal there at the table next to them; Hoover PD detective Laura Brignac next to McDanal; Jeff McCord's attorney, Mike Shores, sat next to his client.

There was a numbing sense of irony present in the room that no one needed to acknowledge. It was just there. Like the hum of the air ducts. Jeff had been in this same position in years past—but on the opposite side of the microphone. Now Jeff was the perp. His story being put on tape. How the tables had turned! And over what? A woman? Jeff McCord felt he was facing charges of double murder because his wife, a woman he had loved—maybe too much—and obeyed—without question—had asked him to help her get rid of a problem.

That turned into two "problems," essentially.

"Mr. McCord," Roger Brown said, "uh . . . I'm going to go over the things we went over a little earlier, and that we discussed with your attorney yesterday."

Jeff nodded. Looked away.

"Um . . . in return for the reduction of charges that we made," Brown continued, "you have agreed to fully disclose to us everything you know regarding the circumstances of the deaths of Alan and Terra Bates, leading up to it and following it."

Brown then explained how he would administer "an oath," and everyone expected Jeff McCord to be truthful. It was that, or the deal was off.

"We may wish to administer a polygraph at a later time to satisfy ourselves of the veracity of what you have to say. Do you understand all that?"

"Yes."

Jeff McCord was ordered to raise his right hand.

They talked formalities first: address, age, former job as a police officer. And then the day—February 15, 2002, a little over a year ago now—which Brown referred to as "the occurrence."

The life and death of two fine people could be refined into two meaningless words of such little value. It wasn't Brown's word, but a professional way to address the murders on tape.

"The occurrence."

Jeff talked about how his day-to-day life was with Jessica, her three kids and the kid they had together. Things seemed all right at first. He loved the woman.

A large truck drove by the window outside as Jeff spoke. Roger Brown waited for the noise to subside, then got back to the interview.

The former Pelham police officer was passive. Quite

taken aback by the process of talking about what led up to the murders, and what actually had happened that day. Brown asked Jeff if he knew Alan Bates at the time Jeff and Jessica got married.

"I knew who Mr. Bates *was*," Jeff said. "No, I hadn't—I don't even think I had met him once at the time."

Jeff married Jessica, and yet he had not met her ex-husband, who had been, according to what Jessica had told Jeff, a violent nuisance in her life. Someone to fear. It was clear from Jeff's responses that Jessica had married him out of spite, wanting to one-up Alan and his then-future marriage to Terra.

Jeff said he met Alan for the first time in August 2000.

"Next to the interstate in Montevallo."

Alan picked up the girls. Terra wasn't with him.

Brown moved on to what had become a pivotal point in the postdivorce relationship between Alan and Jessica: the fact that Jessica withdrew the children from the school system and began homeschooling them. Not because she wanted the children to have a better education, but for the sole purpose of hiding them from Alan.

After Brown asked the question, making reference to the fact that Jessica was hiding the family so Alan couldn't find them, Jeff took a deep breath. Sighed. Shook his head. It was one of those *oh yeah* moments, as if he'd forgotten how devious his wife had become. Because he lived in the situation day in and day out, Jeff speculated, it was harder for him to see what was happening in front of his eyes.

It was just easier to go along with Jessica than to fight her.

Jeff could understand how wrong that all was now. He had gone along with Jessica on all these matters because she was his wife and he believed that's what husbands were supposed to do.

Obedience.

As Jeff explained it, near the time Jessica proclaimed to be homeschooling the kids, somebody from the Hoover central school office, or Green Valley Elementary, he could not recall which, called the house.

"Yes?" Jessica said. "What is it?"

"Due to some sort of bureaucratic snafu, the records weren't in order. The girls cannot continue to be students at the school and have to be removed."

Apparently, the house the McCords lived in on Myrtlewood Drive in Hoover was not on file, Jeff said. It appeared the kids were going to the wrong school. So the school had them removed—which played right into Jessica's desire to hide them from Alan.

From there, she simply decided not to enroll them in another school.

During this same time period, Jeff explained, he never witnessed any animosity between Alan and Jessica regarding the kids or visitations. This was an important point for Roger Brown. The problems leading up to the murders began, by Jeff McCord's account, during the fall of 2000, a year and a half before he and Jessica murdered Alan and Terra.

After Jeff gave a detailed account of the murders, placing himself behind the murder weapon, Brown asked him to go through how he and Jessica disposed of the bodies. It was clear to Brown that Jeff was following Jessica's lead during the entire ordeal. She directed. Jeff listened. Whenever she panicked or lost her head, it was Jeff who took over. The Hoover PD had been close in putting together the murder and cleanup afterward—90 percent of the department's theory proved accurate, as far as Jeff's explanation of that day and night went.

Jeff said that as they were on the way to the dump that Saturday morning to get rid of some of the evidence, his chief phoned.

"I get a call. . . . I get a *call* from . . . work." He was told either to phone the GBI himself or have his attorney do it. "We get back to the house, I call this number I'm given . . . and as it turns out . . . I spoke with [someone from the GBI], identified myself, and he told me he had no clue why I would need to call him."

Brown confirmed with Jeff that Jessica's high-school friend in Montevallo—the house where they had stayed on the night before they were arrested—a guy who was now facing perjury charges for lying during his grand jury testimony—did know where the storage facility was that Jessica had placed some of the evidence in. According to another source that police had interviewed, a cellmate of Jessica's said that Jessica and Jeff rented a storage facility. Inside the small unit Jessica had apparently put plastic bags containing "bloody stuff," along with furniture and the luggage Terra and Alan had with them. Jessica was said to have arranged for her high-school friend Michael Upton and her stepfather to "clean out the storage unit" in exchange for $500 cash to split.

Upton turned around and, according to prosecutors, lied during his grand jury testimony when asked about this same incident.

He, along with another person closely tied to the case, were about to be indicted, Brown told Jeff.

Jeff laughed at that.

As the interview drew to a close, Jeff seemed more relaxed and even in a good mood. Not once during the interview did Jeff McCord express any sorrow for the victims—nor any remorse whatsoever for killing them. He came across cold and calculating, as if he were the one walking away with a win. There were times, as chilling as it sounded, when Jeff laughed out loud. The man had shot at point-blank range two people he had no connection to, two people he did not know the slightest about, and he laughed when telling portions of that story.

Regardless of what family and former friends would later say, that behavior alone said a lot about who Jeff McCord was.

67

On April 25, 2003, shortly after Jeff formally pleaded guilty, Jessica was sentenced to life without parole. In the end the judge took the advice of the jury and signed the Sheriff's Commitment Order, sending Jessica to prison for the remainder of her natural life. She was never going to see freedom again. After Judge Vinson handed down the sentence, she asked Jessica if there was anything she had to say for herself. Maybe some explanation? Sorrow? Remorse?

Jessica declined.

Asked later on by a reporter if she wanted to make a comment, Jessica "smiled," Carol Robinson noted, and said, "Not hardly."

Before being whisked off to prison, Jessica was allowed to spend some time with friends and family, including her mother and grandmother, who were in court for the sentencing. Jessica laughed as she chatted with her family. What was so funny, no one actually knew. But the fact that she would appeal her case was probably fueling Jessica's hostile, defiant attitude. It was still all a joke to Jessica McCord. There's no doubt she saw herself getting out of prison one day when the appeals court heard her plea.

John Wiley was a bit more grounded in reality. He

showed professionalism as he left the court, telling reporters, "The death penalty is wrong in any case and this case is no exception, so we're very pleased and relieved that Mrs. McCord is delivered of that possibility of being killed by the state of Alabama. "She gets to turn her attention now to her appeal, and, hopefully, one day she'll have a new trial and a more favorable outcome."

Jeff and Jessica McCord ended up on the same bus heading out to prison later that day. There was one bus. All prisoners boarded. The males were separated from the females by a fence, but they could still speak to one another.

As Jessica stepped up onto the bus, shackles clanking, a cocky smile across her face, she noticed her husband sitting in the back among a group of inmates.

In her sarcastic way, quite mean-spirited and vile, Jessica stopped, smiled and looked at Jeff. By this time she knew Jeff had come clean with his version of the murders and had cut himself a deal. Up until this point Jessica had had nothing but good things to say about Jeff.

"Hey, everyone," Jessica said as loud as she could, the entire bus stopping to look up, "that's my husband." She pointed Jeff out. "He's a cop!"

Jessica sat down and faced the front.

Due to how high profile my case was, it is rather safe to say that virtually everyone in metro-Birmingham knew that I was a police officer, Jeff McCord wrote to me after he was asked if this verbal assault against his character by Jessica had caused him any problems later on when he got to prison. It's no secret that inmates are not too fond of cops as cellmates.

Overall, I have had no real problems as a result of it or in relation to my former profession. . . . I have been housed in either protective custody or administrative segregation depending on my placement.

68

Roger Brown was convinced Dian Bailey had lied to him while testifying during her daughter's trial. A grand jury believed the evidence Brown had presented in relation to those charges. Now Brown was determined to prosecute Dian Bailey and the McCords' friend, Michael Upton, who, the prosecutor's office believed, had lied during his grand jury testimony. How dare these people think they can lie to the police and prosecutors investigating a double homicide? For what? To protect murderers? Reaffirming Brown's contention that Upton lied about the storage facility, Brown got the results of Jeff McCord's polygraph, and the examiner felt Jeff was telling the truth.

On Tuesday, August 5, 2003, Michael Upton was in court facing a jury on charges of hindering prosecution and perjury for his role in lying during the investigation into the deaths of Alan and Terra Bates. Upton was said to have told varying stories regarding that storage facility and the possibility of potential evidence Jessica had hidden.

Investigators never found the storage unit or the evidence. Still, Upton, a man in his early thirties, sat and listened as prosecutor Doug Davis explained to a jury the state's case against him.

Davis said Upton repeatedly changed his story, which led police to believe he was lying. More than that, Davis was firm in his personal belief that Upton had "decided loyalty to his friends [was] more important than the truth. He chose to cross the line of criminality."

Richard Poff, Michael Upton's lawyer, explained that his client had no idea a storage facility existed; he only knew of a storage unit that Albert Bailey had rented. Apparently, Upton got mixed up in the fiasco when Jessica asked him to help her stepfather move some furniture from Bailey's storage unit over to her mother's house so the kids would have something to sleep on while she was in jail.

"It was a misunderstanding," Poff argued. "This is all a tale of sound and fury signifying *nothing*."

The star witness of the day, after Roger Brown and detective Laura Brignac testified, was one of Jessica's former cellmates. She told police that Michael Upton knew of the "bloody stuff" in the storage unit.

The next day, August 6, Jeff McCord sat and, for the first time publicly, described how he and Jessica had murdered Alan and Terra Bates, and then went about an elaborate plan to try and cover up the crimes.

Listening to Jeff's graphic, detailed descriptions of the murders, Michael Upton sat with a stoic flush of sadness written across his face. At times tears streamed down his cheeks. Upton later said that none of it seemed real until Jeff McCord illustrated the murders so vividly on the witness stand. Upton said that up until that moment, he still held "on to some hope that they (Jeff and Jessica) were still innocent."

Upton took the stand himself and told the jury he

had no idea Jessica had rented a storage facility. He also said he "suffered from memory loss" due to a car accident he was in years before. Because of the injuries he had sustained, Upton testified, he "easily [became] confused under stress, which may have led to a misunderstanding during grand jury proceedings."

Shocking the courtroom, Upton then said that his wife, pregnant with his child, dropped dead of a heart attack just two months ago.

Closing arguments were heard later that afternoon; then the jury was asked to deliberate the case. Perjury, a Class C felony, was good for ten years in the state pen if a judge felt inclined to give such a stiff sentence.

The next morning, after three hours of discussions, the jury found Michael Upton guilty of perjury (the judge dropped an additional charge of obstruction).

Michael Upton was devastated, his attorney said after the trial.

A little over a month later, Upton was sentenced to "spend a year in a work-release program," followed by five years of supervised probation. This meant Michael Upton would spend his nights in jail, but be allowed to leave during the day and work outside the prison.

69

Dian Bailey's alleged crime, although similar to Michael Upton's, might have had far greater implications on Jessica McCord's case, prosecutor Teresa McClendon explained to a jury on the morning of October 27, 2003. The fact that Dian lied during Jessica's trial could have influenced jurors to acquit her daughter, essentially allowing a murderer to escape justice.

That made this particular crime of perjury inexcusable, McClendon suggested.

The prosecutor told jurors how Jeff and Jessica carried out this vicious, premeditated double homicide with callousness and hatred. She spoke of how they lured Terra and Alan into the house. How they made them feel comfortable, using the children as bait. But then Jeff shot them four times each without warning.

These were evil people. Anyone who helped them should be viewed the same.

And so here comes the mother of one of the accused, who had walked into a courtroom some months ago and stomped all over the law. Above anyone else, Dian Bailey should have known better—she had worked for the court system herself for nearly two decades.

* * *

In his opening argument Bill Dawson downplayed his client's responsibility, talking about Dian's emotional state at the time, telling jurors she was "working full-time, caring for a father with Alzheimer's and a mother with pneumonia"—all while taking care of her daughter's four children.

The woman was burned-out. She didn't know up from down, when she had seen her daughter and when she hadn't.

"She told what she *thought* was the truth," Dawson said.

Jeff came in and told his tale of murder once again, stunning another jury with his words. However, nowhere in Jeff's version of the events did he testify to stopping at Dian's house at or near midnight, which was what Dian had told jurors during Jessica's trial.

There was no way to confuse this detail—because it never happened.

Dawson attacked Jeff's credibility, implying that he was now on the state's payroll—so to speak—and part of the prosecution's team, fulfilling his duty as part of a deal he had signed to escape the death penalty.

Jeff could be back on the street, inside thirty years, Dawson said.

Sheron Vance, the Morgan County Sheriff's Office lieutenant who had gone with Bureau agent Kimberly Williams to Dian's house that Saturday morning, said Dian was "visibly surprised" when Jessica told police she had stopped by her mother's house the previous night, near midnight.

An unplanned lie. Just tossed out there.

"I was looking," said Vance, "right at Dian. She had just been standing there, staring into space the entire time." But when Jessica mentioned to Williams that she had seen her mother the night before, Dian "rolled her eyes and took a step back. . . ."

Fifty-eight-year-old Dian Bailey decided against taking the witness stand.

That out of the way, closing arguments were next.

The jury took thirty minutes to convict Dian, completing a hat trick of guilty verdicts for the prosecution. Dian didn't respond to the verdict. She sat, no emotion, dumbfounded and confused.

On December 9, 2003, Jefferson County Circuit Court judge Mike McCormick gave Dian Bailey an eight-year sentence. The courtroom was silent while McCormick spoke. Filled with whispers afterward.

Eight years. *Ouch!*

Jessica's mother would spend one year in a Shelby County work-release program—same as Michael Upton— and an additional seven years on probation, with no actual jail time.

Before he was finished, McCormick asked Dian if she had anything to say for herself.

Like her daughter, Dian said no.

"Apparently," McCormick concluded, "out of some misguided loyalty, you chose to lie. This is a very serious matter."

Finally, during the summer of 2004, after the Klugh and Bates families filed a $150 million wrongful-death suit against Jeff and Jessica McCord, both families won an additional judgment that allowed them to collect any money Jeff McCord might make from a book or movie deal throughout his lifetime.

Then they went after Jessica for the same.

Neither Jeff nor Jessica would ever profit from their crimes.

"This sort of settlement is, first and foremost, to prevent the criminals from profiting from their crime," Kevin Bates told me in closing. "Should any money ever come of selling Alan and Terra's story, we just wanted to ensure that every penny went to Alan's girls—who have truly lost the most from Jeff and Jessica's horrific and selfish actions."

70

Terra's father, Tom Klugh, didn't need to know any more about life than he had learned over the past several years. He had lost his only child to a cruel murder. He was divorced. Then, with all of the trials and lawsuit hearings behind him, Tom Klugh got a call from his doctor.

Prostate cancer.

A rough road didn't even begin to describe those past few years for Tom.

But then others had it worse, Tom knew deep down. There were other people in the world suffering a hell of a lot more than he was. He didn't want people feeling sorry for him. He just wanted to go away for some quiet time and begin to rebuild and recover.

That story of Terra tossing her red boots into the stream back in the early 1970s when Tom and his wife and Terra lived in Cullowhee, North Carolina, kept coming back up for Tom as he went over his life up to this point. Tom had always felt strongly that Terra's life had been spared by God on that day. She was *allowed* to live by her Maker because there was more for her to do. In dying with Alan by the hand of evil, Tom still felt Terra's mission in this life had been fulfilled.

"I had heard from some people who saw Terra and Alan that day of the deposition," Tom recalled, referring to the hours before Alan and Terra were murdered, "when they were leaving a local restaurant, that they never seemed happier. They were walking away from this restaurant across from the Alabama Theatre. . . . I got the feeling that they, well, that they *knew* they were leaving. I know it sounds a little hokey, but they were really, really happy at that time."

The question that bothered Tom was *Why?*

After Terra and Alan's memorial service, Tom took a portion of Terra's ashes, a small bit from the vase, and placed it in a vial. He didn't know what he was going to do with the vial when he took it, but he felt confident that the purpose would come to him someday down the road.

Now, many months after the trials and convictions, with all the madness of the murders behind him, after thinking things through, it was perfectly clear to Tom what he needed to do with that vial of Terra's ashes.

He called his brother. "I need you to come with me."

"Where?"

"Cullowhee."

They took off and made the trip into the Blue Ridge Mountains. It was a pilgrimage, Tom recalled, more than a simple road trip two brothers had embarked on. They headed back to the place where, "by all rights," Tom said, Terra should have been killed nearly twenty-nine years prior—that is, had God wanted to take her home on that day she wandered down by the river. It only seemed fitting to Tom that some of his daughter's ashes be spread over—or returned to—that small creek she had almost fallen into and drowned in so many years before.

An ode to her memory?

Perhaps.

A way to honor her memory?

Maybe.

For Tom, it was more like paying God back—giving Him the respect He deserved. Maybe thanking Him for giving Tom those additional decades with his daughter.

Tom and his brother couldn't really get down to the creek edge because it had grown in so thickly with brush and trees. But there was a small bridge they could stand on. It extended over the water rushing fast underneath.

"There . . . let's go," Tom said.

He opened the vial and said something to himself.

Paused.

Then, standing in the middle of the bridge, he spread the ashes over the water.

Some of the solid, heavier pieces of ash fell into the creek and made small splashes. However, the remainder, which had turned into a large cloud of dust as it headed down toward the water, was "picked up," Tom recalled, "by a gust of wind and carried into the air," as if there were somebody waiting to scoop it up into her hands.

"I get chilly bumps on my skin just thinking about it," Tom remembered.

Looking at this display of what Tom could see only as an angel picking Terra up and carrying her off, he thought of what Terra might have said, had she been there in the flesh standing next to him on that bridge.

In the flesh, of course, because it was so obvious Terra's spirit was there with Tom and his brother that day.

Okay, Dad, you're here; I've done this. . . . Life is good.

The circle of his daughter's life, from where Tom Klugh stood, was complete. She and Alan, Tom was now certain, could rest in peace together.

EPILOGUE

Jeff McCord seemed to express a bit of repentance for his crimes. Yet, in writing to me, Jeff's words of remorse sounded more self-serving than sorrowful. In fact, I sensed a narcissistic tone in Jeff's syntax, and thought this was probably one of the reasons why he and Jessica had gotten along so well and meshed together so effortlessly when it came time to commit murder. That is, when you come down to it, Jeff McCord—no matter what he says now—never once voiced any opposition to Jessica's plan. We could even say that, in many ways, Jeff *fueled* Jessica's desire to kill.

There is NO acceptable reason for my doing what I did to put myself where I am, Jeff wrote to me in February 2009. *[There is an] . . . agony on those who have suffered and continue to do so as a result of my actions. What I did was WRONG! I very much regret my actions and the problems arising from them.*

I'm unclear if Jeff is sorry for killing two people, or for getting caught.

I readily admit, he continued, *that I allowed myself to be unduly influenced by Jessica. Also, I allowed myself to be convinced that my viable options were limited to the one I chose.*

I allowed myself to become isolated. None of that in any way excuses my reprehensible course of action.

Jeff never addressed Terra or Alan by name.

Seeing that he was at least responsible enough to answer my requests for interviews and communicate with me, I asked Jeff why he would not want to sit down and tell me his complete story. Get it all out there. You know, his version of the marriage from the inside. Truly explain to my readers how Jessica had managed to manipulate him into shooting two human beings eight times while they sat in his house.

Jeff had taken an oath to protect and to serve. His job was to help people. Save people. Prevent crime. He had expressed a longing, at one time, to help children. How had the tables turned on him in such a violent manner? Where did everything go wrong?

Jeff's attitude baffled me. I told him he had nothing to lose at this point. His appeal was denied. He was not getting out of prison for, at the least, twenty-five years.

Many convicted murderers hold on to the thinnest thread of hope—thinking that someday some hotshot, enthusiastic young lawyer will take their case and spring them on a technicality or a glitch in the trial, thus rescuing them from the miserable life of prison. With that in mind, I thought Jeff would see things differently because he had been a cop. He knows the law. He understands how the system works. Opening up, giving me the answers to those hard questions, could only help Jeff.

But he refused, and sent me this, instead:

I obviously should have gone about things far differently than I did. I exercised poor judgment and made a plethora of poor and bad decisions. I also readily concede that I could have and should have taken steps to prevent things or to prevent the situation I was in to deteriorate

to the point it did. With all of that said . . . I still made
the choices I made.

Then, in what can be construed as a bizarre choice
of words, Jeff added:

Again, I do not regret my actions and am sorry for the
adversive [sic] impact they had and continue to have on
the Bates, the Klughs, my former step-daughters, my chil-
dren, my family, Jessica's family, the few friends I have
at this point, as well as the other people involved with or
connected to my case in some way. What I did is most
likely inexplicable and inexcusable at least where most
people are concerned.

"Most people"? "Most likely"? The guy did not regret
his actions? What was Jeff McCord saying to us here?
  Jeff McCord is a strange human being. Jeff was a lot
smarter on paper than his behavior would lead you
to believe. Something, somewhere, went wrong for
Jeff. What, exactly, only Jeff McCord knows.

  Jessica is another story. We can see that some of her
behaviors were hardwired into her fragile psyche as a
child. It might seem to an outside observer that Jessica
McCord was a sociopath. She fits rather perfectly into
about 90 percent of the "sociopathic" profile Dr.
Robert Hare and Dr. Hervey Cleckley designed many
years ago. Cleckley outlined sixteen behaviors on a
checklist of sociopathic behavior, including unrelia-
bility, insincerity, suicidal threats and a host of other
behaviors and attitudes that seemed to fit Jessica
McCord quite closely.
  I wrote to Jessica repeatedly. I called and e-mailed
her mother, Dian Bailey, repeatedly. I never heard

from either one of them. I did hear a lot of talk that went on behind the scenes—excuses on Jessica's part regarding why she couldn't talk to me. I guess, in the end, I wondered if Jessica had agreed to interviews, what I could possibly learn or believe. What would she have to say to me? Maybe one of the reasons why she did not want to talk to me is because she understands I cannot be manipulated—that I would be able to see through her lies.

Still, as I was completing this book, I heard from a former cellmate of Jessica's. She expressed a desire on Jessica's part to answer some of my questions: *I am an acquaintance of Jessica . . . [and she] has asked me to contact you. . . . She is currently in segregation. . . .*

(It seemed whenever I spoke to a source inside the prison, Jessica was "in seg." Or in the psych ward. Or complaining about the treatment she was receiving by guards. The universe is a strange, unforgiving, mysterious place, whereby some are inclined to believe that what you give, you get back. It would seem that a majority—not all—of the turmoil and trauma Jessica had caused others in her life on the outside is coming back to her ten-fold now that she is locked up.)

In response to the e-mail I received from Jessica's former cellmate, I sent the following:

Thanks for writing. Please tell Mrs. McCord that I have given her __and__ her mother several opportunities to talk about her case. Time is running out. If she wants to contact me, she should write me a letter and explain all she can in that letter—but she needs to do it quick. I have read her testimony and I find one hole in it after the next. I have interviewed scores of people (former friends, neighbors, former and present inmates, and many, many others) and there's not a lot of her story that checks out.

In her letter, she should tell me about Jeff, the type of person he was, and why he would kill two people he didn't know. What purpose did Jeff have? She should tell me about her childhood. The abuse she suffered at the hands of George Callis. She should talk about why she kept the kids from seeing Alan when the court ordered the visitations (I have hundreds and hundreds of pages of documents from several different courts). I don't want to hear lies. I want truth.

But she needs to do this quickly.

I was told for the next three weeks that Jessica was "in the process" of writing to me. That she was eager to talk. That she wanted to tell "her side" of this story. "Get the truth out." That she had "things" to say about Alan, about Terra, about what "really" happened.

As of this writing, I have not heard from her.

Her behavior here fits flawlessly into the austere, "poor me" image Jessica McCord likes to project of herself. She wants the people around her to think of her in one light, but she behaves in an entirely different manner. She is incapable, at this point, of explaining herself. Unless she comes clean and begins to accept that she has been convicted of double murder, Jessica McCord is only fooling herself.

I'm told from prison sources that Jessica is on Lithium and all sorts of other antidepressant and antianxiety medications. I'm told she is constantly in the medical ward of the prison. That she routinely complains about prison life (what a shocker!), the conditions in which she lives and the treatment she receives behind bars.

Once again, everyone around Jessica McCord seems to be against her.

I was told by a few sources that after I "had called

Jessica's two churches (for interviews) . . . as a result, one church will not replace her Bible that was illegally taken from her when she got sent to seg."

So, therefore, I am the one responsible for Jessica not being allowed to read the Word of God.

Go figure.

From prison Jessica has told people that an agreement she signed with the court prohibits her from speaking about her case. That, incredibly, other agreements having to do with the lawsuit the Bateses filed—which she claims to have been "forced to sign"—will not allow her to talk to anyone until Alan's girls are adults. She even went so far as to say that if she talks to me, she could have her "canteen account" seized under the agreement.

This is all ludicrous, of course. None of it is true. This is Jessica, once again, lying to support her claim that jailhouse rules force her to be silent about her case.

Ridiculous.

I was also told that a family member is sneaking one of her children into the visiting section of the prison when a court order spells out clearly that the child is *not* to be near the prison.

Jessica McCord is playing by her own rules once again.

And yet, throughout it all, she has never once expressed an iota of sorrow for the deaths she is responsible for. Nor has she ever shown a bit of compassion for those who have lost so much in being forced to say an early good-bye to Alan and Terra. This behavior Jessica is showing us behind bars falls right in line with the character of the narcissist: her world is her stage, the people around her the players in a drama she continues to broadcast to those who want to participate still.

* * *

As my narrative spelled out, I wrote to George Callis, Jessica's biological father. He is in prison serving a life sentence for murder. George wrote back— boy, did he ever! A manifesto, to be exact, that is truly unreadable. George is a self-described "born-again" Christian. Every thought, every word, every sentence, every page of what he wrote to me, speaks of some sort of "vision" from the Holy Spirit. He'd begin with the first-person pronoun "I" and then break off into quotes from the Bible. God bless, George; he has found meaning in the Holy Scriptures and feels the Holy Spirit is actively involved in every aspect of his life. He feels forgiven, obviously, for the nightmare he has caused. None of it, though, was helpful in understanding how his daughter might have turned out to be a murderer—*ahem*, like him.

In closing, I'd like to say that in all of the books I've written, in addition to the cases I have researched and studied over the past ten years, I have never seen such a disregard for authority. All murder is, inherently, evil and senseless. We know that. All murderers are, in every respect, coldhearted and immoral. We understand that, too. But when you have two people murdered by a woman who had claimed to love one of them once, and by a man who had been trained to preserve, protect and save lives, there is an additional layer of cruelty, insensitivity and selfishness involved. That is, besides inviting into the conversation the absolute disregard for relative morality.

Remember, Jessica McCord claims to be a Christian. She says she loves her children. Yet, when the facts are reviewed, we can see that Jessica McCord showed that love and dedication to Christ by killing her children's father and stepmother.

ACKNOWLEDGMENTS

First and foremost, I need to thank someone who has been a major part of my career, pushing it forward behind the scenes, talking me up to booksellers and truly promoting the idea that the work I do is worthy of an audience. Doug Mendini, the sales manager at Kensington Publishing Corporation, has worked doggedly promoting me as an author and a journalist, screaming from the sidelines that my books are much more than your average quickie true-crime pulp paperback. Doug is a generous human being with his time and truly believes in the books he works so hard to get out to the buying public.

Court reporters Ann Rushing and Kelly Alexander were helpful. *Birmingham News* reporter Carol Robinson made a few things much easier for me. Carol is one of those rare, honest-to-goodness, old-school reporters writing stories simply because she loves the work. I also appreciate the documents Carol sent me and her insight into the daily nuances of Jessica's trial.

The Bates family and Tom Klugh were tremendous. I am grateful for their courage and also the trust they put in me to share those memories of Alan and Terra, along with those anecdotes that added so much to the narrative.

Jupiter Entertainment producer Donna Dudek was instrumental in helping me gather documents, photos and other research. Donna is one of the most competent and thorough researchers/television producers I have ever met. I cannot thank Donna enough for all the help she has given me throughout the years.

Captain Greg Rector, of the Hoover PD, was especially helpful in setting up interviews and bridging the gap between myself and some of the investigators involved in this case. I owe Hoover PD chief Nic Derzis a special consideration for allowing his fine officers to chat with me about the case. Laura Brignac was extremely helpful. Additionally, I want to thank GBI investigator Kimberly Williams, prosecutor Roger Brown and GBI special agent Tom Davis Jr. Of course, every investigator on this case was helpful, even if I didn't interview him or her. This was one of those investigations that turned out to be a true team effort in every sense of the word. It took several law enforcement agencies to put together a case—in record time—against Jessica and Jeff McCord. That takes professionalism, tenacity, experience. These are fine men and women. They all deserve my respect and admiration.

I've thanked the usual suspects in my previous books. You all know who you are. Without you, I could not do this.

April, Mathew, Jordon, Regina.

I cannot write a book without thanking my readers, who continue to come back book after book. The letters and e-mails I receive are very important to me. I treasure each one of them. Every comment—good, bad or indifferent—is taken into account as I approach each book. I am extremely grateful for every reader. I do this year after year because you keep asking me to do so. I have the best fans in the business!

DEATH TRAP UPDATE 2012

The most common questions that come in after readers finish this book are: "What happened to the children?" and "Where are they now?"

People want to know how Alan Bates's kids made out and where they ended up. I might say that I didn't include this information in the first edition, as I said then, because the families asked me not to do so. I wanted to respect their privacy.

I did reach out to Alan's brothers recently and asked the question, noting how eager readers are to learn more about the kids' lives now. I think the concern by many is that Jessica McCord is somehow seeing and still manipulating the kids.

"Alan's daughters, now a decade beyond this tragedy," Kevin Bates told me in July 2012, "continue to miss their father and stepmother, as they themselves enter adulthood. Samantha manages a popular wine shop and restaurant in the northern suburbs of Atlanta, where she lives with her one-year-old son, who carries his grandfather's name. McKenna recently returned from studies of global leadership in South Africa as she continues pursuing a degree in anthropology with minors in art history and music."

They sound like wonderful kids, who've managed to

grow into productive, healthy, caring and pleasant adults, despite a twisted psychopath having used them as pawns in what was an unspeakable horror. I love to hear of success stories in the face of tragedy. Truly, this is one!

"The families of Alan and Terra Bates continue to enjoy hearing and sharing memories of their loved ones from family and friends that adored them far and wide," Kevin concluded.

I've heard from sources that some of Jessica's younger children visit her in prison and stay in contact with her through Jessica's family members. If true, I find this quite disturbing. In my opinion, I feel that by killing Alan and Terra Bates, Jessica should not have the right to see any of her kids.

Jeff McCord's mother passed away; the prison, I'm told, allowed him to attend the funeral.

Terra's father is doing well.

Now, from what I have heard, Jessica McCord continues to try to manipulate and con her fellow inmates with her wicked ways of lying. I have been told she's tried to manipulate the system from the inside out, but she was quickly found out and punished for her behavior.

"I know that Jessica has gotten pregnant while incarcerated and might have had another abortion," said a source who used to correspond with her. "That figure," the same source added, "of how many abortions she's had throughout her life, I have heard, could be in the neighborhood of twenty."

There is no way to verify this information, of course. However, by studying Jessica's life and looking deeply at her history, I can state without doubt that Jessica McCord is a sociopath who believes that her truth is the only truth, and she will *never* change. So, for me, it is entirely believable that this devastating tally could be accurate.

For more real-life crime drama,
read a preview sample of
M. William Phelps's
next riveting nonfiction thriller,

Bad Girls

Coming soon from Kensington Publishing Corp.

Turn the page . . .

1

"Something bad may have happened."

It was the only fact she was certain of. Beyond that, the woman thought the victim might be "a friend of her niece's." His name "might have been" Bob. But that was all she knew. She feared the worst, however: that Bob Something was dead. She didn't know the exact address where the police could find him, but she could explain how to drive there, and she would escort cops to the house if they wanted to meet her somewhere in the neighborhood.

On a quiet evening, May 5, 2004, forty-eight-year-old Richard "Rick" Cruz called the Mineral Wells Police Department (MWPD) and explained what his wife, Kathy, had just told him. Both Kathy and Rick were in somewhat of a panicked state. Not freaked out. But their feelings were more of a puzzled, what's-going-on—type thing they didn't quite understand.

"Have you heard anything about someone being shot on Eighteenth Street?" Rick asked the 911 dispatcher.

Rick had the street wrong. It was actually Twentieth Street. Still, dispatch wasn't in the business of sharing information with worried callers phoning in to report gunshots fired at people.

"What other information do you have?" the 911 operator asked.

Rick explained the layout of the neighborhood as best he could. He said he and Kathy weren't all that familiar with Mineral Wells and this particular neighborhood where Bob supposedly lived. They had only heard about it.

The operator said they'd send an officer out to Eighteenth Street to check things out.

Rick and Kathy Cruz lived in Graford, Texas, directly next door to Kathy's mother, Dorothy Louise Smith. Graford is about fifteen miles from Mineral Wells, where the shooting was said to have occurred. Kathy and Rick had arrived home at about 4:30 P.M. Rick was driving. As they exited the vehicle after Rick parked, Kathy's mother, Dorothy, standing on her porch next door, waved them over.

"Come here," Dorothy said. She seemed frazzled and agitated, as if in a hurry to get them over there so she could speak her mind about something.

"What is it?" Kathy asked.

Dorothy was "very upset," Kathy Cruz later explained in a police report. Kathy and Rick noticed Dorothy was on the telephone. Apparently, Kathy found out after walking over and assessing the situation, Dorothy was talking to her other daughter.

Something terrible was happening.

"What is it?" Rick and Kathy asked.

A pause. Then a bombshell: Somebody shot Bob.

Dorothy got off the phone and clarified what she knew. As the story went thus far, somehow, Dorothy explained, Kathy's niece (Dorothy's grandchild)—who had been living with Dorothy intermittently throughout the past year—might be involved in the shooting. Nobody really knew how or why, or any of the circumstances surrounding the story. Just that it was urgent someone get over there to this Bob Something's house immediately.

Rick walked into Dorothy's house. Without explaining what he was doing, according to what he later told police, he headed into his niece's room to have a look around.

"You stay here," Rick said to Kathy, who was becoming more upset by the moment. Kathy's niece had lived with the Cruzes for a while as well. Kathy had been close to her.

The idea Rick had in mind was to see if he could find something in the house that might clarify just what the hell was going on. A note. An e-mail.

Anything.

There was probably a simple answer. Usually there was. People overreact. Perhaps Dorothy, in all of her excitement, had totally misinterpreted the situation and blew it out of proportion. Drama—every family, in some form or fashion, had certain members that thrived on drama.

Upon immediately entering the young girl's room, Rick found an empty gun holster. Exactly what he did not expect.

Where is the weapon?

Then he found an unloaded pistol in a second holster.

This alarmed Rick. The report of a shooting. A gun missing from a holster. Another weapon on the bed in a holster. Rick wasn't Magnum, P.I., but then again, he didn't need to be a private investigator to figure out that something was up. And it didn't look good.

Rick ran out of the room, then out of the house. While outside in the front yard, Rick called the MWPD back on his cell phone.

"Have you found anything?" Rick asked the operator. He sounded more serious.

"No. The officers out at Eighteenth Street haven't located anything suspicious." The dispatcher wondered what was going on. Was this guy—Rick—playing games with the MWPD?

Rick hung up. Then he grabbed Kathy's attention. "Listen, we have to head out to Mineral Wells ourselves and find out what's going on."

Kathy thought about it.

Good idea.

They took off.

On the way to Mineral Wells, having no clue, really, where in that town they were headed, Rick phoned Kathy's sister, her niece's mother, Cindy Meyer (pseudonym), and asked for directions to a house in Mineral Wells that Kathy's niece had been hanging out at and even living in lately. There was even some indication that the niece was working with the guy, Bob, who lived there. Cindy had been to the house.

After getting more detailed directions, Rick decided that he'd better stop first at the MWPD and relay to them what he had uncovered.

"I have the gun," Rick explained, referring to the pistol he had taken out of the room in Dorothy's house. "Do you want it?"

The cop was a bit taken aback. "We need to find that house first, Mr. Cruz. And we need to see if anything happened—then we can take it from there."

Kathy's niece was young—nineteen years old. According to Kathy and Rick, she liked to "get on drugs and exaggerate things." Others had said she liked to brag about being a tough, gangsta-type chick. Although she had been in a relationship with a man, engaged to be married, and had a baby, she was an open and admitted lesbian with scores of sexual partners and girlfriends—plus, drugs had become her life. Who knew what she was into now? Could be just about anything.

They left together, the cop following Rick and Kathy.

Rick pulled onto Eighteenth Street first and didn't seem to know where he was going. He was driving slowly past each house, checking to see if he recognized any of them. In back of him, the cop became more impatient as each block passed. The officer threw up his hands, beckoning Rick to tell him what in the hell was going on here. Was this some sort of a joke?

After a time of Rick's stop-and-go game, the cop got on the telephone with Kathy's sister; she talked him directly over to Twentieth Street.

Finally they arrived at the right house.

Bob.

Patrol corporal Randy Hunter, the participating officer, got out of his cruiser and told Rick, "You stay here by your truck and wait." Hunter said he needed to approach the door by himself.

Procedure.

Hunter knocked on the front door as Rick and Kathy looked on.

No answer.

"I'm going around back," Hunter said. "Stay where you are." He held up his hand as to indicate stop. The plan was, Hunter later said, "to check and see if anybody may have been in the backyard, look around. . . ." See what he could find out.

Nobody seemed to be home, but Officer Hunter noticed something peculiar as he focused on the back door of the home.

One of the windowpanes had been smashed.

"Something may have happened inside," Hunter recalled later, speaking about that moment he spied the broken back window, "that we needed to investigate a little further [and] check the welfare of the people inside."

Several additional officers arrived. Officer Hunter approached the house slowly, his weapon drawn, reached for the knob and opened the door.

"Mineral Wells Police Department!" the veteran cop yelled as he walked in. "We're here with Richard and Kathy Cruz. We're coming in."

Not a peep.

Hunter announced himself "four or five times" before heading into the kitchen.

As he made his way through the kitchen stealthily, as if expecting to be ambushed at any moment, Hunter heard music. A radio or television was on.

Coming out of the hallway from the kitchen, Randy

Hunter spied a "subject," as he described the person, "somebody lying on [a] bed. . . ."

He pointed his weapon toward the subject and shouted pointedly: "Mineral Wells Police Department!"

No response.

"The size of the body . . . it appeared to be a male," Hunter recalled.

But Randy Hunter couldn't be 100 percent certain, because the bottom half of the subject was covered with a blanket. And from his neck up, the subject's face was covered with a pillow or bag of some sort.

Randy Hunter carefully approached the subject, bent down, and placed two fingers on the man's carotid artery to check for a pulse.

No sign of life.

Then, as Hunter grabbed his radio to call in additional backup, he saw blood.

"We're going to need an ambulance over here . . . ," Hunter said into his handheld. "Send Captain [Mike] McAllester and Sergeant [Brian] Boetz, too."

Hunter worked his way around the corner from that small bedroom and located a second back bedroom, which he also approached with caution.

The door was slightly ajar. Hunter pried it open slowly and saw a "hospital-type bed . . . with all kinds of stuff piled on it." As he walked toward the bed to check the other side, "an arm fell out from underneath a blanket. . . ."

2

She believed it to be some sort of celestial "sign." Those incredibly vivid dreams invading her sleep were coming "for a reason," she felt. They were fuzzy images, certainly, filled with metaphors of "which path to take," she later explained. In one, Jennifer Jones believed she was setting herself up for failure simply because she had been born (as they might say in Texas) *kin* to Clyde Barrow, half of the infamous Bonnie and Clyde murderous duo. Indeed, according to her grandmother, who was said to have made a shrine in her house dedicated to the old murderer and bank robber, Jennifer had that bad blood of the Barrows coursing through her veins, and there was nothing she could do about it.

Jen's mother before her, Kathy Jones, had set herself on that same path. Kathy was tough as rawhide, a bar bruiser and career criminal, in and out of jail. Kathy had even come close to death a number of times, stabbed and beaten. Jennifer never saw herself in that manner; but coming from that sort of pedigree, a woman can't help but develop a thick exterior and disastrously unhealthy inner dialogue. She would begin to convince herself that she *can't* do anything. And all of those dreams she was having lately, well, they fit right into the madness that had made up her life. She felt doomed, in other words.

Destined to fail, that is.

"I found a list once," one of Jennifer's sisters explained to me. "Jennifer was like just about fourteen. It was a list of all the guys she had slept with. She stopped at one hundred. I asked why [the list abruptly ended]. She said she lost count. The list started with names. As it continued, she dropped the names. I asked why. She said she didn't even know some of the names of the guys she'd had sex with."

Because of that Clyde Barrow connection and a mother she viewed as destructive, unavailable, and quite caught up in a world of drugs and crimes to support bad habits, Jennifer Jones obsessed over the self-prophesized fact in her head that her life had been paved by a road already chosen for her. No matter what she did—no matter how hard she tried—Jennifer believed nothing could get in the way of this tragic evolution that became her fate.

So why fight it? Jennifer decided. Why not embrace its ambiguity and dark side? Years ago, Jennifer wrote about her chosen future in a journal, which had become her best friend at the time. On December 28, 2000, just five days after her sixteenth birthday, Jennifer sat down and confirmed the inevitable: *These dreams are coming to me for a reason. . . .*

The Jennifer Jones of sixteen years old had no idea how visionary—call it wishful thinking, a self-fulfilling prophecy, creating one's own reality, whatever you want—those dreams of her future were to become. The baby-faced, clear-skinned, attractive Texas teen, with long brown hair and a Colgate smile, had set herself on a dangerous and deadly course, indeed. She didn't know it, but in front of Jennifer was a carefully chosen path that her mother had tried to manage before her. It was one that Jennifer had herself predicted years before, and the new "love" of her life—a tomboyish (but deceivingly pretty), petite, butch blonde, whom friends called a "little boy"—would end up becoming the proverbial scapegoat for it.

3

It was 7:30 P.M. on **May 5, 2004**. By most accounts it was a quiet night in Mineral Wells, Texas. Mineral Wells is a mostly white, bedroom community of about sixteen thousand, located in the northern central portion of the state pushing up toward the Oklahoma border. Fort Worth is the closest major city; Dallas and Irving are not too far east from there.

Before Rick and Kathy Cruz had telephoned into the MWPD what appeared to be a murder, the town had enjoyed a near-nonexistent homicide rate for years: between 1999 and 2004, for example, there had been three murders. So people killing one another was not what Mineral Wells residents worried all that much about. When the locals were asked, the main problems in Mineral Wells dated back to 1973, when the military installation known as Fort Wolters transferred its last remaining helicopters out of the popular base and began the economically devastating process of closing. There had been a time when Fort Wolters kept Mineral Wells bustling with all that military money floating around in bars and petrol stations and every other type of financial mainstay holding up a small community.

During what some might call the financial heydays of World War II, some say nearly a quarter-million soldiers filed their way through the Fort Wolters base, with another forty thousand during the Vietnam War. After that last copter and soldier left, however, Mineral Wells felt the hit immediately. All that military money vanished seemingly overnight. Add to that, too, the collapse of the cottage industry of the Baker Hotel, an icon in Mineral Wells since the 1940s and 1950s. As the years progressed, Mineral Wells fell more in line with that familiar poverty-stricken, jobless brand that has become small-town America. It became a burg ravaged by the horrors of what meth and ice can do: robberies, burglaries, auto thefts, and rapes. Not a trade-off, necessarily, for a low murder rate, but it was a fact the locals—many of whom were born and raised in Mineral Wells—could not and would not ever deny.

"Still," one local told me, "Mineral Wells sometimes gets thrown that way"—being a bad place to live—"but it's really not. Probably just like anywhere else, we have the same problems other communities have. We're average people."

The Baker Hotel was a resort, a bona fide destination for many tourists and Hollywood celebrities and curiosity seekers from all over the world. The likes of Marilyn Monroe to FDR attended. Everyone came in search of some of that old "crazy water" said to be tapped in Mineral Wells springs. The town had been founded on a certain type of mineral water that had sprung up, which was thought to have some sort of a therapeutic value. It was said to be the cure for everything from arthritis to insanity, hence the "crazy water" name. As a result, the town became somewhat of a miracle, curing destination. Everybody wanted what was in that water. The Baker Hotel, a rather large landmark in town—now run-down and about to fall in on its own building blocks—became the go-to hot spot. There in the center of town stood a high-rise establishment, with the top floor deck dedicated to mineral baths.

"People came from all over to soak in the baths and then profess it was a cure for anything they had," said one local. "So back in the '50s and early '60s, this was a booming town."

Throughout that time the economy was great; the military was rocking and rolling. The Baker Hotel became like a little Las Vegas, and all was copasetic in town. But then that military base closed and the bottom fell out. No sooner did the Baker Hotel close.

Still, the one fact that MWPD officers and locals would acknowledge all day long was that, despite the downturns throughout the years, Mineral Wells had "one of the lowest, if not the lowest, murder rates in the state."

Indeed, murder was not a call the MWPD got all that frequently.

Randy Hunter and the other MWPD officers who arrived on scene to back him up weren't in the house all that long. When Hunter and the other police officers emerged, Rick Cruz heard additional sirens—other cops and an ambulance heading toward the scene. It all seemed real now to the Cruzes. Something had happened. Something terrible. Something sinister and maybe even deadly. Officer Hunter must have found something inside the house, Rick Cruz surmised, looking on.

Hunter came out and walked over to Rick and Kathy as more cops and an emergency medical technician (EMT) van pulled up. "I'll need that gun, Mr. Cruz."

Rick handed it over. "What's going on?"

The officer didn't say anything.

"What is it?" Rick asked.

The cop said nothing.

Then again, he didn't have to. The look on his face— and all of the arriving officers and emergency medical technicians—said it all. What had started hours earlier as a "maybe" was now something much more serious. Someone had been shot. No doubt about it. And by the look of it, Rick and Kathy Cruz knew while standing there in Bob Something's driveway, sizing up the scene

as it unfolded in front of them, the cop was in no hurry
to help the victim out.

By now, the MWPD believed there were possibly two victims inside what was an absolute dump of a house on
Twentieth Street. Inside, police had found a male and a
female. Or a mother and her son, as it turned out. That
first responding officer, Randy Hunter, knew the man was
dead; as it turned out, the woman was alive—just barely.
The MWPD had no idea what happened: how, why, when,
or by whom. They only inferred that a gun was somehow
involved—that by Rick and Kathy Cruz stating there
might have been guns involved, a gun was somehow involved. Hunter and his team of responding officers did a
cursory search of the house, where they had found the
one man—presumably Bob Something—unresponsive,
lying on a bed, cold to the touch, dead as roadkill.

As Hunter walked into that second bedroom, and the
arm fell off the bed, he heard a groan. And it scared him.

What in the hell? Hunter thought.

Not another DB—dead body.

There was an elderly woman awake in her bed in that
adjacent room, buried under a mound of covers. The
room was a complete mess. "Junked out," said one law enforcement source. There were empty Happy Meal boxes
all over the place. She had been watching television, actually. And when Hunter approached, weapon drawn, ready
and expecting to find her dead, too, she looked at him
quizzically and wondered what in the world was going on.
It was obvious she had been underfed and was perhaps suffering from malnutrition and some form of dementia.

"Out of it," one cop told me later. She was totally obliv-
ious to the fact that the man—her son!—in the room
next to her was dead. "Once she got some fluids in her,
though, she bounced back quickly and was—she let us
know—totally surprised that the cops were in her house."

One report had the old woman sitting up in bed at one

point, saying, *"Is there anything wrong, Officer?"* as Hunter dug her out of the covers she was buried under and realized she was alive.

The responding officers were smart not to touch or meddle with the crime scene. It's amazing how many first responders muck up what can be a slippery slope when walking into a crime scene involving a potential murder victim. It's those first responders, most forensic scientists will agree, that can make or break a case depending on how they go about closing off and securing a scene. In this case the MWPD had trained its officers properly— apparently. There was a protocol, and it was followed.

Thirty-five-year-old MWPD detective Brian Boetz was at home, already done for the day, enjoying his life outside work, when he took the call.

"We have what appears to be a double homicide . . . out on Twentieth Street," dispatch said.

"Got it. On my way."

One murder in Mineral Wells on a Wednesday evening was beyond rare. But *two*? That got Boetz's attention mighty quick. He didn't waste much time hopping up out of his chair, grabbing his weapon and radio, firing up his black Yukon SUV, and kicking stone and dust from his driveway as a siren blared as Boetz found himself heading toward a possible double-homicide scene.

Inside the house Randy Hunter had made sure that the old woman was taken out by EMTs and brought directly to a hospital.

It took Detective Boetz about fifteen minutes to get to the scene. He stepped out of his Yukon, saw Richard and Kathy Cruz standing, looking rather puzzled, and headed into the house. No sooner had Boetz arrived, did his captain, Mike McAllester, pull up.

Boetz was a Texas transplant. He, his mother, grandfather, and grandmother had moved to Mineral Wells from

Denver, Colorado, when Boetz was twelve. "My dad lives
somewhere in Oregon, I think," the detective told me.
"I don't know for sure. I don't keep in touch with him."

Taking a look at the house from outside as they headed
in, Boetz and McAllester astutely determined that no one
had been taking care of the place. They'd seen worse,
sure. But this house was nothing more than a run-down,
dirty, substandard, ranch-style box of decaying wood. It
had been nearly overcome by aggressive, vinelike vege-
tation, with paint peeling off like confetti in droves.

The EMTs were gone by the time Boetz and
McAllester arrived. A cursory review of the neighborhood and it was clear that they were looking at a cookie
cutter series of similar single-family ranch homes on
postage-stamp sects of land. This was part of suburbia
in Mineral Wells. Most homes were kept up as best they
could be under the conditions of the economic times,
and there was not much drive to fix up a community that
had been falling to the ills of the drug culture for years.
Drugs had a way of working themselves into the nicer
communities, once the suburban partiers move on from
weed and booze and into the heavier stuff, like heroin,
crack, and meth. There was no defining line much anymore, separating the "hood" from the "burbs," unless
one was talking exclusive areas of the town. Drugs were
everywhere today.

"The town of Mineral Wells is definitely in decay," one
visitor to the neighborhood told me, "and none of the
homes in that neighborhood will be in *Better Homes and
Gardens*."

An understatement.

"We entered through a back door"—after reaching in
through what was a windowpane of smashed-out glass with
a bit of blood surrounding it, and unlatching the lock—
"and found a victim deceased and an elderly female subject still alive in her bed," Randy Hunter explained to
Boetz as they got together inside and talked.

"No kidding?"

"Yeah. . . ."

"So it's not a double?" Boetz asked. He was confused at first. Dispatch had called in potentially two homicides. Could there be another victim besides the old woman, who had been taken to the hospital?

"No, just the one," Hunter said. He pointed to the room where the body had been discovered.

"Thanks."

The old woman, Hunter further explained to Boetz, was unmindful of what had happened inside the home. She had no idea someone had been shot and killed.

Better yet, her son.

"There's one deceased person inside and one being attended to [at the hospital]," Boetz explained to his boss, Mike McAllester.

It was 8:23 P.M. Boetz had a look around the house before heading into the bedroom with the DB. It appeared that the old woman had lived inside her room and was being *kept*—for lack of a better term—by someone, probably her son, Boetz surmised.

The deceased victim was naked, lying on a bed, half his body covered with blankets (as if he was sleeping), a pillow or some sort of laundry bag over what was left of his face. He had been shot, apparently point-blank, several times; the right side of his jaw had been blown nearly off his face. His cheek was nothing more than ripped, torn, and bloodied flesh.

"Looks like the elderly lady has been neglected," Boetz said. Interestingly enough, there was a lock on the outside of the old woman's door. Whoever was supposedly taking care of her had essentially locked her inside her room. It was clear she hardly—if ever—left that room.

Boetz asked Sergeant Belz, who had just arrived, to position himself at the front door of the residence. "Keep a log of anybody coming and going from the crime scene."

"Will do," Belz said.

Boetz asked Officer Gary Lively to do the same at the back door. "Don't let anyone in."

"No problem, Detective."

Boetz and McAllester took a moment to look around the house. A basic ranch, the front door opened into a small living room, which was "just messy . . . in somewhat disarray," Boetz recalled. There were mattresses on the floor; pillows and blankets and garbage were strewn all over, as if several people had been living in the house and sleeping anywhere they could find an open space. There was a desk with a computer and chair. "Stacked up on top of a stand, where the TV was on, was a bunch of video-tapes. . . ." There was some other furniture spread throughout the room, sparse as it was, but it was old and decrepit, like the inside of the home itself. And there was a lone fan, Boetz took note of, "noisy and running," sitting on a table. This gave the inside of the house a rather eerie, creepy feel, as though the fan was the only living thing left.

Taking a right out of the living room, Boetz started down a short hallway that went into the kitchen on the right and a sitting room (bedroom) on the left. In the kitchen there were dishes and pots and pans stacked everywhere: on counters, in the sink, on the table.

Disgusting. No other way to put it.

Heading toward the back inside the kitchen, Boetz studied the door. One of the panes had been smashed and there was some blood on the glass and door itself. Not a lot, but enough to get a sample. On the floor below were several bits and pieces of broken glass.

Boetz and McAllester walked into the bedroom where the DB waited for them. The pillow—or, as Boetz realized now, "laundry bag"—was still covering the man's face. The idea, Boetz knew, was to "back up for a moment and look at the big picture of what could have happened here." Any good cop will explain: The scene will speak to him if he doesn't stand in its way and interrupt the process.

Looking around, Boetz pointed to the wall. There

seemed to be a few pictures missing. The corners of the photos or pictures were still attached to the wall by tape and staples, but the bodies of the pictures were gone. Boetz could tell by the grime and dust marking an outline of where the picture hung that someone had removed them recently. The walls were a putrid tan color, like coffee ice cream, and smudged with filth and dirt and grease. There was a bureau to the left of the victim, a stereo on top of it. The bed itself was a mattress on the floor. The striped laundry bag covered the victim's face and upper chest area; a floral blanket, with flowery patterns of pink and green and white and yellow, covered the man from the belly button down.

"Gunshot wound on his left bicep," Boetz said out loud, noticing the wound.

"Have you looked underneath the pillow?"

"I haven't removed it, no," Boetz responded.

Both investigators had been told by then that the entire area had been searched, around and inside the house, and "no other persons had been found." The only wound visible to Boetz and McAllester was on the victim's left bicep. It was clear that he had been shot in the arm.

Boetz had Detective Penny Judd come into the room and photograph the wound on the man's bicep.

Looking closer, Boetz noticed a hole through the laundry bag/pillowcase. He could see gunpowder residue.

Judd snapped a photo. And she continued the take photos of the entire room, the victim, and anything else Boetz pointed out.

Standard operating procedure (SOP).

"That gunpowder residue," Boetz said, "means he was shot at close range."

Someone had placed the laundry bag over the man's face and fired—almost like an execution. Organized-crime figures do this. Sneak up on someone while he sleeps, place a pillow over his face, and fire a few shots into the head. Just like in a Hollywood film.

But that wound on the bicep?

Strange.

There was a pair of men's jeans on the floor by the side of the bed. McAllester walked over and, carefully, being certain not to disturb what could be an important piece of evidence, reached inside the back pocket and took out what appeared to be a wallet.

He looked for a license. Found one.

The Cruz family had it right. The guy's name was Robert "Bob" Dow. He was forty-nine, his fiftieth birthday about a month away. Bob had a potbelly stomach on him, but he was otherwise in what was average shape for an American by today's standards. He was butt naked underneath the covers. Either he had been getting himself ready for bed when someone shot him, was already sleeping, or his killer had surprised him.

As Boetz stood near Bob Dow, he looked closer at the walls, where they had spied the missing pictures.

There was blood on the wall.

"Vic's?"

Was it blood spatter from the gunshot wounds?

Boetz and McAllester didn't think so.

It appeared to Boetz that whoever removed the pictures had cut himself or herself during that process and was bleeding.

Over near the northeast corner of the room was a green chest—like a pirate's—sitting on the floor. Boetz bent down and had a look. It seemed that someone had forcefully pried the chest open. With latex gloves on, Boetz had a look inside.

And that was where, Boetz said later, "we found some ammunition and a gun."